# RESEARCH IN THE COLLEGE CONTEXT

## *Approaches and Methods*

**Frances K. Stage,** *New York University*
**Kathleen Manning,** *University of Vermont*
Editors

**BRUNNER-ROUTLEDGE**
NEW YORK AND HOVE

Published in 2003 by
Brunner-Routledge
29 West 35th Street
New York, NY 10001
www.brunner-routledge.com

Published in Great Britain by
Brunner-Routledge
27 Church Road
Hove, East Sussex, BN3 2FA
www.brunner-routledge.co.uk

Brunner-Routledge is an imprint of the Taylor & Francis Group.
Printed in the United States of America on acid-free paper.

Cover Design and Cover Photograph by Pearl Chang.
The Washington Monument loacated near the NYU Campus.

10 9 8 7 6 5 4 3 2 1

Library of Congress Cataloging-in-Publication Data
    Research in the college context : approaches and methods / Frances K. Stage and
Kathleen Manning, editors.
        p. cm.
    Includes bibliographical references and index.
    ISBN 0–415–93579–2 (hard) – ISBN 0–415–93580–6 (pbk.)
    1. Education, Higher—Research—Methodology.  2. Qualitative research.
I. Stage, Frances K.  II. Manning, Kathleen, 1954–

  LB2326.3.R48 2003
  001.4'2 – dc21

                                                          2003002650

This book is dedicated to my parents,
William Bernard and Opal Smith King,
who taught us not only to ask questions
but how to answer them as well.
—Frances K. Stage

This book is dedicated to George Kuh,
who faithfully encourages the scholarship,
writing, and research efforts of his students.
—Kathleen Manning

# CONTENTS

# EDITORS

**Frances K. Stage, PhD,** is Professor and Director of the Higher Education graduate program at New York University. She has taught classes in research design and case study analysis. Her areas of specialization include college student learning, especially for math and sciences and student participation in the math/science majors. She is author or coauthor of books, articles, and book chapters focusing on college students and the methods used to study them. Books include *Theory to Practice: New Case Studies for Working with College Students, Creating Learning Centered Classrooms: What Does Learning Theory Have to Say, Enhancing Student Learning: Setting the Campus Context,* and *Diverse Methods for Research and Assessment of College Students.*

**Kathleen Manning, PhD,** is Associate Professor in the Higher Education and Student Affairs graduate program at the University of Vermont. Her experience with research includes teaching classes in qualitative research, feminist methodology, and research design. Her specialty content areas within higher education and student affairs include cultural pluralism, organizational analysis, and campus cultures. In addition to numerous refereed articles and book chapters, her published books include *Rituals, Ceremonies, and Cultural Meaning in Higher Education, Giving Voice to Critical Campus Issues: Qualitative Research in Student Affairs,* and *Enhancing the Multicultural Environment: A Cultural Brokering Approach.*

# CONTRIBUTORS

**Katie Branch, PhD,** Associate Professor, Human Development and Family Studies, University of Rhode Island, Kingston, Rhode Island.

**Deborah Faye Carter, PhD,** Associate Professor, Educational Leadership and Policy Studies, Indiana University, Bloomington, Indiana.

**Bridget Turner Kelly, PhD,** Assistant Professor, Integrated Professional Studies, University of Vermont, Burlington, Vermont.

**Agnes Kovacs, MA,** Associate Instructor and Doctoral Candidate, Recreation and Park Administration, Indiana University, Bloomington, Indiana.

**Patrick Love, PhD,** Associate Professor, Higher Education, New York University, New York, New York.

**Teboho Moja, PhD,** Professor, Higher Education, New York University, New York, New York.

**Anna M. Ortiz, PhD,** Associate Professor, Educational Psychology, Administration and Counseling, California State University, Long Beach, Long Beach, California.

**Ruth V. Russell, PhD,** Professor, Recreation and Park Administration, Indiana University, Bloomington, Indiana.

**Robert A. Schwartz, PhD,** Associate Professor, Higher Education Administration, Florida State University, Tallahassee, Florida.

**Michelle Thompson, JD,** Doctoral Candidate, History, New York University, New York, New York.

**J. Fredericks Volkwein, PhD,** Professor and Senior Scientist, Center for the Study of Higher Education, Pennsylvania State University, University Park, Pennsylvania.

# PREFACE

Almost two decades ago George Keller (1985, 1986) criticized researchers on college campuses for asking empty, trivial, or esoteric questions that did little to address some of the most burning issues in higher education such as racial and class inequities in access and success, unfairness in tenure and promotion practices, and bias in standardized testing. The critic likened the research being conducted to trees that, despite being carefully tended and nurtured, bore no fruit. Since that time, researchers have focused more closely on issues that hold real meaning in higher education.

Like Keller, we and other critics believe that an overreliance on traditional approaches has limited understanding of the college campus. Quantitative terms require stripping away idiosyncrasies and imply that anything that is important to know about our campus can be reduced to numbers. Details about members of college campuses, their personal lives, and the influences of the college experience are lost. The resulting limitations result in gaps in communication between those who gather information and those who use it. Practitioners working directly with college students, policymakers working with boards of trustees, and decision makers working within higher education cannot ignore details. But many of the research methods employed within education strip away the details necessary to understand campus life, make sound decisions, or determine well-considered policy. With the loss of information that could be gained through less traditional research techniques, our work is often not useful to administrators, educators, and policymakers (Stage, Russell, & Manning, 1992). Fortunately, scholars have increasingly broadened their approaches to inquiry recognizing that the stripping away of idiosyncrasies removes important aspects of the college student experience.

Since the early 1980s, we have seen an expansion in the use of techniques for conducting research on the college campus. As those who studied college students and college environments learned that many of their most burning questions could not be answered through traditional methods (e.g., the survey, structured interview, and standardized instrument), they turned to other disciplines for guidance. Methods borrowed from a variety of fields including anthropology, sociology, political science, business, and other disciplines formed the bases for attempts to learn about higher education, faculty, college students, and their experiences.

At the same time, we have seen an increasing use of computer-based data and the expansion of our capabilities to access and use that data to answer specific questions about colleges and the students who inhabit them. In addition to campus registrar, evaluation, and assessment data, inquiring researchers can use large national databases to answer their questions. These databases have sufficient numbers so that researchers can focus on narrowly tailored groups of students. For example, a recent learning using such data is that theories and models developed based on research in the 1970s and 1980s do not hold up well when nontraditional students are studied (Hamrick & Stage, 1998; Hurtado & Carter, 1997; Nora & Cabrera, 1996). With this broad availability of information, and new ways of generating data, a need exists for researchers and professionals to understand the alternatives they have for the collection of data on the college campus. Additionally, there is a need for consumers of such information to discern high-quality research.

This book was written to meet the needs of those who are beginning the research enterprise, those who use research only sporadically, and those who are seasoned researchers but who are interested in learning new approaches and techniques. This handbook of approaches and methods is most useful to those who conduct research on colleges and college students. The book would be useful as a class text and would serve as a resource for faculty, student, and administrators' research efforts. Techniques discussed in this book can serve as a guide for those who conduct assessment, evaluate programs, write reports, and engage in fact-finding for practical purposes. Graduate students (master's and doctoral) can use this book as they conduct research for theses and dissertations. Finally, it will be useful to those who already conduct research and who are seeking new ways to answer their research questions. We hope to inspire in our readers a broadened awareness of research possibilities.

Methods presented here address practical as well as theoretical approaches to research. Every research approach has its advantages and disadvantages. Overreliance on a few methods, surveys, and analysis of quantitative data, skews knowledge and limits learning. While not all researchers can be proficient at all methods, one can learn from applications of a wide variety of research approaches across the range of higher education topics.

Whether for knowledge generation, action research, or even fact finding, we offer these techniques to expand possibilities for generating useful information. Practical limitations will not allow us to create a compendium of all possible approaches and techniques (as if such a comprehensive list could be generated and agreed to by all the editors and reviewers). Nevertheless, we hope to present a selected set of topics that are broadly used. We seek to provide introductions to approaches and techniques that would be most accessible and useful to those working on college campuses. We hope to motivate readers to explore some of these techniques and others in more detail and to begin to incorporate them into their own work.

Several of the techniques suggested here might be combined to create a more comprehensive understanding of the topic under study. The use of multiple methods in the study of a single phenomenon can shed light on mysteries that can arise in any good research study. Finally, in addition to embellishing their own research, it is hoped that readers of this book will learn, as consumers of research, to discern high quality.

This book is organized into five major sections: developing a context including formulating questions and approaches, a second part on respondent-based methods, a third on document-based methods, a section on the use of preexisting data and resources, and finally a chapter addressing issues regarding reporting results. The emphasis is on general introduction to particular approaches and techniques, advantages and disadvantages, types of research questions that can be addressed using the technique, and standards for conducting and reporting the results. Examples of uses of the method within higher education are briefly described. Finally, recommendations for further reading are provided in each chapter so that the researcher can further develop his or her expertise.

The first chapter focuses on the development of the research question. The reader with a desire to get started in the actual conducting of research might wonder why we devote an entire chapter to the research question. Whether for the development of new knowledge, the performance of professional duties, or merely the satisfaction of curiosity, the honing of a well-developed question or questions is a critical first step in the research process. The research question not only forms the foundation of study, it points to the literature to be reviewed, defines the approach, and even suggests the techniques to be employed. Later chapters explore the decision regarding the research approach, choice of methods or techniques to answer research questions, and presentation of research results.

This book was written as a guide for new and experienced researchers to explore relatively new research methods. We encourage you to take advantage of the information and examples provided in the chapters and then delve as deeply as feasible into the possibilities of educational research. We hope that this book and the encouragement provided herein yield trees with an abundance of fruit.

Frances K. Stage, New York University
Kathleen Manning, University of Vermont

# REFERENCES

Hamrick, F. A., & Stage, F. K. (1998). High minority enrollment, high school-lunch rates: Predisposition to college. *Review of Higher Education, 21*(4), 343–357.

Hurtado, S., & Carter, D. F. (1997). Effects of college transition and perceptions of the campus racial climate on Latino students' sense of belonging. *Sociology of Education, 70*(4), 324–345.

Keller, G. (1985). Trees without fruit: The problem with research about higher education. *Change, 17*(1), 7–10.

Keller, G. (1986). Free at last? Breaking the chains that bind educational research. *Review of Higher Education, 10*(2), 129–134.

Nora, A., & Cabrera, A. (1996). The role of perceptions in prejudice and discrimination and the adjustment of minority students to college. *Journal of Higher Education, 67*(2), 119–148.

Stage, F. K., Russell, R. V., & Manning, K. (Eds.). (1992). *Diverse methods for research and assessment of college students.* Alexandria, VA: ACPA Media.

*Part 1*

# DEVELOPING A CONTEXT
# FOR RESEARCH

*Chapter 1*

# WHAT IS
# YOUR QUESTION?

**Frances K. Stage,** *New York University*
**Kathleen Manning,** *University of Vermont*

A dean of a college of business notices a decline in the number of business majors. He learns from the director of the advising center that many students switched from business to other majors after failing to complete second-semester calculus. He begins to wonder whether second-semester calculus is useful for his students and asks a graduate assistant to gather a variety of textbooks for quantitative courses to evaluate mathematical demand. He also requests records to track the academic progress of those students who switched from business 5 years ago.

The Director of Residence Life has spent the last several years dealing with increasing levels of incivility based on race, ethnicity, sexual orientation, and gender. She asks her assistant director to provide a summary of recent court cases dealing with hate-speech regulation on campuses before she drafts a policy for residence halls to take to the administrative council.

A chemistry professor reads recent articles suggesting that some students learn and perform better when using web-based chemistry lab modules rather than the traditional wet lab. Her department chair has given her permission to perform a limited experiment using the web-based lab to determine whether it might be useful for students in her classes.

A sociology professor is curious about hierarchy and social support in the academy, particularly for untenured professors. He wants to combine a survey on social support with interviews to learn about the experiences of new faculty.

The seeming disconnection of commuting and part-time students troubles the faculty of a small liberal arts college. After enrollments started declining 10 years ago they recruited local students to fill the gap. The faculty senate decides to learn more about these students and the ways the college can serve them.

The director of a college transition program for minority students is writing a report for campus administration. He used focus groups to get students' reactions to the program. Although students who enroll through the program seem to be doing well, their persistence rates still lag below the campus average for new students. He decides to use registrar data to compare success rates between his students and others who enter college with similar test and high school records.

The campus admissions officer, after being directed to cease the practice of race-based admissions, decided to make existing practices explicit and to create targeted geography-based admissions. One year after creating a policy detailing guidelines for admissions based on family alums; gender; athleticism; academic, artistic, and literary talent; and geography, she wants to see what the effects were on the makeup of the new class of students.

In each of the vignettes just described, the individuals in question were about to embark on a research project. Each of them had a question that required acquisition and analysis of information in some form to answer. As demonstrated by these, the term *research* applies to a broad range of activities on the college campus. Analysis of already available institutional data, exploration of legal implications of a campus issue, questions about student learning in classes, research on faculty experiences, needs assessment, evaluation of programs, and monitoring of new policies—all these and more fall under the general rubric of research.

This book discusses the development of a research project beginning with the glimmer of an idea, through the gathering of relevant information and the choice of an approach and a technique for answering the research question. Throughout the book, we stress the importance of the breadth of possibilities faced by the research novice. At the decision stage of a research project the researcher has the opportunity to choose one of a variety of methods or to select more than one method. During the research project the researcher is encouraged to follow closely the advice given by the chapter authors to ensure ethical, high-quality research. Finally, the researcher's responsibility to disseminate findings in ways that enable the research to be viewed by the widest possible audience is discussed.

## DEFINITION AND TERMS

Any discussion of research must begin with a common understanding of definitions and terms that will clarify meaning. Given the possible range and scope of research project activities just described, all of which can loosely be defined as research, shared common terms promote understanding across the chapters.

First, the three overarching terms, *research, evaluation,* and *assessment,* that constitute the subject matter of this book are defined. From that starting point, strategies to guide the reader from a general idea to a well-developed research question are discussed using the preceding vignettes as examples. Elements of a good research proposal follow the discussion of the research question development. Finally, the possible approaches one might take to answering research questions are introduced here and expanded in chapter 2.

1. "Research is simply gathering the information you need to answer a question and thereby help you solve a problem" (Booth, Colomb, & Williams, 1995, p. 6).
2. Assessment is "any effort to gather, analyze, and interpret evidence which describes institutional, departmental, divisional, or agency effectiveness" (Upcraft & Schuh, 1996, p. 18).
3. Evaluation is "any effort to use assessment evidence to improve institutional, departmental, divisional, or agency effectiveness" (Upcraft & Schuh, 1996, p. 19).

In general then, both assessment and evaluation usually involve making a judgment about the future direction, performance, or ultimate usefulness of an educational enterprise. On the other hand, research is typically associated with knowledge generation. The topics and techniques contained in the remainder of the book are useful to all three activities. However, referring to the three activities separately by name throughout the book would be cumbersome. Therefore, unless otherwise noted, the word *research* is used to refer to a range of information-gathering activities used for educational purposes, whether or not evaluative and whether or not knowledge generating. Several additional terms warrant explanation, as their meanings are contested and multiple throughout the research literature.

1. *Authenticity criteria* includes a set of constructivist paradigm (discussed later) based techniques to assure high-quality research. The criteria include fairness, ontological authenticity, educative authenticity, and catalytic authenticity (Guba & Lincoln, 1990; Manning, 1997).

2.  *Trustworthiness* involves a set of techniques, grounded in the conventional paradigm, used by the qualitative researcher to assure high quality research methods (Guba & Lincoln, 1990).

3.  *Constructivist paradigm* is an "alternative to the scientific paradigm" that is also called "interpretive and hermeneutic" (Guba & Lincoln, 1990, p. 39). "Ontologically...[it asserts] that realities are social constructions of the mind. . . . Epistemologically . . . [it suggests] that the findings of a study exist precisely because there is an *interaction* between observer and observed that literally creates what emerges from that inquiry. *Methodologically* . . . it [uses] a *hermeneutic/dialectic process* that takes full advantage, and account, of the observer/observed interaction to create a constructed reality that is as informed and sophisticated as it can be made at a particular point in time" (pp. 43–44, italics in original).

4.  *Naturalistic inquiry* occurs when the "researcher frequents places where the events he or she is interested in naturally occur" (Bogdan & Biklen, 1992, p. 3).

5.  *Positivistic perspective*, also called "scientific inquiry" (Guba & Lincoln, 1990), is a "single-method tradition" embracing the ideas that "knowledge [is] confined to what has been experienced or can be experienced, . . . The adequacy of knowledge increases as it approximates the forms of explanation which have been achieved by the most advanced sciences, . . . Scientific explanation is limited to only functional and directional laws . . . or to only mathematically functional laws" (Polkinghorne, 1983, pp. 18–19).

6.  "*Post-positivistic science* does not propose a unified view of science. . . . The knowledge claims that a community accepts are those that withstand the test of practical argument and use (Schwandt, 1997). Knowledge is understood to be the best understanding that we have been able to produce thus far, not a statement of what is ultimately real" (Polkinghorne, 1983, p. 2).

7.  "*Qualitative research* is an umbrella concept covering several forms of inquiry that help us understand and explain the meaning of social phenomena. . . . Other terms often used interchangeably are *naturalistic inquiry, interpretive research, field study, participant observation, inductive research, case study,* and *ethnography*" (Merriam, 1998, p. 5; italics in original). Interviewing, document analysis, and observation are techniques used to gather data primarily in the form of words and symbols describing and interpreting constructs of interest.

8.  *Quantitative methods* are measures requiring a numerical or other evaluative symbol assigned to the construct of interest.

9.  *Secondary data analysis* uses previously collected data to answer research questions.

10. *Validity* is a concept in quantitative research that determines the extent to which a measure or observation describes what it is purported to describe.

These terms and definitions form a basis for the context of this book. As educational research evolves, multiple and sometimes contested meanings for the same word might develop.

## THE PURPOSES OF THE RESEARCH

Methodologists Marshall and Rossman proposed that the purposes of research include exploration, explanation, description, and prediction (1995, p. 11). Although a new researcher might ambitiously think that his or her research can meet all these purposes simultaneously, the researcher is advised to decide which one or two of these purposes most suit his or her methodological talents and research temperament. Is the researcher interested in idiosyncratic, context-dependent interpretation? Does the researcher believe that study should address broad questions and apply to a large population? Does the researcher want to predict outcomes? Does the researcher prefer to explain and describe events, practices, or actions in more distinct settings? "You will want your research to solve different kinds of *problems*: to entertain them, to help them solve some problem in the world, or simply to help them understand something better" (Booth et al., 1995, p. 18).

The following guidelines (adapted from Rudestam & Newton, 1992) can be considered by researchers when they explore topics for their research.

1. Will the topic sufficiently sustain the interest of the researcher and consumers of the research?
2. Is the topic manageable? Does the researcher have the resources (including the financial resources and methodological talent) to complete the research project?
3. Is the topic linked to an issue with too much salience and emotion for the researcher?
4. Is the researcher attempting to grind a personal ax through the project?
5. Will the research make an original contribution?
6. Will pursuing the research raise any logistical or political issues? For example, is the project to be undertaken at odds with a dissertation committee member's theoretical perspective?

These and other issues can be explored in a journal kept by the researcher as soon as he or she begins to conceptualize a research project. This journal can be used to explore the questions just posed, draft research questions, experiment with topic statements, and explore research project summaries. Through subsequent drafts of the research topic statement, questions, and subquestions, as well as the use of a journal, the purpose of the research will be more clearly expressed.

Not all researchers have a proclivity or talent for all types of research. Individual talents, backgrounds, and education guide thinking about research, its purposes, and the role of the researcher within the individual research project. As the research question, subquestions, and possible methodological choices are determined, individual preferences, talents, and temperament for research must be considered. This exploration on the part of the researcher builds a firm foundation for a successful research project.

## IDENTIFYING THE RESEARCH QUESTION

The first step in any research project is to identify the research question. Methodology faculty, dissertation advisors, and others engaged in research often hear the announcement, "I want to do a qualitative [or quantitative] study. I just haven't decided on my topic yet." Unfortunately, this approach confuses the order of decision-making needed as one pursues a research project. Whether a dissertation, assessment study, or other research project, a study's method is based on which techniques best answer the research question(s).

The research question as the foundation of the study, defines the research paradigm that forms the assumptions of the study, identifies the literature from which the research emerges and to which it contributes, defines the methodology utilized, and suggests techniques to be employed throughout the research. The purposes of higher education include social change that improves the quality of life for participants, expands social justice, and increases democratic participation. Any research conducted, particularly with the use of public resources, can create a greater good, inform social practice, and contribute to the field's knowledge base. Ideally, a research question will be real. It will grow out of the researchers' curiosities, hunches, professional insights, intuitions, biases, and preconceptions but be grounded in practice and the expediencies of the higher education field.

Overall research questions are broad encompassing statements. The foundational research question must be expansive enough to generate subquestions that further define and clarify the research project. The process of writing the research question and subquestions is often an extended, iterative process. Although the researcher may have a general idea of the question to be pursued through the project, the nuances and details of that research question are most often revealed over time. "Real research loops back and forth, moving forward a step or two, going back while at the same time anticipating stages not yet begun, then moving forward again" (Booth et al., 1995, p. ix). Rarely is a question as clear in the beginning of the study as it is at the end.

Some researchers, especially new doctoral students embarking on their first substantial project, formulate questions so broad they could fill an entire career with subquestions to be explored. Other researchers focus narrowly, seeking to answer questions so esoteric that only a handful of people in an exactly similar situation would care or understand the results. To avoid Keller's (1985) admonition about educational research being "trees with no fruit," one must balance the narrow and broad.

## Balancing the Narrow and the Broad

One way of striking the balance between narrowness and breadth is by considering a hierarchy of statements that describe the study—moving from the very broad to more narrow: the research topic, the research problem, and the research question(s). For example, a chemistry professor may want to know more about student motivation to learn. College student motivation to learn may be thought of as a broad research topic, one that has occupied scores of researchers across several generations. In an attempt to narrow the focus, the professor moves from her *broad research topic* to her *particular discipline*, for example college student motivation to learn chemistry. Narrowing the scope further, her *research problem* might be to learn some effective ways to motivate learning in beginning chemistry students. Finally, the chemistry professor designs an experiment that fits within the context of her courses. She then formulates her *research questions*, addressing what kinds of assignments among a handful that she chooses to implement to best motivate her students. Throughout this process the professor relies on her own experience, discussions with colleagues, research literature on the topic, and web postings to broadly inform her decisions.

If the initial research question is very narrow, the inquirer can move in the opposite way, situating the question within successively broader contexts, which have wider interest. As an example, a doctoral student was interested in women in leadership positions on college campuses. Although she had read widely about the importance of mentoring in leadership development, she had not personally seen evidence of such mentoring in her campus administrative experience. As she described her topic—"Do women mentor other women?"—the focus seemed narrow, and the possible "yes" or "no" answer even seemed trivial. By reading the literature on women's leadership and discussing her project with others, she realized that she was actually interested in how women are promoted into high-level administrative positions. She devised a slightly broader question, "How do women learn to lead?" The answer to that question will not only address her question about mentoring, but also may reveal information regarding multiple ways of becoming a leader. Finally, this broader question can significantly contribute to the literature on women leaders in higher education. Answering more complex questions allows the doctoral researcher to learn more about leaders as well as generate information that adds to theory and practice of leadership development.

## Unearthing Research Questions

For the novice, identifying research questions might seem a daunting task. The beginning inquirer is advised to avail him- or herself of the broad array of resources concerning topics of interest. The more familiar the researcher is with the questions, techniques, and answers of others who share similar interests, the easier it is to generate a new level of engaging questions. In addition, question generation is a skill, a habit of mind. Three means to discover relevant and interesting research questions are: (a) reading higher education literature, (b) speaking to practicing professionals, and (c) attending relevant activities (e.g., conferences, meetings) in the field.

### Gaining Familiarity with Higher Education Literature

Regular reading in research journals is the hallmark of a good scholar and researcher. The following questions can serve as a framework for research considerations regarding the article: What has the reader observed about the same phenomena? How does the literature review relate to the statement of purpose and research question? What questions remain unanswered after reviewing the literature? What questions remain at the end of the study? As one reads articles over a period of time and take notes on these questions, similarities and differences between articles covering similar topics emerge. Interesting research questions can be mined from the journal article or book author's "recommendations for further research."

The importance and role of the literature in this process cannot be overstated. Perhaps the topic under consideration in its simplest form has been addressed. Within research, rarely is a question answered definitively or for all populations on all types of campuses. The same topic can be studied using different techniques (including those presented in this book) to provide new ways of answering familiar research questions. These and other research possibilities can be explored through a careful reading of the field's literature.

## Colleagues as a Source of Research Questions

A second way to develop research ideas is to talk to faculty and administrators. In an environment such as a college campus where information is valued, practical questions abound. In each of the research vignettes described at the start of this chapter, campus issues awaited researchers with the skills and motivation to provide guidance for decision making in some cases and for the expansion of knowledge in others. The American Association for Higher Education (AAHE) (2002) annually conducts a research forum composed of scholars and researchers interested in research topics related to higher education. Together the group generates and disseminates a comprehensive list of research questions waiting to be answered. The list is so comprehensive that research papers emanating from the questions would fill volumes (for further information, see http://www.aahe.org).

## Conferences and Meetings as Sources of Research Questions

Research conference attendance might be one of the most obvious ways to engage in research idea development—nevertheless, it works. The critical issue here is to choose a conference that includes a large number of research sessions. Conferences that focus on research related to college campus issues include the American Association for Higher Education, American Educational Research Association: Postsecondary Education Division, Association for Institutional Research, Association for the Study of Higher Education, and, to a lesser extent, the American College Personnel Association and the National Association of Student Personnel Administrators.

Even if the conference consists chiefly of presentations addressing campus problems and practical issues, there are often sessions on research topics where close attention can be paid to the presenters. How do they state their problem in relation to the literature? How do they describe the research questions and methods employed? What are their findings and how are these presented? What suggestions do they have for future research? Conference presentations are often an excellent way to engage in conversation with experienced researchers and practitioners knowledgeable about a topic of interest.

## ELEMENTS OF A RESEARCH PROPOSAL

As one nears a solid determination of the research topic, the elements of a research proposal and the logistics of the project should be considered. The elements of a research proposal (e.g., statement of problem, review of the literature, questions and/or hypothesis, instrumentation, sampling, data collection, data analysis, significance, and research schedule) provide a framework for the researcher. The researcher should have clear but flexible plans for these elements before beginning any study. They are absolute necessities in requests for funding, proposals for a plan of dissertation research, and in the conduct of any research project.

The following suggested sections of a research proposal can assist the thought processes for forming the research question and subquestions:

1. Write a *statement of research problem*. The research statement should not be coy but, instead, explicitly finish either or both of the following statements, "I am studying . . ." or "The problem to be addressed by this study is . . ." Beginning and experienced researchers are advised to state the problem in ways that are understandable to others who are knowledgeable about education issues but uninformed in the area of the study. The research problem statement should "define and delimit the specific area of the research," "foreshadow the hypotheses to be tested or the questions to be raised," and "indicate *briefly* the significance of the study" (Doctoral Advisory Committee, 1983).

2. Compose an overall, *general research question,* which directly states, "I want to find out who/how/why ___" or "The research will address ___." These questions, although broad, must be answered at the end of the project.

3. Write research *subquestions*. These questions emerge from the overall research question and address the subpurposes of the research project. They answer the question, "What related questions will be addressed and answered through the research project?"

4. State the *rationale* for the research project and questions addressed. The researcher should address that the project is being undertaken "in order to understand how/why/what ___" (Booth et al., 1995, p. 44).

5. Throughout this exploration process of topic, questions, and subquestions, the researcher, particularly if new to the research experience, should ask him- or herself the question, "Is this the research I *really* want to undertake?" "Has my topic strayed from my original purposes?" While this may be difficult for the beginning researcher to understand, experienced researchers share that it is possible to lose track of the research purpose and/or question. The original purpose can shift and change as stakeholders, including dissertation chairs and consultant employers, press their agendas and pose unanticipated questions. Although some evolution of the research purpose and/or question is normal and to be expected (especially in qualitative research where the research question is more clearly defined as data are collected and analyzed), the researcher must be ever vigilant to assure that the research purpose and/or question does not evolve in unwanted or unwarranted directions.

## MODEL RESEARCH QUESTIONS

The vignettes introduced in the beginning of this chapter describe various research topics and approaches. Whether for doctoral dissertations, faculty-initiated projects, or administrative based activities (e.g., assessment, policy analysis, satisfaction, quality of campus or work life), research takes a variety of forms. In order to illustrate the various types of research, the vignettes offered earlier are listed in Table 1.1 with accompanying possible research questions and subquestions.

**TABLE 1.1**
**Possible Research Questions Related to Chapter 1 Research Topics**

| Research Topic | Research Questions |
|---|---|
| College of Business Dean and second-semester calculus | General Research Question:<br>   Is advanced calculus necessary or related to other skills in the field of business?<br>Subquestions:<br>   Is there reference in business texts to skills in advanced calculus?<br>   Is success in the business major, as defined as persistence through graduation, related to obtaining advanced calculus proficiency? |
| Director of Residence Life and increasing incivility | General Research Question:<br>   What is the current state of legal rulings regarding campus hate speech?<br>Subquestions:<br>   What is the current state of campus policy regarding hate-speech?<br>   Can a hate speech policy be applied as an intervention to campus incivility? |
| Chemistry professor and web-based chemistry lab | General Research Question:<br>   What are the differences (as measured by class grades and student satisfaction) between traditional wet chemistry laboratories and computer-based lab simulations?<br>Subquestions:<br>   Are students more successful in a wet laboratory setting than in a computer-based simulated laboratory experience? |
| Sociology professor and the experiences of new faculty | General Research Question:<br>   Do hierarchy and social support influence the experience of untenured professors?<br>Subquestions:<br>   What is the nature of hierarchy in a campus environment? What kind of social support is available to untenured faculty members? |

*(continued)*

**TABLE 1.1**
**Continued**

| Research Topic | Research Questions |
| --- | --- |
| Disconnection of commuting and part-time students at a small, liberal arts college. | General Research Question: <br> Do commuting students experience a connection to college in ways congruent with the goals of liberal arts education and healthy campus environment? <br> Subquestions: <br> What are the differences in experience between commuting and residence life students? What are the differences in experience between full- and part-time students? |
| Director of College Transition Program and persistence rates | General Research Question: <br> What are the success rates of students in a college transition program in comparison to similar students not in the program? <br> Subquestions: <br> What is the level of satisfaction among participants in the college transition program? Does satisfaction with the college transition program correlate with increased persistence toward graduation? |
| Campus admissions officer and geography targeted admissions policy | General Research Question: <br> What is the demographic makeup (specifically, race, socio-economic status, and gender) of the present first-year class as compared to last year's first year class? <br> Subquestions: <br> Has the change in admissions policy from a race-based system affected the demographic profile of the incoming students? Can an admissions policy based on family alumni status, gender, athletic ability, academic success, artistic and literary talent, and geography criteria result in a diverse first-year class in regard to race, gender, and socioeconomic class? |

When reviewing the research topics and questions just suggested, it is important to consider alternative questions that could be asked. A fascinating aspect of conducting research is that any topic can yield an almost infinite number of research questions. The nature of the questions asked about the topic leads to the choice of research method. Prior to taking that step in the research process, the researcher should consider the larger context into which his or her research falls. Potential audiences, whether the research was intended for them or not, should also be considered. Both topics are explored in the following sections.

## RESEARCH IN A LARGER CONTEXT

Clark (1986) suggested the following categories as ones into which the majority of research projects could fall. Although there is not space within this chapter to describe each category (and many are self-explanatory), questions that epitomize each research category may assist you to make foundational and methodological decisions about your research.

*Provocative exception.* "Why don't students of color and White students from comparable backgrounds score similarly on GREs?"

*Conflicting evidence.* "Why do students describe a faculty member as an excellent teacher, yet when responses to the standardized teaching evaluation form are examined, the teacher's scores are mediocre?"

*Knowledge void.* "I am interested in faculty spiritual development but I can't find any research on the topic."

*Action–knowledge or knowledge–action conflict.* "Why do faculty members continue to use the lecture method of teaching when it has repeatedly been shown to be ineffective?"

*Action–action conflict.* "Some people prefer to study in groups, others individually . . . I want to study the learning outcomes of different methods."

*Action–theory or theory–action conflict.* "Enrollment management says that student involvement is essential but student discipline systems don't have student involvement as a central tenet of their programs. What are the reasons for this discrepancy?"

*Theoretical conflict.* "Kohlberg's and Gilligan's theories conflict in the ways they describe women's moral development, I want to explore which theory best explains women's development as assessed on the $x$ measure of moral development."

*Policy–action or action–policy conflict.* "I want to determine whether policies regarding tenure add to the success of tenure-track faculty members."

*Policy–theory or theory–policy conflict.* "Alcohol policies are at odds with college student development theory which says that traditionally aged college students take greater risks with their lives. What are the ways in which the policies can incorporate more student development theory?"

With an understanding of the research context into which a project falls, decisions about methodology can be made with more ease, research topics can gain and/or retain clarity, and challenges to research decisions can be more artfully addressed.

## CONCLUSION

The first step in any research project is identification of the research question. As the foundation of the study, it defines the research paradigm that forms the assumptions of the study, identifies the literature from which the research emerges and to which it contributes, defines the methodology utilized, and suggests techniques to be employed throughout the research. Reading literature, speaking with professionals, and attending professional meetings and conferences are all good strategies for discovering relevant and researchable questions. The next stage in the process is identifying the approach to take in answering the research question.

## FURTHER READING

For general information about qualitative research methods and conducting qualitative studies, see Bogdan and Biklen (1998), Denzin and Lincoln (2000), and Patton (2002), and about quantitative research methods and studies, see Gall, Borg, and Gall (1996). Schwandt (1997) provides a resource for terms utilized in discussions of qualitative inquiry. Glatthorn (1998) and Galvan (1999) provide information on writing dissertations and conducting literature reviews. Russell and Stage (1992) provide an argument for the use of multiple methods in research. Scott and Usher (1996) discuss the political and philosophical ramifications of conducting research. Stage, Russell, and Manning (1992) provide an introductory collection of research methods available to the inquirer.

## REFERENCES

American Association for Higher Education. (2002). *Learning in context: Who are our students? How do they learn? A research agenda.* Washington, DC: American Association for Higher Education 2002 Research Forum.

Bogdan, R. C., & Biklen, S. K. (1992). *Qualitative research in education* (2nd ed.). Boston: Allyn and Bacon.

Booth, W. C., Colomb, G. G., & Williams, J. M. (1995). *The craft of research.* Chicago: University of Chicago Press.

Clark, D. (1986). Worksheet A: State of the problem. Unpublished paper from Indiana University, Bloomington.

Denzin, N. K., & Lincoln, Y. S. (2000). *Handbook of qualitative research.* Thousand Oaks, CA: Sage.

Doctoral Advisory Committee. (1983). *The elements of a proposal (adapted from Egon Guba).* Unpublished paper, University of Vermont, Burlington.

Gall, M. C., Borg, W. R., & Gall, J. P. (1996). *Educational research: An introduction* (6th ed). White Plains, NY: Longman.

Galvan, J. L. (1999). *Writing literature reviews: A guide for students of the social and behavioral sciences.* Los Angeles: Pyrczak.

Glatthorn, A. A. (1998). *Writing the winning dissertation: A step-by-step guide.* Thousand Oaks, CA: Corwin Press.

Guba, E. G., & Lincoln, Y. S. (1990). *Fourth generation evaluation.* Newbury Park, CA: Sage.

Keller, G. (1985). Trees without fruit: The problem with research about higher education. *Change, 17*(1), 7–10.

Manning, K. (1997). Authenticity techniques in constructivist inquiry. *Qualitative Inquiry, 3*(1), 93–115.

Marshall, C., & Rossman, G. B. (1995). *Designing qualitative research* (2nd ed.). Thousand Oaks, CA: Sage.

Merriam, S. B. (1998). *Qualitative research and case study applications in education.* San Francisco, CA: Jossey-Bass.

Patton, M. Q. (2002). *Qualitative research and evaluation methods* (3rd ed.). Thousand Oaks, CA: Sage.

Polkinghorne, D. (1983). *Methodology for the human sciences: Systems of inquiry.* Albany: State University of New York Press.

Rudestam, K., & Newton, R. R. (1992). *Surviving your dissertation.* Thousand Oaks, CA: Sage.

Russell, R. V., & Stage, F. K. (1992). A case for triangulation. In F. Stage et al. (Eds.), *Diverse methods for research and assessment of college students* (pp. 123–138). Alexandria, VA: ACPA Media.

Schwandt, T. A. (1997). *Qualitative inquiry: A dictionary of terms.* Thousand Oaks, CA: Sage.

Scott, D., & Usher, R. (Eds.). (1996). *Understanding educational research.* New York: Routledge.

## Chapter 2

# WHAT IS YOUR RESEARCH APPROACH?

**Kathleen Manning,** *University of Vermont*

**Frances K. Stage,** *New York University*

The researcher's task in choosing a technique through which to answer a research question is one of the most important decisions of a research project. In undertaking this task, the researcher needs to consider the topic, general and subquestions, and the paradigmatic basis upon which he or she bases the methodological choices.

## MATCHING RESEARCH QUESTIONS AND PARADIGMS

When choosing a method with which to conduct the research, the inquirer should consider the goals of the research in the broadest possible terms. Will the researcher seek to refute, confirm, test, or build a theory? Will the findings be interpretations primarily useful at the site in which the research was conducted? Will the researcher generalize the findings across a wide range of populations? Will the study be based on one or several individuals, a group or groups? Will the data be gathered from a random sample? Will purposive sampling be used? Will the results be aggregated across a wide sample? Will the results make sense only when viewed in the original research context? Will the research findings be used across a wider variety of contexts and settings? The answers to these questions can be used to determine the paradigm from which research is conducted.

Over the last 20 years, two major paradigms, the conventional or positivistic and the emergent or constructivist, evolved into the predominant perspectives from which research is conducted. Although additional paradigms are sure to emerge, the criticalist paradigm is gaining currency (Denzin & Lincoln, 2000; Lincoln,

Smart, & Talburt, 2002), this chapter focuses on the conventional and constructivist paradigms. The choice of paradigm, discussed below, dictates the system to be followed to seek answers to the research question. When the researcher chooses his or her paradigm, choices are made about the ontology, epistemology, and methods available (Guba & Lincoln, 1990). These choices affect the scope, findings, focus, data, and results of the research conducted. Table 2.1 depicts several continua at play across various research issues (i.e., scope, findings, focus, data, and results) as the researcher considers the two main research paradigms. As can be seen in the table, the two paradigms serve different purposes, are based on divergent assumptions, and contribute in valuable and unique ways to knowledge regarding educational institutions and individuals. No one research process exists at either extreme of a given continuum. Instead, there are shades of gray and variations across the continua among the various research considerations (quantitative and qualitative).

## The Traditional Research Paradigms

As researchers consider the methodological choices, they must first understand the paradigm into which their thinking falls. The two traditional paradigms discussed within this chapter are the constructivist (also called emergent and postmodern) and the conventional (also called traditional, positivist, and postpositivist).

### Constructivist Paradigm

The constructivist paradigm, a long-established worldview through which research can be conducted, has meaning and understanding as its end goals (Lincoln & Guba, 1985; Manning, 1999). The constructivist paradigm is a highly effective perspective on which to rest research when individual, idiosyncratic meaning and depth are the goals of the effort. The researcher should consider the following questions

### TABLE 2.1
#### Research Issues Within Emergent and Conventional Paradigms

| Research issues | Emergent paradigm | Conventional paradigm |
|---|---|---|
| Scope | In depth | Broad |
| Findings | Interpretive | Generalizable |
| Focus | Individual | Group |
| Data | Idiographic | Aggregate |
| Results | Context dependent | Context independent |

to assess whether the research to be conducted is congruent with the constructivist paradigm: Is the researcher interested in exposing the multiple perspectives within the phenomenon under study? Do the researcher(s) and respondents interact closely? What values are inherent in the research? Does the researcher wish to generate themes (i.e., grounded theory) from the collected data? Will the findings be interpretations inductively generated from the data? (Lincoln & Guba, 1985). If the researcher answers yes to any of these questions, a constructivist approach to a research project is warranted and should be considered.

**Constructivist Paradigm Particulars.**   Researchers employing the constructivist paradigm work with categories and interpretations that are grounded in the data, analyze data through inductive means (i.e., interpretations emerge from the data), and concern themselves with the discovery of meaning. This meaning making can entail the ways of being of individuals within an organization or characteristics and behavior of groups who occupy a particular culture. Assumptions about the nature of reality, inquirer–respondent relationship, purpose of the inquiry, nature of explanation, and the role of values within the constructivist paradigm are discussed next (Guba & Lincoln, 1990; Lincoln & Guba, 1985; Manning, 1999, 2000).

*Nature of Reality.*   Reality, from the point of view of constructivism, is multiple and socially constructed. Due to this phenomenon, inquiry often raises more questions than it answers. With a multitude of realities (and the perspectives that emanate from those multiple realities), prediction and control (the goal of much traditional research) are unlikely. Instead, one is able to build theory "grounded" in the specific context of the research setting. This context is represented in the data (i.e., words, symbols, respondents' interpretations) collected by the researcher. This theory, interpretive and descriptive, aids the researcher and others to understand and/or make meaning of the phenomenon under study. This understanding is limited to the context, or similar contexts, in which the understanding was built. Interpretations to contexts that differ from the original are often a stretch—an inaccurate, erroneous use of the research findings (Guba & Lincoln, 1990; Lincoln & Guba, 1985; Manning, 1999, 2000).

*Inquirer–Respondent Relationship.*   The researcher and participants in the research project affect and influence one another through a process of mutual interaction. Because the subject of the inquiry is a human being, an organization of humans, or other human phenomenon, there is no way to fully and completely isolate the influence of the researcher from the researched. In fact, such isolation is unwanted because it is specifically the human interaction that results in high-quality data, findings, and interpretations (Guba & Lincoln, 1990; Lincoln & Guba, 1985; Manning, 1999, 2000).

*Purpose of Inquiry.* The goal of research from a constructivist point of view is to build a time- and context-dependent body of knowledge that is expressed as interpretations (Guba & Lincoln, 1990; Lincoln & Guba, 1985; Manning, 1999, 2000). In other words, the action studied and resulting interpretations of that action must be viewed within the situation from which it arises. The nature of the human behavior (including the outcome or products of that behavior) warrants the belief that difference is as interesting as similarity.

*Nature of Explanation.* Action is explained and interpreted through the research process in terms of multiple interacting factors, events, and processes. The researcher is not searching for a singular variable or set of variables that causes a result in each and every case or even in nearly every case. Rather, all actions are mutually and simultaneously shaped by other actions and circumstances. In fact, even the tiniest of effects can cascade into significantly large outcomes (e.g., the "butterfly effect"). One cannot possibly find or isolate any "effect" from its "cause." Singular and multiple causes result in singular and multiple effects. The interpretations and descriptions that compose the research findings take this mutual, simultaneous shaping into account (Guba & Lincoln, 1990; Manning, 1999, 2000). The result is a richer account of human action.

*Role of Values.* Inquiry, by the nature of its human component, is value bound and dependent. Values must be considered across a wide context, including the researcher's values, underlying theory, paradigm choice, methodology, and research context. In addition to these individual value-laden contexts, the researcher must consider the overall value-congruence across these research contexts (Guba & Lincoln, 1990; Lincoln & Guba, 1985). Ethical and logistic questions that arise from this value consideration include the types of research that can practically be conducted by particular researchers. For example, what are the value considerations when a White graduate student conducts research on a sample of Black students at a predominantly black campus? What considerations of researcher and respondent need to be taken into account in the research process? Is it ethical to conduct research on a topic or topics about which you are fundamentally and ethically supportive or opposed?

**Weaknesses of the Constructivist Paradigm.** Weaknesses of constructivist approaches include Lincoln's (2002) observation that it may be difficult to separate the researcher's values from what he or she "sees" in a research context. For example, the close researcher–respondent relationship necessitated by the constructivist paradigm can result in researcher advocacy that may conflict with the research purposes. The researcher's advocacy might result in overlooking data not deemed relevant in the data collection process. When these data go unreported, the goals of a rich, meaning-endowed account may be compromised. This "weakness" is also strength in the ways that advocacy can result in research findings more closely aligned with the needs of the respondents.

A second weakness of a constructivist approach is the lack of generalizability of constructivist studies. This characteristic of constructivist research limits the applicability to policy in an expansive context. Although the interpretations and findings may have extensive application to the site under study (or sites very similar to it), constructivist researchers are often queried about the uses of their research. Without generalizability to wider contexts, many are asked the question "So what?" when they discuss or present their research findings.

Constructivist paradigm researchers are concerned about meaning, researcher–respondent rapport, co-construction of the research findings by the researcher and respondents, practical application of research findings, and reciprocity between and among researcher and respondents. Constructivist methods are particularly useful when depth is desired from the research project. Qualitative methods discussed in this book that may be conducted from a constructivist perspective include the ethnographic interview (chapter 3); focus groups (chapter 4); some aspects of nonreactive measures (chapter 5); document analysis (chapter 6); historical methods (chapter 7); visual methods (chapter 8); legal issues (chapter 9); and policy analysis (chapter 11). Constructivist paradigm methodologies that are excellent choices in many research projects although not discussed in this book include naturalist inquiry, life histories, participant observation, field research, phenomenology, case analysis, hermeneutics, symbolic interactionism, action research, and feminist research.

### Conventional Paradigm

The conventional approach to educational research has its basis in scientific approaches to learning about the world. The basic assumption of the paradigm is that data are collected and examined statistically vis-à-vis a theory or hypothesis (Burns, 2000). The researcher should consider the following questions to assess whether the research to be conducted is congruent with the conventional paradigm: Is the phenomenon under study viewed in the context of a singular reality? Is the research based on hypotheses to be supported or unsupported by the research findings? Is the researcher–subject relationship independent, objective, and separate? Will the research findings be based on a priori theory and/or categories? Can the researcher isolate his or her values, the values of the underlying theory and methodology, and those of the subjects from the research context? Answers of yes to even one of these questions indicate a conventional approach to a research project.

**Conventional Paradigm Particulars.** The conventional paradigm is concerned with categories assigned a priori and specified before the analysis of data begins.

Statistical comparisons are made within and across categories. The influence of the variables considered form the basis of analysis. Results are interpreted on the basis of preestablished categories and recommendations. Findings from conventional studies can include changes in practice for relevant populations, policy recommendations, and demographic or attitudinal information about particular groups. Below are the characteristics of the conventional paradigm in terms of the nature of reality, the inquirer–respondent relationship, the purpose of the inquiry, the nature of explanation, and the role of values.

*Nature of Reality.*  Reality is viewed as objective and understandable. The conventional paradigm adheres to the idea that reality can be modeled and explained. Within this paradigm, human commonalities in characteristics and experiences are examined for their influences on human experience and processes.

*Researcher–Respondent Relationship.*  The researcher and subjects are independent, detached, and separate. In an attempt to avoid bias, an objectivist stance is adopted such that the researcher has no influence on the researched (Gall, Borg, & Gall, 1996). Extensive procedures called controls (both physically, as in experiments, or statistically) are employed to methodologically avoid any researcher influence. Controls are also applied to remove the simultaneous influence of many variables to isolate cause and effect (Burns, 2000).

*Purpose of Inquiry.*  The purpose of conventional paradigm research is to illuminate generalizations that are by definition applicable to a wider population than the individuals who are being studied (Gall et al., 1996). These broader statements of practice and theory are aggregated to a larger population. It would be difficult to identify one archetypical person among those researched who exactly fits the theory. Likewise, it is often hard within the larger population to find one person whose experience follows the theory as precisely as written. This one to one correspondence is not the purpose of inquiry. The purpose is to describe a generalized pattern of behavior that helps develop practice and policy for large numbers of people.

*Nature of Explanation.*  In the conventional research paradigm causes are sought for human behaviors and effects are attributed to causes (Gall et al., 1996). Typically, theories or hypotheses are examined within which particular, especially singular, effects traced to specific, clearly differentiable and definable causes are the goal. When causality is found consistently across an array of studies and samples and/or the accumulation of a body of research points to an underlying causality, then practice, policy, and the environment can be shaped in beneficial directions. Practices, therefore, are not anecdotally based but, instead, supported by research that describes that certain actions likely lead to certain results.

*Role of Values.* The conventional paradigm's emphasis on bias, objectivity, and methodological procedures, which support separation and detachment, are underscored by the assumption that research should be value free. The values of the researcher, context, theory, and methodology are to be limited if not eliminated completely. An unbiased and objective point of view is the goal. If this ideal is achieved, results are assumed to apply to a broad population.

**Weaknesses of the Conventional Paradigm.** Similar to the constructivist paradigm, the conventional paradigm contains weaknesses inherent to its assumptions and approaches. Although the scientific method, the mainstay of conventional paradigm research, results in remarkable discoveries (particularly in the sciences), the findings in the human sciences (including education) are less remarkable. Absolute belief in the findings or theories generated through the research is unwarranted. When findings are generalized to a large group of people, the range of what can be said about any one individual or small group of individuals narrows. For example, examining relationships for statistical significance relies on the experiences of the majority of those studied. Individuals in the sample who differ significantly from average (for example, older students, or ethnic minority students on a predominantly White research university campus) are unlikely to find their experiences represented unless the data are collected in a manner that deliberately seeks to represent large numbers of these students.

As postmodernism has risen to the forefront of intellectual thought, few researchers hold absolute belief in the infallibility of their chosen paradigm. The conventional paradigm entails a concern about a priori categories, bias, and deductive analysis (conclusions deduced from theory). It is a highly effective perspective on which to rest research when generalizations and breadth are the goals of the effort.

The conventional methods discussed in this book include aspects of nonreactive measures (chapter 5), secondary analysis of data (chapter 10), aspects of policy analysis (chapter 11), and surveys and questionnaires using local data (chapter 12). Quantitative methodologies that are excellent choices for many research projects, depending on the focus and research questions asked, include quasi-experimental design, survey research, correlational studies, cross-sectional designs, and longitudinal studies.

The researcher is urged to consider his or her choice of paradigm simultaneously with the choice of method. Both paradigms employ overlapping techniques (e.g., interviews, policy analysis, and document analysis can be conducted from either paradigm stance) with vastly different purposes and outcomes. A helpful exercise is for the researcher to examine his or her underlying assumptions (including worldview and the underlying assumptions of the supporting theory) prior to starting a research project. It is hoped that researchers will recognize the values in both approaches. Neither paradigm, conventional or constructivist, can teach us all there is to know about human interaction, learning, and human behavior.

## METHODOLOGICAL CHOICES AND CONSIDERATIONS

As surely as any singular research project cannot satisfy all purposes, different research methods better meet different purposes. Questions to ask when considering research questions and subquestions include: What are the available research method options? What questions cannot be answered by certain methods? What are the strengths and limitations of any research method? How can the method be used to produce optimal research results?

### Method Considerations

Although there is not space in this chapter to review all research methods, several common ones are listed below. Table 2.2 presents a partial list of research methods (right column) matched to research projects represented by particular characteristics (left column). The lists in this table are certainly not all inclusive.

Depending on the assumptions of the research process, the methods in the top half of the table are congruent with the assumptions of the constructivist paradigm. The methods listed in the bottom half of the table, depending on their implementation, are congruent with the conventional paradigm. Several methods listed here are described more completely in the chapters of the book. As suggested throughout this book, similar or nearly identical methods can be used under the auspices of either the constructivist or conventional paradigm. The difference depends on the underlying assumptions of the researcher, use of a priori theory, and data analysis techniques.

## ANSWERING RESEARCH QUESTIONS

In the first chapter, Stage and Manning introduced several vignettes and accompanying research questions. The questions and subquestions posed (see Table 1.1) could possibly be answered through several different research methods. Examples of those different means are offered in Table 2.3. It is important to consider that the methodology selected may answer the question but in a nuanced and different way than for an alternate choice of methodology. It is equally important to realize that some methodological choices will never answer particular research questions.

Obviously, the suggested approaches under Possible Methods represent a few of the myriad possibilities available to answer the research questions posed in the

**TABLE 2.2**
**Characteristics of Research Paradigms and Associated Methods**

| Character of the topic under study | Possible methods |
|---|---|
| Constructivist paradigm interests: | |
| Dense | Case study |
| Deep | Ethnography |
| Detailed | Constructivist |
| Descriptive | Action research |
| Interpretive | Historical |
| Inductive | Philosophical |
| | Feminist research |
| Conventional paradigm interests: | |
| Aggregate | Survey/questionnaire |
| Explanatory | Experiment |
| Broad | Quasi-experiment |
| Generalizable | Correlational study |
| Deductive | Evaluation |
| | Secondary data analysis |

scenarios. The nearly infinite variability in approach to answering research questions supplies the rich literature base of educational research.

## ADVICE TO NEW RESEARCHERS

Although many want to conduct research of the highest quality, research methods can be confusing and complicated. This section offers advice to new researchers, particularly doctoral students, as they embark on their first major research project.

### Matching Research Question and Method

Many beginning and experienced researchers struggle with choosing a method that adequately addresses their research question. The expertise and detailed thought required to make this choice cannot be overemphasized. One often becomes an expert in a particular statistical approach or qualitative method during the dissertation or first major project undertaken. Although graduate-level classes and advanced study in particular methods are crucial, one cannot fully understand the use of ethnographic interviewing, analysis of variance (ANOVA), constant comparative method of analysis, $t$-tests, measures of statistical validity, or content

TABLE 2.3
Possible Research Methods for Vignettes from Chapter 1

| Scenario and topic | Possible methods |
|---|---|
| College of Business Dean and second-semester calculus | *Document or content analysis* of quantitative research texts for mathematical requirements.<br>Random sample the academic records of students who switched from business to perform comparison (anova) with business majors (*nonreactive measures*). |
| Director of Residence Life and increasing incivility | *Legal research* of court cases pertaining to incivility on campus.<br>*Policy analysis* of policies implemented at other campuses. |
| Chemistry professor and web-based chemistry lab | *Experiment* with students randomly selected to take the wet lab class or the web-based class. Compare grades using a *t*-test.<br>*Survey* students to assess the level of satisfaction with wet lab class versus the web-based lab class.<br>Perform a *document or content analysis* of the lab reports written by students to assess quality and quantity of learning that occurred.<br>Conduct a *focus group* with students from each class to determine level of satisfaction and performance. |
| Sociology professor and the experiences of new faculty | *Survey* new faculty using a nationally normed instrument to determine the nature and quality of their experience as new academics.<br>Conduct individual *ethnographic interviews* of new faculty to gain an understanding of their experience as a new academic.<br>Conduct *focus groups* interviews with new faculty.<br>*Observe* the orientation and year-long professional development activities of new faculty. |
| Small liberal arts college faculty and disconnection of commuting and part-time students | Conduct a quality-of-life *survey* of all students and disaggregate the findings by residence life, commuter, and part-time students.<br>*Ethnographically interview* a purposively sampled population of commuting and part-time students.<br>Conduct *focus group* interviews of commuting and part-time students. |
| Director of college transition program and persistence rates | Using *nonreactive measures*, statistically compare the academic records of students who have similar admissions rankings.<br>*Ethnographically interview* students of different races but with similar admissions rankings to understand their campus experience.<br>Conduct *focus groups* of students involved in the transition program to collect data about their decision to stay or potentially leave the institution.<br>By phone, *interview* students who no longer attend the institution to assess their reasons for leaving the institution. |

**TABLE 2.3**
Continued

| Scenario and topic | Possible methods |
| --- | --- |
| Campus admissions officer and geography-targeted admissions policy | Using *institutional records,* statistically compare the racial, class, gender, and socioeconomic status of the first-year class over the last 5 years. Interview (*ethnographic interviews or focus groups*) the admissions staff to determine the implications of the admissions policy change. |

analysis until the first research project is undertaken. As such, no beginning researcher should despair. Instead, one should take advantage of the rich array of resources available concerning methods.

## Consulting Experts

As soon as the research topic is considered, consult with a methodologist, whether quantitatively or qualitatively oriented, about what method(s) will answer the question(s). If the researcher is a doctoral student, he or she is well advised to have a methodological expert on his or her committee. Even without dissertation committee involvement, statistics professors, faculty with expertise in particular methodologies, and doctoral students particularly gifted in certain methods are often readily available for consultation. The details and nuances of research methods warrant this close consultation with someone well versed in those methods. Many a journal manuscript has been rejected on the grounds that the research method employed could not possibly address the research question posed.

## Using the Literature

A second consideration in choosing a method is accessing the literature on that topic. Published studies conducted on similar topics to the research question provide a wealth of information about methods and techniques used to get results and answers to research questions. Although original research is valued and all researchers want to undertake studies based on imaginative ideas, theory in higher education is enriched and expanded through replication of research previously conducted. The experience of researchers in areas similar to or vastly different from the research topic being considered can provide a wealth of expertise and knowledge about possible research choices.

## Developing Expertise

Third, the researcher is strongly advised to develop expertise prior to using a particular method. Although thorough expertise cannot be gained until the doctoral student or new researcher undertakes his or her first independent project, the skills and knowledge necessary to use particular methods must be gained in advance of the study. This is particularly the case with qualitative methods. Few would consider undertaking a statistical study without a class or classes in those methods. However, the interpersonal nature of qualitative research has led some to erroneously assume that these methods, unlike quantitative analysis, can be completed on a learn-as-you-go basis. Although such seat-of-the-pants researchers will most likely complete the research projects, time lost, opportunities missed, and incomplete analysis are often the result. As discussed throughout this book, researchers have an ethical obligation to use the time and resources provided by respondents, research site gatekeepers, dissertation committee members, and others involved in the research in the most effective and fair way possible. This ethical responsibility includes being well versed in the methods employed so surveys do not have to be readministered, results are not rejected due to lack of statistical power, and interviews do not need to be repeated because of errors in the method.

## CONCLUSION

This chapter discussed the considerations one must undertake in choosing a methodology for a research project. The researcher must have a clear research topic and question in advance of any consideration of the chosen methodology. After that step of the research process, methodological choices—including the research paradigm to be used during the study, the specific procedures employed, and the consideration of processes to undertake the study—follow from that original question.

Any researcher should have significant expertise in methodology prior to embarking on a study. The following chapters review of a variety of techniques, an excellent first step to learning the methodologies. The recommended readings at the end of each chapter can provide even more sources of information about those techniques.

## FURTHER READING

For general information about the conventional approach to research, see Gall et al. (1996), Kerlinger and Lee (2000), and Pedhazur (1997). For information on approaches to data collection see Babbie (1990) and Dillman (1999). For theoretical and philosophical foundations to consider in research, see Broido and Manning (2002); Erlandson, Harris, Skipper, and Allen (1993), Bogdan and Biklen (1998), Merriam (1998), and Patton (2002). Manning's (1999) edited collection of case studies provides examples of constructivist inquiry. For discussions of critical approaches to research, see Denzin and Lincoln (2000).

## REFERENCES

Babbie, E. R. (1990). *Survey research methods* (2nd ed.). New York: Wadsworth.

Bogdan, R. C., & Biklen, S. K. (1998). *Qualitative research for education: An introduction to theory and methods* (3rd ed.). Boston: Allyn and Bacon.

Broido, E., & Manning, K. (2002). Philosophical foundations and current theoretical perspectives in qualitative research. *Journal of College Student Development, 43*(4), 434–445.

Burns, R. B. (2000). *Introduction to research methods.* Thousand Oaks, CA: Sage.

Denzin, N. K., & Lincoln, Y. S. (2000). *Handbook of qualitative research.* Thousand Oaks, CA: Sage.

Dillman, D. A. (1999). *Mail and Internet surveys: The tailored design method.* New York: John Wiley & Sons.

Erlandson, D. A., Harris, E. L., Skipper, B. L., & Allen, S. (1993). *Doing naturalistic inquiry: A guide to methods.* Newbury Park, CA: Sage.

Gall, M. C., Borg, W. R., & Gall, J. P. (1996). *Educational research: An introduction* (6th ed). White Plains, NY: Longman.

Guba, E. G., & Lincoln, Y. S. (1990). *Fourth generation evaluation.* Newbury Park, CA: Sage.

Kerlinger, F., & Lee, H. (2000). *Foundations of behavioral research.* New York: Holt, Rinehart and Winston.

Lincoln, Y. (2002, November). *On the nature of qualitative evidence.* Paper presented at the annual meeting of the Association for the Study of Higher Education. Sacramento, CA.

Lincoln, Y., & Guba, E. (1985). *Naturalistic inquiry.* Beverly Hills, CA: Sage.

Lincoln, Y. S., Smart, J., & Talburt, S. (2002, November). *Verifying data.* Symposium conducted at the Association for the Study of Higher Education, Sacramento, CA.

Manning, K. (Ed.). (1999). *Giving voice to critical campus issues: Qualitative research in student affairs.* Latham, MD: University Press of America.

Manning, K. (2000). *Rituals, ceremonies, and cultural meaning in higher education.* Westport, CT: Greenwood Press.

Merriam, S. B. (1998). *Qualitative research and case study applications in education.* San Francisco, CA: Jossey-Bass.

Patton, M. Q. (2002). *Qualitative research and evaluation methods* (3rd ed.). Thousand Oaks, CA: Sage.

Pedhazur, E. J. (1997). *Multiple regression in behavioral research* (3rd ed.). Orlando, FL: Harcourt, Brace.

*Part 2*

# RESPONDENT-BASED
# METHODS

## Chapter 3

# THE ETHNOGRAPHIC INTERVIEW

**Anna M. Ortiz,** *California State University, Long Beach*

Ethnographic interviews give researchers unique insight into the lives and experiences of the individuals most affected by the educational problems and issues under study. Entire qualitative studies have been conducted on the strength of respondent interviews. Clearly, interviewing is one of the most popular research methods, in both the emergent and conventional paradigms. Ethnographic interviews allow the researcher to explore a topic in a way that yields rich data impossible to obtain through surveys, document analysis, or observation.

This chapter discusses the process involved in planning and conducting ethnographic interviews. Steps in the process include decision making about the type of interviews to conduct, the selection of research participants, the design of interview protocols, data analysis, and methods to ensure the trustworthiness of results. Throughout, attention is paid to the diverse setting in which the research may occur and the ways in which the position of the researcher (e.g., administrator, doctoral student, educational researcher) may affect the research process.

## RESEARCH NEEDS AND INTERVIEWING REALITIES

As is evident in this volume, different research questions require varying methods and techniques to answer them. The expense in time and human and financial resources required of ethnographic interviewing necessitates that researchers and administrators interview only when this method most appropriately addresses the research purposes. If research questions involve classical quantitative terminology (e.g., "correlation," "leads to," "relationship with"), then a survey may be more appropriate. If the researcher is interested in what happens in a place on campus, behavior in a classroom, or student organization, than participant observation may be more appropriate. For example, Rhoads's (1994) study of gay and bisexual college men is an example of using participant research to study a student organization.

Questions that seek to discover the meaning individuals make of their experiences are well suited for the interview method. If one suspects that there may be variation in meaning among specific groups of students, faculty, or staff, the ethnographic interview may be the best way to learn about the meaning held by different constituent groups or people. Learning how graduate students experience socialization into academic careers is a question that seeks meaning defined by the individual (Austin, 2002). When thick description of a complex topic is sought, interviews accompanied by ethnographic observation may be most appropriate. Campus climate issues for any constituency group, studied through interviews, have the potential to illuminate nuances and highly important and sensitive information often overlooked through quantitative methods.

Exploratory questions that may not be well researched and that may eventually be answered by other methods (e.g., quantitative survey design) often benefit from initial explorations through interviews. Data from these interviews can then be used to design or select survey instruments. An example of this is a doctoral dissertation study conducted to discover the experiences of underrepresented students in online courses (Mina, 2000). The preliminary data, collected through interviews, may assist administrators to design or acquire a survey instrument.

## Ethnographic Interviewing

Ethnographic interviewing reflects the characteristics of traditional data collection techniques established through early efforts in sociology and anthropology. The subject is studied in situ or "in place." As such, the complexity of behavior and meaning making are closely intertwined within the social systems where individuals interact. Heyl (2001) defined ethnographic interviews as a method where there is an on-going respectful relationship with interviewees characterized by "genuine exchange of views" (p. 369) that elicits the meaning interviewees make of the world around them. Ethnographic interviews must be of sufficient length and duration to nurture the relationship between the researcher and the interviewee so that an understanding of how culture shapes and influences the lives of participants is discovered. Thus the interviewee becomes a coconstructor of the interview and the research itself. In order to achieve these goals, ethnographic interviewers must be acutely aware of the necessity to establish a climate where respectful listening is paramount and where there is an understanding of the role he or she plays in how the interviewee constructs meaning through the research process (Heyl, 2001). Kvale (1996) suggested that all knowledge produced during the interview is in fact a product of the interaction between both research participants. The notion of the interviewee as collaborator in ethnographic interviews continues throughout the research process through the use of data validation techniques such as member checks (Linclon & Guba, 1985) and participant involvement in data analysis.

Because ethnographic interviews uncover the meaning participants make of their experiences, the context in which they live is a central feature of investigation. Researchers seek to gain the perspective of the participant that is informed by social context and the participant's position within that context. Therefore, ethnographic interviews often generate discussions about the influence of race, gender, class, and other sociohistorical forces on the experiences of participants and meaning made of those experiences. With sustained interaction in the social setting, researchers discern themes and patterns that represent collective understandings that include diverse perspectives.

## DESIGNING AND CONDUCTING ETHNOGRAPHIC INTERVIEWS

Prior to conducting ethnographic interviews, the researcher must have access to the setting, the training necessary to conduct the research, and the familiarity and knowledge of the setting and culture under investigation. When the researcher is studying his or her home culture (e.g., a U.S. citizen studying college culture), the familiarity with the setting is often assumed. Most faculty, administrators, doctoral students, and institutional researchers are highly socialized to the culture of higher education and thereby assume that their immersion in the setting makes them knowledgeable of the subcultures or questions they intend to study. This assumed familiarity might be in error, though, as the subtleties of student, faculty, and administrative culture warrant a need to be familiar with specific environments.

In order to undertake a sound research program as well as build rapport with the participants, the researcher must have knowledge about the events, history, and perspectives that shape campus meaning. Frequently visiting and observing the setting before the interview protocol is developed or research participants identified accomplishes this. Through these visits the investigator learns about the context and gains a better understanding of the problem or question being investigated.

## Gaining Access

The researcher will typically need administrative approval for access to participants in addition to human subject permission (see individual procedures at the home institution as well as the institution under study). The manner in which entry is gained is the precursor to the trust and rapport critical to the quality of the interview conducted and data gathered. Researchers should carefully plan how they are introduced to potential respondents.

Campus visits can serve the purpose of building rapport with participants in two ways. First, the researcher can use the visit to convey knowledge and preliminary understanding of the participants' context. Second, observation prior to conducting interviews allows the researcher to become a familiar part of the environment. This may increase participants' willingness to participate in the study. This is especially important when the researcher is studying problems or environments where mistrust of social researchers is a part of the group or individual's sociohistorical experience (Dunbar, Rodriguez, & Parker, 2001). Although this step is often ignored in practice, gaining participants' trust is crucial to yielding high-quality interview data and enhancing authentic data analysis and interpretation.

## Sampling or Selecting Interview Participants

Ethnographic observation assists the researcher to select interview participants who represent a broad spectrum of experiences in the setting. Purposive sampling (Patton, 2002) requires that the researcher identify the method and rationale for selecting individuals prior to the interviews. The rationale behind the sampling enables the researcher to meet the goals of the study and answer the research questions.

One method of purposive sampling is maximum variation sampling where the goal is to interview participants representative of the diversity of the setting (Patton, 2002). For example, the researcher may interview formal and informal campus leaders, as well as individuals from specific populations within the university. Participants whose experiences are clearly divergent from or in stark contrast to the cultural norm are excellent sources of rich data. These represent a second type of purposive sampling, extreme deviant case sampling (Patton, 2002) or negative case sampling (Lincoln & Guba, 1985). The exposure of a diversity of perspectives shows how various stakeholders experience the issue being researched differently. Patton identified other types of purposeful sampling: typical case sampling (selects the "norm" from the environment to study), homogeneous sampling (selects participants from a specific group for in-depth study), critical case sampling (examining one setting that is particularly experienced with the research topic), criterion sampling (selecting participants based on a specific, relevant characteristic), and snowball sampling (identifying participants based on the recommendation of other members of the sample selected).

Other sampling methods used in higher education include recruiting students in lower division social science courses to participate in interview studies and granting extra credit as an incentive (Ortiz & Santos, forthcoming). Participants can be recruited via newspaper ads with compensation as an incentive. Other incentives include discounts or gift certificates to bookstores or local merchants and drawings to "win" a large sum of money, sought-after item (e.g., personal data assistant), or gift certificate. Interview participants may also be recruited through administrative offices on campus. The student affairs staff may recommend students to be interviewed; the provost may assemble faculty members for participation in a particular study.

However the respondents are recruited, the researcher must be careful to sample such that both rich data and a wide variety of perspectives are obtained. Without careful attention to who is being recommended, the provost may only provide the names of faculty who are likely to speak favorably about the issue under investigation. The student affairs staff may provide access to student leaders rather than a full range of student ability and involvement status. Students who self-select to participate may be motivated by their favorable attitudes and experiences with the research topic. Those who are rewarded for their participation may be participating only for the remuneration. During selection of participants the researcher needs to ask, "Whom and what perspectives am I missing by gathering my participants in this way?" By concretely identifying missing perspectives, the researcher should continue to purposively sample for the type of individuals missing. This can be achieved by directly asking a third party or gatekeeper about needed respondents. The researcher can also use snowball sampling (i.e., ask interview participants for his/her recommendations of other respondents). Throughout data analysis and interpretation, the implications of sample selection must constantly be considered. The researcher must constantly question whether the data collected is representative of a wide range of campus experiences and individuals.

Higher education research often requires that the researcher investigate aspects of his or her environment. This is especially the case if the investigation is conducted on one's campus. Therefore, researchers need to develop and maintain equitable interviewing relationships with their participants. In no case should the respondents be made "unduly vulnerable by participating in the interview" (Seidman, 1998, p. 35). Ethical practice requires that the researcher avoid any dual relationships with participants. As such, researchers should not interview acquaintances, employees whom they supervise, or friends. In general, the sample must be large enough to generate rich data, which culminates in results that are deemed trustworthy by the consumers of the research.

## Sample Size

Availability of resources often affects the number of interviews conducted. Methodologically, two constructs help to determine how many interviews are needed in a study. *Sufficiency* is met when the numbers of interviewers reflect the range of experiences in the site. *Saturation* is met when the same information is heard repeatedly throughout the interviews; the researcher is "no longer learning anything new" (Siedman, 1998, p. 48). Kvale (1996) suggested that saturation is typical with no less than 15 interviews. Seidman cautioned to err on the side of more interviews rather than less. Once the researcher leaves the site, it may be difficult, if not impossible, to regain access to gather data discovered to be missing during data analysis. Kvale focused on interview quality rather than quantity and favored fewer well-prepared and well-planned interviews.

The researcher must consider all the factors just outlined in selecting the number of interviews to conduct. A small research sample of in-depth case studies may contribute significant theoretical understanding to emerging issues in higher education, but may achieve little credibility from administrators or policy makers who will use the research to inform policy decisions. Likewise, data derived from large interview studies using brief interviews with little depth may be attractive to administrators and policy makers, but rejected by the higher education research community.

## Creating an Interview Protocol

A carefully constructed protocol can assist the researcher to ask important questions, pose easy to understand questions, or posit probing questions yielding productive data. Once the participant walks out of the interview the researcher never gets that time back, so asking well-considered, thorough questions the first time is critical. The time and resources to conduct interview research leads many methodologists to recommend a minimum of 60 minutes for any interview. This length allows enough time for the researcher and respondent to explore issues in depth. Furthermore, the length takes full advantage of the time and effort it has taken to design the interview, gain access, and arrange the other logistics of the interview.

Interview protocols are best designed to flow from low-risk questions to high-risk questions. The priority during the beginning of the interview (or for the first interview if there are multiple interviews of individual participants) is to build rapport between the participant and the researcher. Part of this relationship building is to communicate the purposes of the research, negotiate the consent form, and discuss other procedural issues. Questions related to rapport, access, and informed consent can be included on the protocol so that they are attended to each time a new respondent is interviewed.

Broad open-ended questions related to the research topic are best asked early in the interview. High-risk questions are asked later in the interview with the assumption that the participant will be more likely to disclose after being familiar with the interviewer. However, if the interviewer never establishes rapport or has difficulty communicating questions and responding to the participant, the order of questions may have little effect on the quality of responses provided. It is important that researchers pilot interview protocols so that they can receive early feedback about the clarity of questions, flow of the questions, and skill of the interviewer.

## Semi-Structured Interviews

For novice researchers, the semistructured interview protocol is most appropriate. In a semistructured interview a series of open-ended questions addressing the research questions are created. These questions encourage the participant to respond with in-depth responses. Asking "how" rather than "why" is another way to enrich what is gained through open-ended interviews. Each question should have an accompanying number of "probes" to assist the participant to answer the question more fully. It is quite possible that the subject will answer all the probes with the first question. This is ideal and may mean that a good initial question was written and that the participant is cooperative and knowledgeable about the research topic. Including probes as a part of the protocol also helps the researcher manage nervousness that might arise early in the research process.

## Unstructured Interviews

Unstructured interviews use more open-ended protocols that require the interviewer to be highly skilled and experienced so that helpful probes and direction can be offered intuitively. This type of interviewing is commonly used in the field, when ethnographic observation is the principal method used. In these cases the researcher takes advantage of unique opportunities for data collection, such as a particular cultural event, political situation, or

peculiar interaction. These spontaneous interviews seldom have a precon-
ceived protocol and are highly specific to the situation. Open-ended protocols can be committed to paper, using "grand tour" questions (Spradley, 1979).
If a written protocol is used, it becomes a road map for the interview with
the questions deviating from the protocol when interesting data and data
streams arise during the interview. If using a more conventional paradigm
style, the same questions should be asked at each interview. If using a more
emergent paradigm style, questions can be asked more intuitively.

## Interviewer Selection and Training

A common assumption is that a researcher can "just do" interviews without
attention to the interviewer's characteristics or without special training. Both
interviewer selection and training have a direct impact on the quality of interview data collected, the initial interpretations the interviewer makes in
the follow-up questions asked, and the field notes recorded. In addition to
the generation of richer data and interpretations, a well-trained interviewer
is less likely to "do harm" through the course of the interview. Kvale (1996)
stressed the importance of interviewer skill: "Interviewing is a craft: It does
not follow content- and context-free rules of method, but rests on the judge-
ments of a qualified researcher" (p. 105).

The positionality of the interviewer in terms of gender, ethnicity, administrative relationship to the participant, and age has the potential to influence the level of disclosure that the participant displays. When possible,
research designers should match interviewer and participant characteristics
to create a situation where, because the interviewer and interviewee are well
suited, rapport can be established easily with a rich array of data resulting.
This is especially critical if the research topic is one where identity and power
differences illuminate unique variations in the experiences of the population. However, Dunbar et al. (2002) reminded us that "the simple common
ground of race provides no guarantee that the . . . respondents will honestly
relate their experiences" (p. 281). Indeed, additional characteristics such as
socioeconomic status and cultural variation may affect the interview process even if the interviewer and participant share the same ethnic background.

In higher education, as in other educational studies, the position or role
the interviewer plays in the environment should be considered and discussed
as part of the rapport setting stage of the interview. This is especially the case
in program evaluation or institutional assessment. If there is an authorita-
tive relationship between the interviewer and participant, the latter may be
less likely to share pertinent information that contrasts with the perceived
expectations of the interviewer.

Although a complete treatment of interviewer training is not possible in this chapter, the research designers should consider three areas of training for interviewers: basic communication skills, skill in using the research protocol, and data gathering techniques.

## Conducting the Interview

The decisions the researcher has made up to this point have a strong impact on the quality of data collected during the interview. In many ways, the actual interview signifies the end of the planning stage and commencement of the data analysis phase. Interpretation and analysis often begins at the moment the exchange between the researcher and participant takes place. This section outlines important features of the interview setting and data recording techniques used during the interview.

### Interview Setting

The setting for the interview is a part of the interview technique. Seidman (1998) recommended that the interviewer establish equality in the interview by conducting the conversation in a neutral, nonthreatening place. Privacy is an important consideration of building trust as well as a requirement of the human subjects review process. The topic under study (e.g., highly sensitive or less sensitive) dictates the amount of privacy needed. Less sensitive topics can be discussed in a wider range of interview locations. Regardless of the subject, it is important that the comfort and wishes of the participant take precedence over the convenience of the interviewer.

### Interviewing Skills

Active listening and intense concentration are the most important interview techniques. Seidman (1998) identified three levels of listening: (a) actively listening to what the participant is saying, (b) listening for what is said beneath the stated words, and (c) listening to how the interview is progressing. Active listening is hard to achieve when the interviewer is concentrating on what question to ask next or attending to logistics of the interview such as the audio equipment or surroundings. Listening to the meaning beneath the words requires that the interviewer attend to the private and public voices being expressed. This approach requires an ear for hearing what is not being said as well as what is being voiced (Seidman, 1998).

The interviewer attends to process by monitoring the energy of the participant, remaining cognizant of the time, identifying probes and other techniques to move the interview forward, and knowing how to redirect the interview if a tangent has diverted its course (Seidman, 1998). To help participants tell their stories, interviewers can borrow basic helping techniques from counseling. Judiciously sharing experiences through self-disclosure can help build rapport and model for participants the kinds of stories to share. Probes and follow-up questions can urge participants to share a deeper understanding and clarification. Interrupting the participant and finishing his or her sentences should be avoided as this can overly guide the interviewee by positively or negatively reinforcing the participant's responses. Silence and leaving time for reflection is an effective active listening tool.

## Human Subjects Issues and Ethics

Standard practice, federal guidelines, and ethical considerations prescribe certain behavior and techniques for qualitative researchers. Informed consent and issues of confidentiality should be carefully planned prior to data collection.

**Informed Consent and Protection of Study Participant.** Each college or university has a human subject review procedure to be followed. All researchers conducting studies, assessment, or evaluation must consult the policies at their institution for specific guidance. At minimum, each interview needs to be prefaced with a conversation with the respondent about informed consent. This human subjects requirement is typically discussed with and granted by the respondent through a consent form that he or she signs. This form becomes a part of the research record. The respondents need to understand that their participation is voluntary, they can refuse to answer any question, they can choose to end the interview at any time, and if they withdraw from the study they can have their data returned.

**Confidentiality and Anonymity.** Most human subject review processes require researchers to delineate how confidentiality is maintained through the project including data storage. Typically, pseudonyms guarantee that names are not used in the research project. Participants can be invited to choose their pseudonyms. As much as possible, participants need to feel assured that negative personal consequences will not result from the research project. When sensitive topics (e.g., student eating disorders, drug or alcohol abuse among faculty) are explored or exposed during the interview, questions asked may invoke unintended responses. The interviewer should therefore have referral information if participants need support or consultation.

**Reciprocity.** Participants need to feel that they are respected members of the research process rather than tools for obtaining data. Researchers can create this impression in a number of ways. Minimally, participants should be thanked for their participation via a letter or card. The final research report (or an executive summary of the same) can be shared with participants.

## Data Collection Techniques and Issues

Audio recording and written field notes are the primary data collection techniques used during interviews. Most researchers use these techniques in tandem, rather than relying on either method exclusively.

**Audio Taping.** Because it is impossible to take notes on everything that transpires during the interview, interviews should be tape-recorded whenever possible. Researchers should exercise caution and never totally rely on tape recorders, which frequently malfunction. Regardless of any use of audio equipment, field notes should be simultaneously taken by hand during the interview. Malfunctions can be partially avoided with the use of high-quality recording equipment. If the interview is tape recorded, respondents need to give permission. Written field notes during and after the interview provide a record and interpretation of the data expressed during the interview. An interview protocol designed with a spacious amount of white space can facilitate note taking during the interview. When the interview is completed (at minimum, within 24 hours of the interview), the interviewer should record, expand, and interpret his or her field notes and recollections of the interview. The interviewer can also record the nonverbal elements of the interview that may not be apparent from the tape recording or subsequent transcription of the interview.

**Data Transcription.** Technology can be used in the interview transcription process. When transcribed verbatim, word-for-word interview transcriptions become the primary documents used in data analysis. Be warned that transcribing is very time-consuming; one hour of interviewing requires four hours of transcription time. Professional transcribers are commonly hired to perform this time-consuming task. Regardless of who does the transcription, the interviewer should insert into the final field notes nonverbal communication, interpretations, and other important data and interpretations that cannot be picked up via the audio recording.

Voice recognition software is an additional way to transcribe interviews. After "training" the software to recognize the researcher's voice, the researcher, in essence, reads the interview to the computer. This method has great potential for reducing the expense of transcription as well as increasing researcher contact with the data.

## DATA ANALYSIS

The goal of analysis is to reduce the data into meaningful constructs that best represent the experiences and understandings of the study participants. This is typically accomplished through the constant comparative method (Lincoln & Guba, 1985). In this method data (e.g., interview transcripts) are unitized (i.e., isolated) into meaningful pieces where one idea, response or concept is captured in the interview. After data are unitized, these meaningful pieces are organized into thematic categories that reflect the emergent themes in the study. This categorization is accomplished by comparing unitized pieces of data to other data already represented in the category (thus, the constant comparison). Decisions about the categorization of unitized data are made on the basis of similarity between the data being evaluated and those already present in the category. The researcher can ask the question, "Does the unitized piece being considered look or feel like other data in the category?" Data that do not fit into an established category are assigned a new category, placed in a miscellaneous category, or remain uncoded in a "dead pile." The miscellaneous category data is reconsidered at the end of the process. Lincoln and Guba (1985) recommended that no more than 5 to 7% of data be left uncoded. Finally, at the end of the unitizing and categorizing process the data and the categories into which they were sorted are reexamined for overlaps within and among the constructs or themes. Piles of data in categories can be combined or placed close together into subcategories if closely related.

Computer software programs are also available to assist with data analysis. These programs facilitate data coding (i.e., labeling) and reduction. Many commercial software products (e.g., Nvivo, Ethnograph) are available, all with varying levels of sophistication and theoretical underpinnings. Researchers should seek the advice of colleagues who use such programs and evaluate which product best suits their needs. Many established qualitative researchers continue to rely on hand-coding methods with assistance from conventional word-processing programs. In fact, first time qualitative researchers are advised to hand code their data in order to gain intense familiarity with the themes and patterns emerging during data analysis.

### Trustworthiness and Authenticity

Several procedures are recommended to enhance the trustworthiness and authenticity of the research process (Ely, Anzul, Friedman, Garner, & Steinmetz, 1991; Lincoln & Guba, 1985; Manning, 1997). First, a written audit trail of all research procedures and decisions (e.g., sample selection, completion of interviews, data analysis, etc.) should be established. Often this is accomplished through a reflexive journal kept by the researcher. Peer debriefing is employed to review or check the data analysis process by a non-participating research peer. This provides feedback to the researchers about the soundness of interpretations made during data analysis. Member checking (i.e., forwarding the transcribed field notes and themes to the respondents) provides another review of the data, themes, and interpretations.

## CONCLUSION

The strength of ethnographic interviewing as a research method lies in its capacity to gain deep understanding of educational problems and issues as experienced by the many constituent groups in higher education. Embarking on ethnographic interview studies requires astute assessment of the context to be studied, training research staff in the art of conducting interviews, and careful attention to authenticity in the data analysis process. It is also important that the protection of human subjects is attended to throughout the research process, including both consent procedures and the minimization of ill effects from dual relationships. All researchers, whether they are administrators, doctoral students, institutional researchers or faculty, can enhance the quality of the work and increase the educational impact of their efforts through the mastery and use of ethnographic interviewing techniques.

## FURTHER READINGS

For general information on conducting ethnographic interviews, see Denzin and Lincoln (2000), Gubrium and Holstein (2002), and Rubin and Rubin (1995). Case studies and/or ethnographies using interview methods include Dilley (2002) on the topic of gay men in the history of higher education, Wallace (2001) on mixed heritage students, Tierney and Bensimon (1996) on faculty promotion and tenure, Arnold (1995) on valedictorians, and Rhoads (1997) on community service.

## REFERENCES

Arnold, K. D. (1995). *Lives of promise: What becomes of high school valedictorians: A four-teen-year study of achievement and life choices.* San Francisco: Jossey-Bass.

Austin, A. E. (2002). Preparing the next generation of faculty: Graduate school as socialization to the academic career. *Journal of Higher Education, 73,* 94–122.

Denzin, N. K., & Lincoln, Y. S. (Eds) (2000). *Handbook of qualitative research*. Thousand Oaks, CA: Sage.

Dilley, P. (2002). *Queer man on campus: A history of non-heterosexual college men, 1945–2000*. New York: Routledge/Falmer.

Dunbar, C., Jr., Rodriquez, D., & Parker, L. (2002). Race, subjectivitiy, and the interview process. In J. F. Gubrium & J. A. Holstein (Eds.), *The handbook of interview research* (pp. 279–298). Thousand Oaks, CA: Sage.

Ely, M., Anzul, M., Friedman, T., Garner, D., & Steinmetz, A. (1991). *Doing qualitative research: Circles within circles*. New York: Falmer Press.

Gubrium, J. F., & Holstein, J. A. (Eds.) (2002). *Handbook of interview research: Context & method*. Thousand Oaks, CA: Sage.

Heyl, B. S. (2001). Ethnographic interviewing. In P. Atkinson, A. Coffey, S. Delamont, J. Lofland, & L. Lofland (Eds.), *Handbook of ethnography* (pp. 369–383). Thousand Oaks, CA: Sage.

Kvale, S. (1996). *InterViews: An introduction to qualitative research interviewing*. Thousand Oaks, CA: Sage.

Lincoln, Y. S., & Guba, G. E. (1985). *Naturalistic inquiry*. Newbury Park, CA: Sage.

Manning, K. (1997). Authenticity techniques in constructivist inquiry. *Qualitative Inquiry, 3*(1), 93–115.

Mina, L. (2000). *Technology in the Classroom: The Experience of Minority Business Students*. Poster presentation at the 27th Annual Meeting of the Association for the Study of Higher Education, Sacramento, CA, November 16–19, 2000.

Ortiz, A. M., & Santos, S. J. (forthcoming). *The ethnic experience of college: Creating diverse campus communities*. Sterling, VA: Stylus.

Patton, M. Q. (2002). *Qualitative research and evaluation methods* (3rd ed.). Thousand Oaks, CA: Sage.

Rhoads, R. A. (1994). *Coming out in college: The struggle for a queer identity*. Westport, CT: Bergin & Garvey.

Rhoads, R. A. (1997). *Community service and higher learning explorations of the caring self*. Albany, NY: State University of New York Press.

Rubin, H. J., & Rubin, I. S. (1995). *Qualitative interviewing: The art of hearing data*. Thousand Oaks, CA: Sage.

Seidman, I. (1998). *Interviewing as qualitative research: A guide for researchers in education and the social sciences*. New York: Teachers College Press.

Spradley, J. P. (1979). *The ethnographic interview*. Orlando, FL: Harcourt Brace Jovanovich.

Tierney, W. G., & Bensimon, E. M. (1996). *Promotion and tenure: Community and socialization in academe*. Albany: State University of New York Press.

Wallace, K. R. (2001). *Relative/outsider: The art and politics of identity among mixed heritage students*. Westport, CT: Ablex.

## Chapter 4

# FOCUS GROUP INTERVIEWS

**Bridget Turner Kelly,** *University of Vermont*

While serving as a committee member at a dissertation oral defense, one of my colleagues asked the doctoral student to defend her use of both focus groups and individual interviews in a qualitative research design. The student began by explaining that focus group data would be collected after the individual interviews to help understand consensus among the participants. When one of the committee members suggested that consensus could be ascertained from analysis of the individual interview data, the student replied that she was conducting a focus group because it was a more convenient and time-efficient way to interview participants. Again the committee member countered that it usually was easier to schedule interviews with individual participants than to schedule a time when all of the participants could meet together. As other committee members pushed the student for the true reason she opted to include focus group data, she replied that focus groups were the only other qualitative method she had heard of in addition to individual interviews. The student reluctantly stated that she chose to conduct focus group interviews because she believed having two methods of data collection would strengthen her research design.

After the somewhat lengthy and awkward exchange, it became clear that the student did not understand the reason to conduct focus group interviews. This chapter is written to address the reasons for and significance of conducting focus group interviews. The audience is practitioners, researchers, and doctoral students studying the college environment.

## FOCUS GROUP INTERVIEWS AND HIGHER EDUCATION

Developed over 30 years ago in business to conduct market analysis, focus group interviews are a relatively recent technique in higher education research

(Vaughn, Schumm, & Sinagub, 1996). Many college practitioners, research-ers, and students may not be as familiar with conducting focus group inter-views as they are with survey methods, questionnaires, qualitative interviews, and other data collection methods. Yet focus group interviews can be par-ticularly useful in a college setting where students naturally form in groups for classes, student organizations, and athletic teams. Thus, students are used to bouncing their ideas off one another and forming opinions based on con-versations with others. Understanding the use of focus group interviews may help us better understand the college environment and all of its members.

This chapter first describes the characteristics of qualitative focus group interviews and techniques associated with conducting them. Second, it ex-plains how focus groups can be used in higher education research. The third section of the chapter identifies the types of research questions that the fo-cus group method can address. In the fourth section are examples of focus groups conducted in higher education studies that illustrate the concepts shared. Finally, this chapter concludes with a list of recommended readings to aid readers who wish to explore the focus group method in greater depth and detail.

## DESCRIPTION OF FOCUS GROUP INTERVIEWS AND TECHNIQUES

Focus group interviews are designed to elicit perceptions, information, atti-tudes and ideas from a group in which each participant possesses experience with the phenomenon under study. The interviewees are often members of a program, class, department, college, or university—in other words, those closest to the phenomenon under study are the most informed people about experience in that setting. Focus group interviews allow a researcher to tease out the strength of participants' beliefs and subtleties about the topic that may be missed in individual interviews (Campbell, 1988). The key in focus group data is capturing participants' ideas and attitudes as they develop through group interaction and exchange.

### Focus Group Dynamics

Focus groups are distinguishable from a one-on-one individual interview in that participants of focus groups have the opportunity to clarify and modify their ideas through discussion and challenge with other participants. Rather than simply having a discussion between an interviewer and interviewee, fo-cus groups often involve disagreement and discussion among participants.

This dynamic creates a great opportunity for the researcher to view the participants' commitment to their views (Weiss, 1998). As Walston and Lissitz (2000) noted, "Focus groups are most useful when all members participate and when members feel free to disagree, so that the full range of experiences and opinions of the group are expressed" (p. 476). One participant may have to defend or provide further explanation for his or her belief because it directly conflicts with another participant's experience. The publicly expressed statement of disagreement, conflict, and conviction allows the researcher to interpret the meaning possessed by the participant. This conviction is not always as clearly expressed in a one-on-one interview setting. When participants publicly defend their responses in the presence of others and within the context of challenges expressed by fellow group members, the researcher witnesses the strength of the convictions held. This dynamic adds to the richness of the data as well as the power and meaning of the study's findings.

### Focus Group Settings and Format

Focus groups are typically face-to-face discussions led by a facilitator and among approximately eight to ten participants around a specific issue or concern (Patton, 2002). The participants usually sit around a table, or in some circular fashion whereby all participants can see each other and the facilitator. The focus group sessions usually begin with introductions by the facilitator who explains what he or she hopes to gain from the session. At this time the facilitator also asks participants to sign a consent form giving the researcher (who is often not the facilitator) permission to record and use the data gathered in the focus group interview. Focus groups are normally audio recorded and then transcribed into verbatim field notes. It is the direct transcripts from the focus group interview that become the data that researchers use to analyze, interpret, and report their findings.

The focus group facilitator typically has four to seven questions prepared for a session of an hour and a half to two hours (Mertens, 1998). The questions follow an interview guide and are structured to allow for follow-up and group-generated questions. The discussion that ensues takes place not only between the facilitator and participants but, more importantly, among the participants as they interact with each other. In this case, notably different from the individual interview, the tacit understanding or meaning of the phenomenon is often contained within the dialogue among participants as opposed to between facilitator and participants. Next is an interview guide used in a study to understand the influence a racial dialogue class had on students' racial views and interactions (Turner, 2001).

## Case Example 1: The Racial Dialogue and Action Project

The Racial Dialogue and Action Project examined the influence of a particular class on students' racial views and interactions. The overarching research question was, "How, if at all, does the Racial Dialogue and Action Project influence students' racial identity development?" Using focus group interviews enabled me to explore the strength of participants' beliefs about the influence of this racial dialogue class, being offered for the first time. Furthermore, this technique allowed me to generate insights about the class experience from the group responses and interaction. Finally, the focus group interview generated different discussion-oriented data than the in-depth individual interviews, which were also conducted.

Focus group data were utilized in conjunction with other data collection methods (e.g., attitude scales, individual in-depth interviews, and document analysis of course writing and journal assignments) to understand if and how a racial dialogue class influenced seven (four African American and three White) female student participants' racial views and interactions. After the initial individual interviews were conducted, the students engaged in a focus group. Each student completed a consent form before we began. The data generated through the two-hour focus group, which I facilitated, helped build understanding about students' convictions concerning their experiences in the class. In addition, questions to ask participants in individual interviews were generated.

**Focus Group Interview Guide for the Racial Dialogue and Action Project.** Interview guides allow researchers to map out questions to yield the richest data possible from the time together with participants. These questions, based on literature about the topic being discussed, are clearly phrased, appropriately sequenced, and explicitly aligned with the study's conceptual framework. Thus, the interview guide ensures that the questions posed will elicit responses that address the study's research questions. The interview guide prepared for the Racial Dialogue and Action Project is given in Table 4.1.

Although focus group interviews follow a structured guide, the group discussion dynamic tends to make the focus group experience more informal than formal. "The goal of focus group interviews is to create a candid, normal conversation that addresses, in depth, the selected topic" (Vaughn et al., 1996, p. 4). In the preceding example, I, as the researcher and facilitator, began the focus group with a situation to set a conversational tone as well as to draw out more than one-word responses from students. My format included probing after each question and improvising during the focus group, which encouraged candid and interactive discussion. These probes, whether planned or improvised, allowed the students to express more detail and to

### TABLE 4.1
#### Interview Guide for the Racial Dialogue and Action Project

#### Mapping Influence on Racial Views

1. Several racial and ethnic incidents have happened on our campus and others since our class. On this campus, our Black SGA president and other Black students were specifically targeted because of their race. They received threatening letters and emails saying they did not belong in leadership positions on campus. The campus police also intercepted anti-Semitic letters targeting Jewish students.
   a. What do you think about these incidents?
   b. Has your thinking changed from how you would have responded before the class? If yes, can you describe the changes? How did they come about? If no, why do you think your views have remained the same?
   c. Anyone else want to add any comments or points of view?
2. We've been engaged in this racial dialogue class for a year.
   a. What has it been like to try and develop meaningful relationships with members of other races? Does anyone have any examples or instances of friendships you've created with someone of a different race after or while you were in class?
   b. What about interracial relationships? Have you felt support? If so, how was it conveyed? Other reactions? How were they conveyed? From whom did you receive these reactions? Family? Other friends? Others?
   c. Anyone else?

#### Accounting for Influence on Racial Views

1. Did you feel safe to express your ideas and experiences in class?
   a. What made you feel safe (unsafe)?
   b. Were there times you felt safe and times you felt unsafe? Why were these feelings evoked? What were the circumstances?
   c. Anything particular about the class make you feel safe? Retreats? How so? Ground rules? How so? Other classmates? How so? Anything else? How so?
   d. Anyone else?
2. Can you describe your best and worst experience with the class?
   a. What made it the best?
   b. What made it the worst?
   c. Anyone else?

provide specific examples. Since participants in focus groups are not required to answer each question posed, when I asked "anyone else?" during the interview their responses tended to be spontaneous and substantial. As such, the focus group more closely resembled a candid conversation than might be the case in a formal interview (Vaughn et al., 1996).

Because I conducted individual interviews after the focus group experience, I followed up on responses students made in the group setting. After transcribing the individual and focus group interviews verbatim, I used the conceptual framework of the study to categorize the document data into themes regarding changes in racial identity development. The themes were used to generate narratives of each student's experiences with race, prior to and upon completion of the class. The findings of the study revealed that the class produced modest changes in students' awareness and knowledge of race, although students' experiences with the class did increase their desire to seek out meaningful relationships with people of other races.

## Facilitator's Knowledge and Role

In the preceding example the researcher and the facilitator were one and the same. I was also the instructor for the Racial Dialogue class. I, as the researcher, examined the influence of a class I was teaching on students. Although there are some limitations in studying one's own class (e.g., researcher closeness to the subject matter, scope), a key strength is the knowledge and experience I had of the both the topic and the student participants. In the preceding interview guide I identified which questions would yield specific data in part by breaking the questions into two parts: (a) mapping influence of the class on students' views and (b) accounting for that influence. In order to obtain the data needed to address the research questions, the facilitator needs to focus on and return to the central research questions throughout the interview. This technique can be incorporated more fluidly when the facilitator knows the participants.

    The facilitator has to be aware of which comments are relevant to the study and which may veer the group into areas unrelated to the study. Often the participants have a limited amount of time for the focus group, and if the group spends too much time talking about topics not germane to the research study, the researcher may need to convene another focus group and collect additional data. The facilitator is responsible for keeping the conversation centered on the phenomenon under study. Although this responsibility is not unique to focus group interviews, it is more difficult in the group setting because there are more people participating than in an individual interview (Carnaghi, 1992).

    The facilitator also has the challenging task of assuring that every participant has ample opportunity to contribute to the conversation. If one member of the group is dominating the discussion or another is not responding, the facilitator must act to redirect the conversation and invite participation from a quiet participant. Facilitators can change the dynamic by turning away from the participant monopolizing the interview; he or she can smile or nod at reluctant participants or in some other way create a means for them to offer their point of view (Walston & Lissitz, 2000). Again, the better the rapport between the facilitator and the participants, the more the focus group interview will be enjoyable for the participants and useful to the researcher.

## STRENGTHS OF FOCUS GROUPS

Focus group interviews can help researchers get different data than they might from an individual interview. As such, the assumption made by the doctoral student discussed in the introduction was partially correct. She chose to conduct focus groups because she believed they are more time efficient. Because all or most of the participants are being interviewed at one time, a significant amount of data often emerges through the interaction of the participants in a focus group interview.

But efficiency alone is an insufficient reason to include focus group interviews in a research design. The strength of the data gathered is the compelling reason to conduct focus group interviews. Rich data can be generated as one participant's reaction to a question draws out another's response. A comment made by one person may jog another's memory about a particular experience shared in the class or through a college program. Rossman and Rallis (1998) described the strength of focus group interviews:

> The interaction among the participants is the critical characteristic of this type of interviewing. This technique assumes that an individual's attitudes and beliefs do not form in a vacuum: People often need to listen to others' opinions and understandings to clarify their own. (p. 135)

## LIMITATIONS OF FOCUS GROUP INTERVIEWING

The strengths of group interaction throughout an interview are matched by the limitations of this data collection technique. Participants can sway each other's opinions, resulting in "group think" (Janis & Mann, 1977). The facilitator may lose the subtleties of individuals' ideas as participants simply nod in agreement or shake their head in disagreement with what others have said. When these instances occur the facilitator has to be vigilant about drawing out specific examples from individuals and following up on participants' nonverbal responses with probes for more detailed responses.

Group interaction may also discourage participants who are reluctant to reveal their experience in front of other participants. This is particularly the case with issues that are traditionally taboo (e.g., racism) or, at the very least, reluctantly discussed in public. Sometimes, "traditional focus groups, like other social interactions, are settings in which many people are reluctant to disclose embarrassing or sensitive information about themselves" (Walston & Lissitz, 2000, p. 459). Participants who are withdrawn and introverted may have difficulty speaking up in the focus group interview setting. This reluctance increases if they believe their comments are being evaluated or are in conflict with others in the group.

Another limitation of focus groups is that one or two participants can dominate the conversation. In face-to-face focus groups, skilled facilitators can usually encourage less active or assertive participants but the facilitators usually need the help of other participants, to create a safe and comfortable environment. If a safe environment is present during the focus group interview, participants can trust the group members, examine their own ideas and feelings, and openly and honestly express their responses (Douvan & Veroff, 1993). A new strategy for addressing this limitation is computer-mediated focus groups whereby all communication between the facilitator and the participants occurs via a computer in real time. Next is an example of a computer-mediated focus group within a college setting.

## Case Example 2: Academic Dishonesty on Campus

A research study on academic dishonesty is used to illustrate the differences between face-to-face focus groups and computer-mediated focus group interviewing (Walston & Lissitz, 2000). The goal of the study on academic dishonesty was to account for "ways that students cheat, their attitudes about cheating, . . . [and] reports of tactics that teachers use that successfully or unsuccessfully discourage cheating" (Walston & Lissitz, 2000, p. 465). The researchers conducted a traditional face-to-face (FTF) focus group as well as a computer-mediated (CM) focus group. The researchers sought to test whether a computer-mediated focus group would encourage students to more freely report higher levels of academic dishonesty than they may be inclined to in a face-to-face setting.

In addition to the focus group data collection method, the researchers had 32 undergraduate students complete a paper-and-pencil questionnaire survey about their past cheating incidents. This survey was administered before the focus groups. For comparison between the focus group methods, two CM focus groups (one with eight members and the other with nine members) and two FTF focus groups (one with seven members and the other with eight members) were conducted. All students were assured that their comments would be kept confidential. To assure this confidentiality, each student chose a pseudonym before the focus groups began.

The CM focus groups took place in a large room with 20 computers arranged in rows. Students sat at computers with an empty computer between them and the facilitator sat at a computer in the front of the room.

Students participating in the FTF focus groups sat around a large table with the facilitator. Upon completion of either the FTF focus group or the CM focus group, students completed two paper-and-pencil questionnaires. One questionnaire asked students about their experience in the focus group and the other asked students to estimate the number of times they participated in a series of academically dishonest behaviors while in college. Based on the questionnaire, all but one student admitted to at least one incident of academically dishonest behavior (Walston & Lissitz, 2000). The transcripts of both focus groups revealed that the undergraduate students did not consider cheating a serious offense. An excerpt from the nine-member CM group illustrates the candid nature with which students discussed their cheating behavior (Figure 4.1). The excerpt reflects the discussion, which occurred in both the CM and FTF focus groups. The researchers note that the focus groups "left the impression that . . . honor codes are not taken very seriously, instructors should anticipate cheating, and to curb it in their classes, they should be very explicit and specific about its consequences" (Walston & Lissitz, 2000, p. 475).

As to the question of whether students would reveal more academic dishonest behavior in the CM focus group as compared to the FTF focus group, Walston and Lissitz found that students who used the computer method were less concerned about what the facilitator would think of them if they gave honest answers. Students reported that they were less likely to withhold information they believed to be embarrassing about themselves. The findings also revealed that of the two CM focus groups, every student provided answers for all of the questions. In contrast, of the two FTF focus groups, at least two members in each of the focus groups made very minimal contributions (Walston & Lissitz, 2000). Additional benefits of the CM focus groups included instantaneous transcripts from the interview, accuracy as to who made each comment, and the ability to participate in a focus group without traveling to the site.

---

Moderator: "Would you report someone that you saw cheating? Why or why not? Under what circumstances?

June: "No, because I've done it before."

Monkey: "No, because I have probably been in the same spot."

Rose: "No, it doesn't really bother me . . . I understand the pressure. But it shouldn't be a habit."

Joplin: "If I really dislike the person maybe . . . but otherwise no."

(Walston & Lissitz, 2000, p. 473)

---

**FIGURE 4.1.** Computer-moderated group transcript excerpt.

Although there are real advantages to utilizing CM focus groups, particularly in an age where college students are computer savvy, one drawback is the lack of group dynamics communicated through nonverbal behavior observed in FTF focus groups. The CM focus group facilitator is unable to observe nonverbal cues from participants or gather a "feel for the group." Researchers exploring issues in the field of higher education will likely need to investigate various focus group methods and make the best decision in the context of their study. Questions about appropriateness of the CM or the FTF method have to be driven by the research questions and how to best gather the data needed to answer those questions.

## Type and Scope of Research Questions Addressed in Focus Groups

Focus group interviews are most effective when the researcher or research community knows very little about the issue or topic being studied (Buttram, 1990). Exploratory or explanatory research questions are best addressed by the focus group interview research method. When a method, program, or class is relatively new, the participants may be the best sources of knowledge (Campbell, 1988). The case example of the Racial Dialogue and Action Project represented a program that was in its first year, and the focus group interview allowed me to gather the participants and discover ways the program worked, how it could be modified, or how it fell short of the desired goals.

Focus group interviews can also effectively interpret unexpected effects of a program or class. For instance, if an English professor discovered from student evaluations that student sessions at the writing center did not help students with their grammar, a focus group interview conducted with these students could reveal why. The professor could also conduct a focus group with the writing center staff to obtain results. "The focus group interview can both unravel fairly complex problems to be pursued through further research procedures and address fairly simple issues" (Vaughn et al., 1996, p. 6). Although the preceding example of the writing center could be relatively simple to examine, a fairly complex problem could involve investigating the reasons for low retention of students or a phenomenon such as binge drinking.

In the following example, I illustrate how focus group data assisted me and another researcher to explore the following research question:

> What academic and social experiences shape the experiences of Black students at a predominately White and a historically Black higher education institution? (Fries-Britt & Turner, 2002).

## Case Example 3: HBU and PWI Campus Contexts

Sharon Fries-Britt and I sought to examine the influence of a particular college environment on successful Black students. In particular, we wanted to understand what contributed to Black college students' success at a predominantly White institution (PWI) and a historically Black university (HBU). Given the extensive literature on the low retention and graduation rates of Black students at PWIs (Bennett & Okinaka, 1990; Wilds, 2000) compared to the relatively high graduation rates of Black students at HBUs (Allen, 1992; Fleming, 1985), we conducted a study of how some Black students who were academically successful were both academically and socially integrated into their college environments (Tinto, 1993).

We believed the students themselves were the most knowledgeable about their experience. Therefore, we utilized the focus group setting to obtain data about academic and social programs as well as experiences that facilitated or blocked their success. We conducted four focus groups, two at the HBU campus and two at the PWI campus. The focus group interviews involved approximately six students each. While one member of the research team took notes and processed group interactions, the other member facilitated the focus group by asking the students open-ended questions, such as:

(a) What challenges have you encountered to your academic and social life on campus?
(b) Has a topic ever come up in class that you felt you couldn't express your opinion on?
(c) How have you connected socially to the campus? And, what do you do when you need academic help? (Fries-Britt & Turner, 2002, p. 318)

The recorded data was transcribed verbatim and analyzed into two emerging themes. The first theme, "Establishing support and campus involvement," captures the academic and social integration of the students at the HBU as compared to the isolation experienced by students at the PWI (Fries-Britt & Turner, 2002, p. 319). The second theme, "The cultivation or diversion of energy," focuses on how Black students' energy is either cultivated or diverted by their interactions on campus (p. 319). These themes are discussed in more detail.

**Establishing Support and Campus Involvement.** One theme evident during the focus groups conducted at the HBU was the close connection and sense of familylike atmosphere that the students exuded in their interactions with each other. Individual interviews may have communicated the degree of closeness the Black students felt with each other at the HBU. However, the focus group setting allowed the researchers to witness the looks of pride, smiles, high-fives and genuineness exhibited as the students responded to comments other participants made. The group interaction indicated the feelings and attitudes expressed in the actual stories of support and involvement the Black students shared. One such student from the HBU stated, "[The HBU] is like a family. In class people are friendlier . . . If you need help the person sitting next to you would help" (Fries-Britt & Turner, 2002, p. 319). Another student commented, "[At this HBU] everybody is working together. You know who you are and where you come from" (p. 320). The research team hand-wrote notes about the nonverbal cues during the focus group in addition to tape recording the comments students made. These signs of meaningful engagement were noticeably absent from the focus group data conducted at the PWI.

**Cultivation or Diversion of Energy.** The findings of strong support and high involvement at the HBU were in stark contrast to the findings of dispersal of energy at the PWI. The students described their energy being taken away from their studies in the classroom and into efforts to combat isolation resulting from the lack of racial and ethnic diversity. One student stated it plainly, "Most of the time I am the only one. All the professors in the American Studies department are White . . . I feel like I am the Black voice" (Fries-Britt & Turner, 2002, p. 326). This student's comment represents the tone of the focus group data from the PWI. The Black students expressed feelings of discomfort at being one of a few Black students in most classes. They also reported feeling as if most of the activities on the PWI campus were primarily geared for White students. Again, the strength of the data came through in the words of the students as well as the atmosphere of the focus group. During the PWI focus group interviews, knowing glances of shared frustration were exchanged. Heads nodded in agreement about different coping strategies used by students to defray the effects of racist comments or situations.

   We used individual and focus group interviews to capture the voices of academically successful Black students at an HBU and a PWI. Nonetheless, the strength of the group interaction showed during the HBU focus group interviews, where we observed a distinct "uplifting" atmosphere and a contrasting "coping" atmosphere we observed during the PWI focus group. Thus, as a data collection method, the focus group interviews helped us more fully understand the varying experiences students described on each campus.

## CONCLUSION

A fuller understanding of whether and how focus group interviews (FTF or CM) enhance research of higher education phenomena must be considered in the context of the research project being undertaken. My hope is that the information provided in this introductory chapter will assist not only doctoral students, such as the one described in the beginning of the chapter, but also anyone with limited understanding and experience with focus group interviews. Focus groups are more than a convenient and time-efficient method to gather data. They are a primary means to gather the rich array of data necessary to answer research questions on complex higher education topics. Through the discussion of focus group techniques with their strengths and limitations as well as the presentation of examples of focus group data, my goal was to enhance interest for students, professors, administrators, and others in using focus group interviews. Along those lines, the next section of this chapter includes a list of recommended readings to provide more information about focus group interviews and to generate ideas for inclusion in your future research designs.

## FURTHER READING

For general information on conducting focus groups, see Bertrand, Brown, and Ward (1992), Carnaghi (1992), Flores (1995), Greenbaum (1993), Lederman (1990), Krueger (1998), and Morgan (1997). Information on a variety of qualitative approaches to research can be obtained from Bogdan and Biklen (1998), Glesne and Peshkin (1992), and Merriam (1998). Guidance on data analysis and interpretation can be obtained in Miles and Huberman (1994). For information on evaluation methods, focus groups, and qualitative research, see Weiss (1998).

## REFERENCES

Allen, W. (1992). The color of success: African-American college student outcomes at predominantly White and historically Black public universities. *Harvard Educational Review, 62*(1), 26–44.

Bennett, C., & Okinaka, A. (1990). Factors related to persistence among Asian, Black, Hispanic, and White undergraduates at a predominantly White university: Comparison between first and fourth year cohorts. *Urban Review, 22*(1), 33–60.

Bertrand, J., Brown, J., & Ward, V. (1992). Techniques for analyzing focus group data. *Evaluation Review, 16*(2), 198–209.

Bogdan, R., & Biklen, S. (1998). *Qualitative research for education: An introduction to theory and methods* (3rd ed.). Boston: Allyn and Bacon.

Buttram, J. (1990). Focus groups: A starting point for needs assessment. *Evaluation Practice, 11*, 202–212.

Campbell, D. (1988). *Methodology and epistemology for social science.* Chicago: University of Chicago Press.

Carnaghi, J. (1992). Focus groups: Teachable and educational moments for all involved. In F. Stage & Associates (Eds.), *Diverse methods for research and assessment of college students.* Alexandria, VA: ACPA Media.

Douvan, E., & Veroff, J. (1993). Social psychology. In D. Schoem, L. Frankel, X. Zuniga, & E. Lewis (Eds.), *Multicultural teaching in the university* (pp. 219–230). Westport, CT: University Prager.

Fleming, J. (1985, November). *Black colleges–The right stuff.* Paper presented at the Black Student Retention in Historically/Traditionally Black Colleges and Universities National Conference, Orlando, FL. (ERIC Document Reproduction Service No. ED 316608).

Flores, J. (1995). Using focus groups in educational research. *Evaluation Review, 19,* 84–101.

Fries-Britt, S., & Turner, B. (2002). Uneven stories: Successful Black collegians at a Black and a White campus. *Review of Higher Education, 25*(3), 315–330.

Glesne, C., & Peshkin, A. (1992). *Becoming qualitative researchers: An introduction.* White Plains, NY: Longman.

Greenbaum, T. (1993). *The handbook for focus group research.* New York: Lexington.

Janis, I., & Mann, L. (1977). *Decision making: A psychological analysis of conflict, choice, and commitment.* New York: Free Press.

Krueger, R. (1998). *Analyzing and reporting focus group results.* Thousand Oaks, CA: Sage.

Lederman, L. (1990). Assessing educational effectiveness: The focus group interview as a technique for data collection. *Communication Education, 38,* 117–127.

Merriam, S. (1998). *Qualitative research and case study applications in education.* San Francisco: Jossey-Bass.

Mertens, D. (1998). *Research methods in education and psychology: Integrating diversity with quantitative and qualitative approaches.* Thousand Oaks, CA: Sage.

Miles, M., & Huberman, A. (1994). *Qualitative data analysis: An expanded sourcebook* (2nd ed.). Thousand Oaks, CA: Sage.

Morgan, D. (1997). *Focus groups as qualitative research.* Thousand Oaks, CA: Sage.

Patton, M. (2002). *Qualitative evaluation and research methods* (3rd ed.). Newbury Park, CA: Sage.

Rossman, G., & Rallis, S. (1998). *Learning in the field: An introduction to qualitative research.* Thousand Oaks, CA: Sage.

Tinto, V. (1993). *Leaving college: Rethinking the causes and cures of student attrition* (2nd ed.). Chicago: University of Chicago.

Turner, B. (2001). *Women's racial identity development: College student perceptions of an antiracism intervention.* Unpublished doctoral dissertation, University of Maryland, College Park.

Vaughn, S., Schumm, J., & Sinagub, J. (1996). *Focus group interviews in education and psychology.* Thousand Oaks, CA: Sage.

Walston, J., & Lissitz, R. (2000). Computer-mediated focus groups. *Evaluation Review, 24*(5), 457–483.

Weiss, C. (1998). *Evaluation methods for studying programs and policies* (2nd ed.). Upper Saddle River, NJ: Prentice Hall.

Wilds, D. (2000). *Minorities in higher education 1999-2000: Seventeenth annual status report.* Washington, DC: American Council on Education.

*Chapter 5*

# UNOBTRUSIVE MEASURES

**Ruth V. Russell and Agnes Kovacs,** *Indiana University*

Colleges and their students and faculty are researched and assessed frequently and extensively. Whether motivated to use college students as a convenience sample, or to understand faculty as a unique group, researchers from numerous disciplines have at least some data from the college setting. Inquiry about students in particular from the psychologist, the sociologist, the economist, the educator, the political scientist, and others converges to provide a rich profile of this population's characteristics, preferences, attitudes, motives, and behaviors that administrators, staff, and faculty in higher education can put to work.

What best predicts a student's decision for a major? What types of information are most persuasive to college choice? Has a new campus policy been successfully implemented? Are students enthusiastic about a change in support services in the residence halls? What role do faculty play in student retention? Answers to these questions may be found in abundance in the research literature of these social science areas, as well as in the assessment files of campus offices.

How have these answers been derived? Questionnaires and interviews are the typical sources for answering questions about those in the college setting; in fact, today the dominant mass of higher education research is based on these sources. By themselves these methods are useful, but what is lamentable is an overdependence upon them. Further, interviews and questionnaires intrude as a foreign element into the normal college setting. That is, most often these measurement strategies, and the motives behind them, are obvious to students and faculty. They run the risk of producing atypical information—of creating as well as measuring attributes. In short, such measurement tools as questionnaires and interviews are reactive.

Reactive measures can set into motion atypical and false responses. For example, a questionnaire that asks college faculty about their attitudes toward international students can inspire, at least long enough to be measured, more positive attitudes than usual simply because the responding faculty are aware of the "desirable" response. This is a source of invalidity brought about by reactivity to the measurement. Such responses may be a better indicator of the success of campus civility initiatives than existing attitudes. Other, less reactive, ways to measure faculty attitudes toward international students might be to count the number of faculty who participate in programs of the campus international student center. Using measures that are not reactive simply means doing some creative thinking about gathering information.

Based on the work of Webb and associates (Webb, Campbell, Schwartz, & Sechrest, 1966; Webb, Campbell, Schwartz, Sechrest, & Grove, 1981; Webb, Campbell, Schwartz, & Sechrest, 2000), alternatives to collecting data on college campuses—ones that are not obvious to students and do not run the risk of yielding invalid information—are available. Webb and the others recommend incorporating unobtrusive measures into inquiry designs in order to avoid the reactivity of the customary measures. Although reactive measures call on students and faculty either to respond to a stimulus presented by the researcher (for instance, a question), or to cooperate with the researcher by carrying on "as usual" while their "natural" behavior is being observed, unobtrusive measures call on the researcher either to find naturally occurring data, to observe unobtrusively, or to create situations in which the students and campus staff are unaware of being parties to research.

For example, in chapter 1 of this book, the situation of a director of residence life was presented. She has spent the last several years dealing with increasing levels of incivility based on race, ethnicity, sexual orientation, and gender. Her goal is to draft a policy on hate speech for residence halls. But, first she wants to understand the extent and nature of this incivility on her campus. There are many ways she can gather this information. She can, of course, ask students about their campus experiences with hate speech, such as through a questionnaire distributed randomly via e-mail. Since asking students directly about this may create responses that are a result of being asked, such as exaggerations or secretiveness, she will also want to add an unobtrusive approach to understanding the existence of hate-speech on campus. For example, she can analyze the hate speech content of bathroom graffiti, or she can study case records involving hate speech from the campus judicial office.

Although the initial reaction by some campus researchers and administrators to adding unobtrusive methods to their inquiries may conjure up images of the classic television series *Candid Camera*, and even though others may declare such approaches a lost art (Page, 2000), the point of this chapter is to demonstrate that these reactions and perspectives are unnecessary.

Using unobtrusive measures is not a difficult approach; in fact, we all collect information nonreactively every day. For example, a favorite illustration of this is a study of radio station listening preferences (Trochim, 2001). Rather than conducting an obtrusive survey or interview about favorite radio stations, the researchers went to local auto dealers and garages and checked all cars that were being serviced to see what station each radio was tuned to.

## THE RATIONALE FOR UNOBTRUSIVE MEASURES

The number of transcripts sent to other undergraduate institutions by the registrar's office may help assess student satisfaction; so might "letters to the editor" in the campus newspaper. The caseloads at the psychological counseling service at the student health center may assist with finding out the timing of stress on campus. Second-hand clothing shop records showing student activity in the selling, but not buying, of clothing could help campus researchers understand periods of financial distress across the year. Library usage rates could add to what is known about students' intellectual curiosity, and technology use could contribute to an understanding of student aptitudes. Used simultaneously with more typical measures of studying college campuses, unobtrusive measurement strategies offer an additional, validating source of information.

No data collection approach is without bias—there is more than one way of knowing. Thus, the reason for using unobtrusive measures is the ability to avoid the same sources of invalidity. Even though unobtrusive measures have their own innate biases, they counterbalance the systematic invalidity characteristics of standard procedures because their bias is different. Adding unobtrusive measures to an assessment or research design increases confidence in those data that may be similar even though they emanate from different measurement methods. Measuring student beliefs about altruism for a dissertation, for example, is more valid if assessed not only by questionnaires and interviews that ask about this belief, but also by nonreactively counting participation in civic and humanitarian student organizations.

Threats to both internal and external validity can be considered as coming from one of three sources: bias associated with the respondent, bias associated with the researcher, and bias derived from the research design. Invalidity that comes from the respondent includes awareness of being tested, role selection, measurement as a change agent, and response sets (Webb et al., 2000). Invalidity derived from the researcher often results from interviewer effects and change in the research instrument. Finally, invalidity from the research design refers to population restrictions, population stability over time, and population stability over areas (Webb et al., 2000).

## Validity Problems Due to the Respondent

Invalidity situations that are due to the respondent, a source of error for many types of measures but minimized by unobtrusive measures, include:

1. Awareness of being tested. Respondents may reply or act in an unusual fashion because there is focus on them. Such a "guinea pig effect" (Selltiz, Jahoda, Deutsch, & Cook, 1959) can result in abnormal behaviors or responses. College students who are studied frequently may become bored and thus lazy in giving responses, or those who are newcomers to serving as research respondents may be self-conscious and give incomplete responses. Observing faculty in their classrooms may mean students are treated to a more (or less!) entertaining session than usual. This source of invalidity may produce inaccuracy, defensivness, or dishonesty in responses.

2. Role selection. Another way in which the respondent's awareness of the research process produces differential reaction involves selecting among many "true" selves or behaviors. Orne (1962) demonstrated that respondents place themselves into false roles as they try to be "good subjects" or "bad subjects." For example, if the researcher asks students how well they like the food in the residence halls, some may give exaggerated negative responses because they perceive it is their proper role as college students to complain about the food.

3. Measurement as change agent. Even if respondents are completely honest and represent true roles, there can still be a reactive effect from the measurement. This threat to validity occurs when the data collection method produces real changes in what is being measured. Also called "pretest sensitization" (Campbell & Stanley, 1963), or the "preamble effect" (Cantril, 1944), attitudes are formed through the process of being measured. For example, college students might score higher on a racial awareness scale if they have previously taken similar scales. They have "learned" from the first testing of the variable.

4. Response sets. A final measurement error due to the respondent, which could be minimized by unobtrusive measures, involves tendencies to respond in a particular way regardless of the question asked. One type of response set, acquiescence, suggests respondents will more frequently agree with a statement than disagree with it. Other response sets include preferences for strongly worded statements or a tendency to use a particular response pattern (such as all third choices). Some college administrators have learned what the media want to hear and developed useful strategies for answering questions in an automatic fashion.

## Validity Problems Due to the Researcher

Sources of potential invalidity in reactive measurement tools due to the researcher include:

5. Interviewer effects. Interviewees respond differentially to visible cues provided by the interviewer, as well as by characteristics of the interviewer. These might include the interviewer's voice tone, eye contact, age, race, ethnicity, gender, physical size, apparent social class, and occupation. Imagine, for example, how a college student might react to an interviewer who is a college administrator as opposed to one who is a classmate.
6. Change in the measurement instrument. When the measuring instrument is an interviewer or a participant observer there are likely changes over time. For example, an interviewer can become more skilled, better able to establish rapport, more expectant of particular responses, or more bored. This might be particularly true if using student interviewers or participant observers who are simultaneously training in research methods and collecting data.

## Validity Problems due to the Research Design

Finally, bias derived from sampling procedures, respondent selection, or population delimitation can result in invalidity that unobtrusive methods can help control.

7. Population restrictions. Even when researchers select a sample that is representative of a population, often they have not randomly selected the population. Populations are selected for inquiry because they are available to be sampled. There is no better example, of course, than the use of college students as respondents by doctoral researchers in many disciplines because they are conveniently accessed.
8. Population stability over time. Just as interviewers change over time, so do the populations studied. Administering a questionnaire over several days, weeks, or even seasons can result in differences in the data collected simply because of changes in respondents due to the passage of time. For example, interviewing students at football games can be impacted by differences in the weather, mid-term exam schedules, and national or international events across the August through November football season.
9. Population stability across areas. Populations may vary from region to region, city to city, or, in the case of college campus inquiry, class to class.

Thus, in a chapter 1 vignette the director of a college transition program for minority students may discover opinions of the program by focus group participants that are specific to those students who were willing to join the group, rather than the opinions of other students who were not, because they are different populations.

Although unobtrusive measures are not free of their own sources of invalidity, they do increase confidence in the validity of the study when they yield similar results as reactive methods. Convergence of findings about a particular phenomenon among alternative assessment methods elevates an inquiry's believability.

## TYPES OF UNOBTRUSIVE MEASURES

How do unobtrusive measures counter the potential for invalidity? They accomplish this because they do not react with the respondents, the researcher, or the research design. There are many ways to measure nonreactively. For example, Webb et al. (2000) presented such tools as natural erosion measures, controlled accretion measures, actuarial records, the mass media, government records, sales records, physical signs, physical location, conversation sampling, and time sampling. For ease of presentation these measures are grouped into the categories of physical traces, archives, and observation.

### Physical Traces

Physical tracing is a study of the physical evidence—those pieces of data not specifically produced for the purpose of a research study. The debris left from a fraternity party provides a trace of what went on; graffiti in campus restrooms offer a clue to student political attitudes or sexual insecurities; and food wastage in the cafeteria adds to our knowledge of menu popularity.

One illustration of the usefulness of physical traces comes from a study of academic misconduct (Pullen, Ortloff, Casey, & Payne, 2000). In this study, discarded cheat sheets were analyzed. The investigators used a cheat sheet to demonstrate an intent to cheat and the possession of disallowed information in testing areas—behaviors that are clearly delineated and condemned in academic misconduct codes. Over the course of several years, crumpled discarded cheat sheets were retrieved from academic building classrooms, hallways, the trash, and outside bushes and walkways. The information extracted from these physical traces included disciplines most frequently represented (business), kinds of information recorded on cheat sheets (facts, concepts, definitions, and formulas), how cheat sheets are constructed (grouped lists—mnemonic devises were rare), and how cheat sheets are concealed and used (concealed in the palm, used more near the end of the term). The investigators also recommended the use of focus groups, interviews, and questionnaires to further explain these findings and to understand the motivations and need for cheating in college courses.

Webb et al. (2000) distinguished between two broad classes of physical traces. First are erosion physical traces, which can be either natural or controlled. And there are accretion physical traces, which can also be either natural or controlled.

*Natural erosion measures* focus on the degree of selective wear on some material. Such a measure could be the wear over time displayed on floor tile in front of various campus exhibits or bulletin boards as an index to each exhibit's popularity. The degree of concern by students about AIDS could be measured by the rate at which informational brochures about the disease need to be replenished in the waiting area at the student health center. Libraries have often measured the utility of different titles by noting the wear on the books, particularly on the corners where the page is turned, but in the sections where there are dirt smudges and fingerprints.

*Controlled erosion physical traces* suggest that the researcher has positioned or adapted the space or material to be better able to pick up the physical trace. For example, floor wax is not applied to the exhibit area floor, or easily destroyed floor mats are placed in front of bulletin boards, to speed the rate at which floor surfaces are worn.

*Natural accretion physical traces* involve the deposit or accumulation of material. For example, counting the number of alcohol containers left in the football stadium after the game could indicate students' level of compliance with the administration's "no containers" policy. The contents of informal bulletin boards throughout campus might add to data about the political tenor of a student body, or the discipline of tutors most often sought by students can reveal weaknesses in teaching or learning in certain disciplines. In addition, the number of newspapers left after class might disclose lack of student involvement or satisfaction with class material or instruction.

Just as with erosion measures, it is sometimes desirable for the researcher to tamper with accretion materials. An example of the use of *controlled accretion physical traces* to evaluate usage of admissions booklets might include inserting a small glue spot on booklet pages, placed close to the binding. These "controlled" brochures are left in the prospective student and family waiting area of the admissions office. After a point in time the brochures are checked to see whether or not the seal is intact for each pair of pages. Or, within the context of the World Wide Web, the number of clicks on links to opportunities on a university web site can also provide traceable information. For example, a student online newspaper may contain links to arts and entertainment events, athletic events, auditions, career development opportunities, forums, lectures and seminars, instructional opportunities, meetings, musical performances, recreational opportunities, religious life, special events, and volunteer options that all can be clicked on, and therefore counted.

Although including physical trace measures in a research design might enthuse the Sherlock Holmes in all of us, there are limitations to their usefulness. First, certain accretion measures vary in their survivability and in their tendency to be deposited. For example, graffiti and paper trash vary in durability. Also, many variables influence the nature of traces left. For instance, the brochures about AIDS may be located in a very public place, thus inhibiting student and faculty willingness to be seen taking or reading them. Another limitation is the scant knowledge available about the persons producing the traces; their anonymity, the very nonreactivity of the measure, prohibits us from knowing anything else about them. What did the students observe most as they stood in front of the student union display case? Were men or women more drawn to the display? What were their reactions? Did the display change an attitude or behavior? These questions can only be answered by more reactive measures, such as interviews and questionnaires. This is why partnerships between reactive and nonreactive data collection measures are recommended.

## Archives

Archives are written records produced for other than research purposes, but that can be used as an unobtrusive measure. Besides the low cost of acquiring even a massive amount of data, one common advantage of archival material is its nonreactivity.

To illustrate, we cite a study on the way students use information technology conducted by Briggs (1997). The study took advantage of the advent of object-oriented technology and the integration of this technology into tools like spreadsheets and databases. The work patterns of 627 students on four class assignments in an introductory business computing course were analyzed. Students had complete control over the length and persistence of their computer supported work sessions on the assignments. The coding of the software made it easy to measure the "when" and "how long" of student work, as well as the correctness of that work. From this, conclusions could be drawn about procrastination, persistence, efficiency, and effectiveness in using technology.

Webb et al. (2000) considered two forms of archives: the running record, and the episodic and private record. *Running records* are the ongoing, continuing, and routine records that are particularly useful for longitudinal studies. Running records tend to be public. Examples include actuarial records (e.g., birth, death, marriage), political and judicial records (e.g., votes, court proceedings), other institutional or governmental records (e.g., city budgets), crime records, mass media archives, and so on. In addition, for college inquiry specifically, examples are admissions figures and faculty salary averages.

*Episodic and private records* tend to be more discontinuous and seldom are in the public domain. Examples include personal documents (e.g., diaries, letters, drawings) and sales records. For college inquiry, examples include class attendance, classroom occupancy, grade, and disciplinary action filed data. The buy-back records of the college bookstore could offer a clue to the value students place on higher education as career preparation.

One archival indicator of faculty patterns of social conservatism could be a charting across years of lecture topics in an introductory sociology class. Others could include analysis of issues discussed in a university-sponsored web chat room as a measure of student quality of life; an assessment of the book titles most frequently checked out at the library as a rough clue of student literary sophistication; parental attendance during summer orientation sessions for new students as a measure of the extent of parental interest and support; and the number, size, and participation rates in formal student organizations that have some specific academic purpose, as compared with clubs that have athletic, entertainment, or social purposes, as indicator of the importance students attach to the life of the mind. Or, class attendance on Monday mornings and Friday afternoons—compared to other days—might reveal something about student propensity to value weekend diversions over academic pursuits.

As suggested by Terenzini (1996), the distribution of courses taken by size and type of instruction (e.g., lecture, seminar, lab, independent study) might reveal the nature of the formal educational process experienced by students. For example, how many opportunities were there for graduating seniors to study in small numbers with a faculty member? Green, Prather, and Sturgeon (1983) used archives to evaluate the performance of college teachers. The indicator was the degree to which teachers developed a following among students, measured by how often students returned to teachers for additional electives courses.

Most colleges and universities are wealthy with archival data, and when used in conjunction with other methods, these data can add to a study's validity. Limitations of archival records, however, can be authenticity, representativeness, and accuracy (Goodwin & Goodwin, 1989).

Authenticity concerns whether the records are real. What is the history of the document? How was it obtained? Was it complete or abridged? Representativeness concerns the record's ability to yield a true likeness of the issue. Such factors as selective recording and selective survival of the records affect their representativeness. For example, letters praising a college or an academic unit are more faithfully filed than are critical letters. Also, how certain statistics are kept can change across time. Finally, the accuracy of archival records is of particular importance. Who prepared the records, using what information sources, and for what purpose? The biases of the author or the perspective of the college could be crucial.

## Observation

A third type of unobtrusive measure, observation, simply refers to watching behavior without the knowledge of those being watched. To be unobtrusive, those being observed must be unaware of the measurement purpose. A variety of mechanical recording devices, such as one-way mirrors, still and video cameras, audio tape recorders, infrared film, radio transmitters, television cameras, bugging devices, and eye or body movement recording devices are available for help in keeping the observation unobtrusive. Two approaches suggested by Webb et al. (2000) are simple observation and contrived observation.

*Simple observation* requires that the observer has no control over the behavior being observed and plays a passive role in the situation. For example, the type, length, fabric, and size of students' clothing could be observed across disciplines to understand different expectations for future occupations. Students might also be better understood by observing library study-group interactions, seating patterns in class, and their alcohol-induced behaviors at sporting events

To illustrate, observational data were gathered from a university cafeteria during lunch for a period of 22 days to determine the frequency with which Black and White cashiers were selected (Page, 1997). The arrangement of the cafeteria was such that once food items were collected and before entering the main eating area, students and campus staff must select a cashier from (usually) three choices during peak lunchtime hours. Distances to each cashier, from food item locations, were approximately equal. Cashiers for the study period were three females; two were White and one was Black. They varied nonsystematically in their location from day to day. The investigator kept a daily record from an observation post partially obscured from view from the cashier area. Notations were made of the number of non-Black customers paying for food at each cashier. A chi-square analysis indicated a significant tendency for patrons to select less frequently a cashier who was Black (Page, 1997).

On the other hand, *contrived observation* involves an active measurer who deliberately varies the setting or uses mechanical devices rather than human observers. Still, these interventions are nonreactive: People do not detect them and the apparent naturalness of the situation is preserved.

To illustrate, and staying with the research question of racial discrimination, a study by Tyson, Schlachter, and Cooper (1988) focused on game playing by South African students. Observing the behaviors of racially mixed game teams, the researchers concluded that both Black and White students cooperated to a greater extent with a Black co-player, revealing an apparent reverse discrimination and paternalistic approach on the part of some of the White players.

Of course, there are limitations to both simple and contrived observation measures. For simple observation these include the chance that much of what is observed may not be relevant. Further, normally only limited random sampling is possible, and populations available for observation fluctuate by time and location (Goodwin & Goodwin, 1989). For contrived observations the cost, size, and obviousness of some recording equipment can be a limitation. Analyzing and reporting results can be difficult and expensive too, if actual photographs, films, or tapes are involved. The most important limitation for contrived observations, however, concerns a host of ethical issues. These are discussed in a later section of this chapter.

## A DEMONSTRATION IN COLLEGE INQUIRY

Unobtrusive measures provide distinct advantages to the researcher. Their primary rationale is that as supplementary measures they ameliorate an over-reliance on any single, or primary, method. As one component of a multimethod approach, unobtrusive methods are especially useful because of their freedom from the same sources of error that threaten reactive methods. In this section, a prototype of a college inquiry demonstrates this rationale and the operationalization of unobtrusive measures.

Suppose we are interested in studying the life of international students on our campus. Because large numbers of international students study in U.S. colleges and universities, and because there is growing concern about alienation and its affect on retention, academic success, and satisfaction with time spent in the United States, this represents an important area of inquiry.

To investigate the level of alienation on our campus, we decide on the following procedure. We randomly select the names of 200 international students from our registrar's list. We mail to them two questionnaires: one that elicits demographic information and another that measures feelings of alienation and levels of social contact.

In the demographic questionnaire we ask about marital status, home country, hometown size, gender, and length of stay in the United States. On the alienation and social contact questionnaire the international students are asked questions about those with whom they generally spend their time outside class and how frequently, social interactions with faculty, and involvement in campus activities, as well as items assessing feelings of powerlessness, meaninglessness, and social estrangement.

Suppose, however, we are worried that students might overstate their frequency of social contacts in order to make their academic work and progress in the United States seem successful. Or perhaps we suspect they may understate their feelings of estrangement to avoid appearing a social failure.

To help counteract these problems, we supplement the questionnaires with unobtrusive methods. Possible options include (1) unobtrusively observing the group makeup of students during randomly chosen time periods in the campus commons, (2) studying the client records from the student counseling center to determine frequency and nature of usage by international students compared to other students, (3) counting the number of international students in non-international-focused campus organizations, and (4) assessing the proportion of international students in campus social clubs made up of members from primarily their own home culture.

In reporting our results and drawing conclusions, the data derived from the unobtrusive methods are treated in the same manner as those from the questionnaires. Suppose, for example, we find from our questionnaires that students from Asia, followed by those from Africa and the Middle East, have higher alienation scores than students from West European countries. We express this result, most likely, by reporting the means and standard deviations, along with the correlational statistics among the various demographic and alienation variables.

Also imagine that by studying the student counseling center records we learn that African and Middle Eastern students are more likely to receive psychological counseling. From studying the composition of noninternational-student-focused campus social clubs we learn that Asian students are least represented. In handling these data, we can use descriptive statistics. For example, we could report the percentages of students utilizing psychological counseling services according to nationality, or the mean number of international students involved in noninternational-focused clubs.

The conclusions for our report likewise should reflect the total data set. That is, we report that Asian students are most likely to experience alienation on our campus and less likely to go to campus-sponsored units for support or help. The point in this is the triangulation of results so that there are multiple confirmations. What do we do when multiple confirmation yields conflicting or inconsistent results? As Webb et al. (2000) explained, "[while] awkward to write up and difficult to publish, such results confirm the gravity of the problem and the risk of false confidence that comes with dependence upon single methods" (p. 5). Contradictory results are explained in the report and usually those findings that have the least amount of extraneous variation are given greater weight in the conclusions. Yet, as Prosser (1964) observed, no one "would not accept dog tracks in the mud against the sworn testimony of a hundred eyewitnesses that no dog had passed by" (p. 216).

This means that in addition to discussing the potential inaccuracies in our questionnaire data due to potential over- or underresponses, we must also report the potential inaccuracies in data derived from our unobtrusive methods. For example, it may not be easy for the unobtrusive observer to properly identify the internationality of student groupings in the campus commons.

## CAUTIONS IN THE USE OF UNOBTRUSTIVE MEASURES

Unobtrusive measurement enables the collection of naturally occurring data about the college environment. In comparison to more overt and direct measuring procedures, the nonreactivity of these methods carries less risk that those studied will react abnormally to measurement. Plainly stated, this means that the study "participants" do not know they are being studied and their permission to be studied is not acquired. This is why these methods reduce the chance of errors stemming from the bias effects of studying cooperative respondents in unnatural situations. Yet because of these advantages of nonreactivity, unobtrusive measurement can raise both validity and ethical concerns of its own.

First, an important concern for using unobtrusive methods is that the data collected might not actually measure the variable of focus. Do Friday afternoon class attendance figures really indicate students are going home for the weekend? Because the researcher remains unobtrusive, respondents cannot be asked about the meaning of the data they provide (Adler & Sedlacek, 1988).

For example, in studying racial discrimination in a college football program (McGehee & Paul, 1984), a simple unobtrusive approach might be to use team records for the racial makeup of the teams. Do any patterns emerge about what positions are played by students of different races? Have Black students ever consistently assumed leadership roles such as quarterback? In concluding that discrimination does exist, there is a risk that the data do not mean this at all. Alternate explanations for the racial makeups of past teams might be that the school has difficulty attracting minority athletes or that no minority quarterbacks were available to be recruited.

Concern with unobtrusive measurement has to do with access to explanatory information. Nonreactive data can thus require more extrapolation and interpretation by the researcher. Data on colleges collected in this manner are rarely complete owing to natural human and social tendencies (for instance, the inconsistencies with which colleges keep records). The solution to these validity concerns, of course, is in the use of unobtrusive methods not as a replacement for other research methods but rather to supplement and cross-validate them.

Ethical considerations are also of concern in the use of unobtrusive measures. Are privacy and the right to informed consent violated when students and campus staff are not aware of the data collected about them? This is a tough call because researchers are on one hand properly reluctant to make surreptitious observations, and on the other hand worried about the fidelity of information collected otherwise. There are several defenses to such ethical concerns, however.

First, while it might be desirable to collect information in ways other than nonreactively, some information is simply not available any other way (Page, 2000). By definition, the value of nonreactively obtained data derives from the very conditions of unobtrusive measurement. Compliance with dry campus regulations may not be available from students in ways other than checking the physical traces of alcohol containers left at campus facilities, studying campus police records for illegal consumption charges, or observing student behavior at campus gatherings.

A second defense of ethical concerns is that perhaps it is time to recognize that the doctrine of informed consent has been asked to play too great a role in some research situations (Page, 2000). In many instances, protection of participants' rights may be applied to such an extent that much research could not even be undertaken. Some go so far as to suggest that as long as the individuals remain unidentified and the information being collected is of minor importance relative to privacy, informed consent is not necessary (Atwell, 1982). Such questions of the appropriate use of informed consent can be the responsibility of thoughtful and accountable review boards and other scientific community expert panels.

A final defense is that unobtrusive methods vary in their degree of ethical concern, and may at times be criticized more because of their stereotype than because of any inherent ethical transgression (Page, 2000). The broader need for validity must be weighed against the ethical inelegance of, say, a telephone call to a landlord with a realistic though nongenuine request for student rental policy information. The call does not harm, embarrass, or otherwise disadvantage the person called.

Webb et al. (1981) concluded that the right to privacy falls on a continuum, from observing public behavior of public figures to spying on private behavior in private places. It was clear to them that one extreme in the continuum is not an invasion of privacy and the other extreme is. The middle of the continuum, of course, provokes the most controversy. A key question for Webb and associates (2000) was whether the people being observed clearly expected that their behavior would be unregarded. For example, observations in public campus restrooms might be considered an invasion of privacy because students and faculty enter such restrooms with the expectation "that their behavior will be studiously ignored" even though they are in "public" places (p. 147).

A case in point about the ethical considerations of unobtrusive measurement comes from a study by Willner, Hart, Binmore, Cavendish, and Dunphy (2000). Working with youth, these researchers faced complex ethical considerations in their direct observation of alcohol sales to adolescents. The study assessed the ease with which adolescents in the United Kingdom were able to buy alcohol. In two urban locations, pairs of 13- and 16-year-old boys and girls were trained to attempt the purchase of alcohol from retail outlets.

The study showed that alcohol was readily available to underage users, an important finding, but the study also presented a number of interesting ethical issues that required consideration. First, the nature of the study made it impossible to implement the usual benefits extended to research participants. For example, the observed vendors did not provide informed consent, they could not withdraw from participation, and they were rarely debriefed. These conditions, as well as the element of deception, were justified during ethical review of the project by reason that the procedures were essential to achieving project aims, and even necessary for protection of the adolescents. The authors also argued that the expected benefits from the study outweighed the potential risks. For the vendors, the collected data were held in strict confidence.

Considering the involvement of young people in this study, strict safeguards were imposed to ensure their physical and moral safety. First, parents were involved at every stage of the research, and their consent and active cooperation were important in order to (1) ensure that the teens selected were of good character and were not driven to participate by financial hardship or antisocial tendencies, (2) monitor and assure their well-being during test purchase sessions, and (3) provide an additional source of longer term monitoring and support. Second, although some might argue minors were taught skills that they might subsequently use to purchase alcohol outside the framework of the study, the careful screening in selecting teens of high moral character, the extensive training provided for them, and the debriefing to discourage any such illegal activity were employed to prevent participants' alcohol purchase in the near future.

Finally, the researchers were concerned about possible adverse effects of participation on the teens' mental health. The researchers attempted to minimize emotional distress by empowering the adolescent confederates to control their part in the research: (1) They chose which days and times they wished to work; (2) at every venue, they were asked if they were happy to enter the premises, and if they were not comfortable the purchase attempt did not take place; (3) those who chose to enter the shop understood that they could abort a purchase attempt at any time and for any reason; and (4) after every purchase attempt they were debriefed and asked if they wished to continue, with the session terminating if they did not. In all this, the usefulness of an internal review board is considerable in determining ethicality.

## CONCLUSION

The case for unobtrusive measures in college inquiry is strong. As stated by Brown (1986), it is important for those conducting research on college campuses to continue to expand their research efforts. Unobtrusive measures can have a useful confirmatory role in this expansion.

A revival of these measures would enable college and university research to move beyond its dependence on reactive data. The advantage is perhaps findings of real significance and generalizability to real-life situations. Further, using some form of nonreactive measures has the potential to generate results that are striking and counterintuitive, resulting in hypotheses that run counter to common knowledge and thus have unique value. As Mahoney (1978) pointed out, findings consistent with a theory cannot prove its truth value, but findings inconsistent with a theory are much more useful since they can and do bear logically on its validity.

So, after you have scored the questionnaires, and transcribed the interviews, get out of the office and on to the campus and see what is really going on!

## FURTHER READING

To learn more about how to use unobtrusive data collection measures see Webb, Campbell, Schwartz, and Sechrest (2000). For examples of college inquiry using unobtrusive methods see Page (1997) and Pullen, Ortloff, Casey, and Payne (2000).

## REFERENCES

Adler, R. M., & Sedlacek, W. E. (1988). Nonreactive measures in student affairs research. *Journal of College Student Development, 29,* 158–162.

Atwell, J. (1982). Human rights in human subjects research. In A. Kimmel (Ed.), *Ethics of human subject research*. San Francisco, CA: Jossey-Bass.

Briggs, C. M. (1997). *Understanding the way students work: Unobtrusive measures and the effect of effort on performance*. <http://hsb.baylor.edu/ramsover/ais.ac.97/papers/briggs2.htm> (9/10/01).

Brown, R. (1986). Research: A frill or an obligation? *Journal of College Student Personnel, 27*, 195.

Campbell, D. T., & Stanley, J. S. (1963). *Experimental and quasi-experimental designs for research*. Skokie, IL: Rand McNally.

Cantril, H. (1944). *Gauging public opinion*. Princeton, NJ: Princeton University Press.

Goodwin, W. L., & Goodwin, L. D. (1989). The use of nonreactive measures with preschoolers. *Early Child Development and Care, 41*, 173–194.

Green, J. E., Prather, J. E., & Sturgeon, J. (1983). *Using administrative data as unobtrusive indicators of teaching performance*. Paper presented at the Annual Forum of the Association of Institutional Research, Toronto, Ontario.

Mahoney, M. (1978). Evaluation of experimental outcomes in psychology. *Journal of Consulting and Clinical Psychology, 46*, 660–672.

McGehee, R., & Paul, M. (1984). *Racial make-up of central stacking and other playing positions in southeastern Conference football teams, 1967-1983*. Paper presented at the Conference on Sport and Society, Clemson University, Clemson, SC.

Orne, M. T. (1962). On the social psychology of the experiment: With particular reference to demand characteristics and their implications. *American Psychologist, 17*, 776–783.

Page, S. (1997). An unobtrusive measure of racial behavior in a university cafeteria. *Journal of Applied Social Psychology, 27*(24), 2172–2176.

Page, S. (2000). Community research: The lost art of unobtrusive methods. *Journal of Applied Social Psychology, 30*(10), 2126–2136.

Prosser, W. L. (1964). *Handbook of the law of torts*. St. Paul, MN: West.

Pullen, R., Ortloff, V., Casey, S., & Payne, J. B. (2000). Analysis of academic misconduct using unobtrusive research: A study of discarded cheat sheets. *College Student Journal, 34*(4), 616.

Selltiz, C., Jahoda, M., Deutsch, M., & Cook, S. W. (1959). *Research methods in social relations*. New York: Holt, Rinehart & Winston.

Terenzini, P. T. (1996). The case for unobtrusive measures. In J. Stark & A. Thomas (Eds.), *Assessment and program evaluation*, ASME Reader Series. Boston: Simon and Schuster Custom Publishing.

Trochim, W. M. K. (2001). *Unobtrusive measures*. <http://trochim.human.cornell.edu/kb/unobtrus.htm> (9/10/01).

Tyson, G. A., Schlachter, A., & Cooper, S. (1988). Game playing strategy as an indicator of racial prejudice among South African students. *Journal of Social Psychology, 128*, 473-485.

Webb, E. K., Campbell, D. T., Schwartz, R. D., & Sechrest, L. (1966). *Unobtrusive measures: Nonreactive research in the social sciences*. Chicago: Rand McNally.

Webb, E. K., Campbell, D. T., Schwartz, R. D., Sechrest, L., & Grove, J. B. (1981). *Nonreactive measures in the social sciences*. Boston: Houghton Mifflin.

Webb, E. J., Campbell, D. T., Schwartz, R. D. & Sechrest, L. (2000). *Unobtrusive measures*. Thousand Oaks, CA: Sage.

Willner, P., Hart, K., Binmore, J., Cavendish, M., & Dunphy, E. (2000). Alcohol sales to underage adolescents: An unobtrusive observational field study and evaluation of a police intervention. *Addiction, 95*(4), 1373–1388.

*Part 3*

# DOCUMENT-BASED
# METHODS

## Chapter 6
# DOCUMENT ANALYSIS

**Patrick Love,** *New York University*

Newspapers, maps, menus, bills, and billboards, numerous documents swirl about us. Flyers, magazines, instructions, postcards, and contracts are no longer merely methods of communication or documentation; documents are part of the fabric of our world. The quantity and pervasiveness of documents in society have grown throughout history. The development of writing instruments and paper caused one surge in the number of documents being produced, the printing press another. During the past century, the advent of radio, television, video, compact disks, and cyberspace has extended and enlarged the definition of document. However, despite predictions about the demise of the printed word, advances in recording, production, printing, reproduction, storage, and retrieval capabilities have provoked an exponential growth in both the number of written documents and the pervasiveness of the role of documents in the functioning of everyday life.

The same can be said for work in higher education and with college students. Memos, e-mail, manuals, flyers, handbooks, web sites, evaluations, incident reports, annual reports, accreditation reports . . . documents are a way of institutional life. Lincoln and Guba (1985) argued that there is hardly an activity in modern life that does not leave some documentary trail. Qualitative research is often a process of sorting, categorizing, and synthesizing multiple and conflicting voices, and differing and interacting interpretations (Hodder, 1998). In such an endeavor, documents provide an important avenue of voice, interpretation, and meaning. Therefore, when conducting qualitative research in a collegiate environment with the goal of understanding something about student, faculty, academic, or administrative life, failure to include document analysis may indeed be leaving a gap in the ability to fully understand the issue or question at hand. Yet, as Silverman (2001) pointed out, interview data is often privileged over written documents (i.e., when in conflict, something someone says almost always refutes what has been written). Another way in which documents differ from interviews is that in most cases they were not produced in response to research questions (Merriam, 1998). Except for historical research, a study of some aspect of higher education based solely on documents is rare. Instead, document analysis is most often used to enhance and enrich research utilizing other qualitative methods. Document analysis can both triangulate and point out discrepancies in data being collected in alternate ways, suggest questions for participants or additional participants, and identify analytical categories.

This chapter addresses a variety of the elements of document analysis. It begins by providing examples and identifying types of documents available for the researcher. It reviews the strengths and limitations of such an analysis. It explains how to incorporate document analysis into a research study through the methods of collecting, cataloging, contextualizing, and assessing authenticity, and finishes with the analytical procedures of categorizing, coding, and content analysis.

## EXAMPLES AND TYPES OF DOCUMENTS

Although document analysis can be conducted on photographs, physical traces, video, and cultural artifacts, the focus of this chapter is on written or printed documents. The lists here identify examples of documents related to higher education and aspects of student and administrative environments. These lists are representative, not exhaustive.

1. *General*: listserv, e-mail, Usenet groups, or chat-room archives; flyers and other public postings; web sites; correspondence; files; telephone call logs; organizational charts; rosters.
2. *Student*: student newspapers, student handbook, incident reports, judicial records, class papers and journals, portfolios, student information systems, survey or census data.
3. *Student organization*: agendas, meeting minutes, policy and procedure manuals, strategic planning documents, budgets and financial records, proposals, progress reports.
4. *Academic*: faculty handbook, academic calendar, course catalog, course schedule, faculty vitae, class rosters, program worksheets, administrative forms, application forms, academic procedures manual, accreditation self-study reports, faculty newsletters, course syllabi.

5. *Administration*: meeting agendas, annual reports, mission and value statements, evaluations, accreditation reports, brochures, press releases, institutional newsletters, policy and procedure manuals, training materials, strategic planning documents, financial records, memos, correspondence, staff journals (e.g., by resident assistants), progress reports, directories, personnel records, interim reports, working papers, document drafts, contracts.

These documents can be sorted into various categories. In fact, one of the steps of document analysis (described later) is categorization. Categories vary depending on the focus of the research; however, there are some general categories into which documents can be sorted. The first is differentiating between records, general documents, and personal documents. Lincoln and Guba (1985) argued that a *record* is any formal statement prepared by or for an individual or organization for the purpose of attesting to an event or providing an accounting. Budget and financial records, manuals and handbooks, contracts, and annual reports fall into this category. Public records often form the paper trail linking events and decisions. Documents, according to Lincoln and Guba, are any written or recorded material that was not prepared specifically in response to a request from an inquirer or for some official accounting. For the purpose of this classification, they are referred to as *general documents*. These include such examples as newspapers, newsletters, training materials, and strategic planning documents. Merriam (1998) further refined the definition of document to the notion of *personal documents*, those that provide some indication of the inner thought process of the individual. Personal documents are also dependable sources for participants' attitudes, beliefs, and views of the world. They provide the participant's perspective and include journals, letters, e-mail, and class papers. The boundaries between and among these particular categories are not always clear. For example, an incident report written by a resident assistant about a policy violation or some type of disturbance is a formal, public record. However, it may also be a personal document if it is written in such a way as to reflect the thought processes of the staff member and provide some indication about the individual's beliefs about the incident.

## STRENGTHS AND LIMITATIONS

Although documents are pervasive on college campuses and can assist in enriching virtually any research conducted on higher education related issues, any document analysis must be conducted recognizing both the strengths and the limitations involved.

## Strengths of Document Analysis

Lincoln and Guba (1985) pointed out that among their strengths, documents are typically available, usually of low cost (especially important for dissertation research), and stable—that is, they can be reviewed repeatedly without physically changing. Documents are a rich source of information, contextually relevant, and grounded in the contexts they represent. Their richness includes the fact that general and personal documents appear in the natural language of that setting and therefore can often provide the vocabulary or rules of grammar of a cultural scene or community. Understanding the language of a particular cultural scene is especially important when studying the distinct subcultures that cohabitate on a college campus, such as those of college students and faculty.

Documents provide the researcher with information about things that cannot otherwise be observed or about which the researcher was unaware (Patton, 2002). They may uncover events that took place before the research began and have endured across time, and documents can encapsulate long periods of time, many events, and many settings (Merriam, 1998; Yin, 1994). Personal documents may include private exchanges between organizational actors or behind-the-scenes information to which the researcher would not otherwise be privy (Patton, 2002).

Documents are unobtrusive data (Merriam, 1998; Yin, 1994), and another advantage is that, especially in the case of formal records, they tend to be precise, containing names, references, and details of an event or policy (Yin, 1994). Finally, documents can suggest a particular focus to research-related observations, serve to stimulate interview questions, and assist in triangulating or problematizing other data being collected.

## Limitations of Document Analysis

The most significant drawback to documents as a source of data is that they are noninteractive and nonreactive; that is, where meanings can be immediately checked with an interview participant, documents remain silent. This results in a situation where documents sometimes cannot be checked for accuracy (e.g., through triangulation), analytic interpretations are often not open to rebuttal, and there is usually no opportunity to gain an emic (insider) perspective on the document (Hodder, 1998). So although texts and documents can be "interrogated," "deconstructed," and analyzed, often they have been disconnected from their creation so it is not possible to explore original meanings and intent with absolute confidence. Even if there are participants who can be asked about original intent of a particular report or document, they are in actuality producing another meaning constructed at a different time and from a different perspective (Hodder, 1998).

Other limitations of documents are that they are possibly unrepresentative, lacking in objectivity, of unknown validity, and possibly either deliberately deceiving or self-deceptive (Lincoln & Guba, 1985). Documents also privilege certain preserved viewpoints over those not preserved. For example, a review of documents of a critical incident on a college campus often preserves the administration's points of view, perceptions, and interpretations, but not those of the students. This is but one example of biased selectivity. Yin (1994) pointed out that retrievability can be low or access may be deliberately blocked. In the case of formal records this may be due to concerns about privacy, confidentiality, and anonymity (Hodder, 1998), such as in the case of judicial or counseling records. There are also the issues of incomplete collections of documents and any unknown bias of the author of a particular document. There may also be cases where determining the authenticity and accuracy of the document is difficult (Merriam, 1998). In using documents as a part of a process of inquiry, researchers need to keep in mind that no document is a literal recording of an event (Yin, 1994).

## INCORPORATING DOCUMENT ANALYSIS INTO THE RESEARCH PROCESS

Just as interviews and observations must be planned for and scheduled, time needs to be allotted for the search, collection, and cataloguing of appropriate documents. Creating a system of organization that allows for quick retrieval of needed documents is imperative. Additionally, prior to conducting formal analysis on a document, the context in which the document was created needs to be determined and the authenticity of the document needs to be assessed. Actually, none of the steps identified in this section or in the analysis section that follows are discrete procedures. In fact, it can be argued that document analysis actually begins with the processes of cataloging, determining the document's context, and assessing its authenticity, because judgments and assessments are being made related to the document. However, the particular steps in this section have been separated from analysis because these are the steps typically taken prior to addressing the specific questions of interest in the research process. In processes described in this section the documents are treated as entities still somewhat separate from the analysis process.

### Collecting Documents

Data collection, be it by interview, observation, or document analysis, is guided by questions, educated hunches, and emerging findings (Merriam, 1998). Therefore, a preliminary list of potential documents should be compiled to assist in the search for documents related to the research in question. This search should be systematic but also open to serendipitous discoveries (Yin, 1994). For example, if one's dissertation is focused on faculty socialization, a preliminary list of potential documents compiled before speaking to anyone could include faculty vitae, the institution's faculty handbook, and any faculty orientation agenda and materials. Also, a list of individuals to ask about the existence of other related documents can be compiled. Typically, the researcher will ask participants for documents related to the research in question. However, additional methods to consider for a thorough search include exploring the setting itself for unanticipated documents, asking individuals related to the scene but not participating in the research, advertising among alumni and other constituents, placing ads in newspapers and newsletters, and searching institutional files and archives (Merriam, 1998).

Given the pervasive and abundant nature of documents in society in general and in higher education especially, the question may well arise as to how many documents is enough or how many becomes too much. There is no clear answer to the question. It is suggested that at least two sampling techniques be employed. The first is purposive sampling, which means identifying any documents that make conceptual sense for including in the study. In a study of organizational planning and transformation, all documents related to formal planning processes should be included in the analysis. The other strategy is to analyze documents until the point of data or analytical saturation. For example, in a study of student affairs discourse (Love & Yousey, 2001) a research team sampled texts from a particular time period and analyzed texts until no new analytical categories emerged. A deeper analysis of documents, such as conducting a content analysis versus merely categorizing the documents, will result in fewer documents being utilized in the analysis.

## Cataloguing

Cataloguing documents is done when they are collected so that they can be easily retrieved. Cataloguing involves assigning a unique alpha or numeric code to the document that can be used to track the document, its contents, and any analytic statements associated with it throughout the research process. Miles and Huberman (1994) also suggest that part of the process of cataloguing should include creating a document form that indicates the source of the document, the date acquired, from whom and where the document was acquired, the name of the document, any event or contact associated with document, a note about the significance or importance of document, and a brief summary of contents. Some of these items overlap with those suggested for determining the context of the document.

## Determining Context

The researcher needs to ask many different questions of the documents related to the research problem; therefore, the particular context of any document needs to be ascertained to the greatest extent possible (Merriam, 1998). To that end, it is important to determine as much as possible about the document, including its origins and reasons for being written, its author, its intended audience, the influences and conditions under which it was produced, and the temporal, political, historical, and economic contexts in which it was written (Merriam, 1998; Yin, 1994). Fully understanding the context of a particular document may involve searching for additional documents or gathering this information from the participants of the study.

## Assessing Authenticity

The authenticity of any discovered documents must also be assessed (Merriam, 1998), and the first step of determining the degree of authenticity of a document is to identify the context in which it was created. The more information collected, the greater is the confidence in the contents of the document. Once the context has been established, the researcher needs to consider the following questions (adapted from Clark, 1967):

> How did the document come into the possession of the researcher?
> What guarantee is there that it is what it appears to be?
> Has it been tampered with or edited?
> Is it an original or is it a reproduction?
> What were the author's sources of information?
> What author biases might have influenced the creation of the document?
> To what extent was the author likely to want to tell the truth?
> What documents or other evidence might exist to corroborate assertions of fact on the part of the author?

Once documents have been collected, catalogued, contextualized, and assessed for degree of authenticity, more in-depth analytic procedures can be undertaken.

## ANALYTIC PROCEDURES

Although the previous steps represent important aspects of analysis, this section presents techniques that engage in deeper forms of analysis. Again, any analysis of documents is done in conjunction with the overarching study in question. The focus of the study drives the search and collection of documents, but the analysis of collected documents will also create additional interview questions, indicate events to be observed, and suggest other documents to be secured. The steps of analysis discussed in this section are those of categorizing, coding, and content analysis.

### Categorizing

Although similar in focus to the processes of cataloguing and determining context, this process identifies a priori analytic categories. These categories may be used later in the process of analysis to sort documents as a way of searching for different patterns among the categories. Perhaps the most important category is whether the document is a primary document or a secondary document. Primary documents are those where the author of the document is recounting firsthand experience with the phenomenon of interest (Merriam, 1998). These include student organization minutes, student or staff journals, incident reports, course syllabi, and listserv or e-mail archives. Secondary documents are reports of a phenomenon by those who have not directly experienced it. Examples of secondary documents can include (depending on the relationship of the author to the event in question) newspaper or newsletter articles, annual reports, and press releases. Other dichotomous a priori categories can include whether the document was solicited or unsolicited, comprehensive or limited, edited or unedited, anonymous or signed, spontaneous or intentional (Lincoln & Guba, 1985). Other nondichotomous a priori categories that may be important for subsequent analysis can be generated from the cataloguing and contextualizing processes and could include the source or author of the document, the date of creation, the reason or motivation for writing, and the intended audience.

### Coding

Coding is the process of breaking down, classifying, comparing, and conceptualizing the data contained in the documents (Strauss & Corbin, 1998). Categorizing is a form of coding, but differs from the process described in this section in that categories of interest and anticipated importance are identified before beginning the analysis. Altheide (1987) recognized this difference by indicating that "although categories and 'variables' initially guide the study, others are allowed and expected to emerge throughout the study" (p. 68). The coding described in this section is an inductive process that involves identifying "concepts relevant to the data rather than to apply a set of pre-established rules" (Dey, 1993, p. 58). Coding also goes beyond categorizing in that it involves assigning meaning to the contents of a document. As Geertz (1973) indicated, analyzing texts involves a process of "guessing at meanings, assessing the guesses, and drawing explanatory conclusions from the better guesses" (p. 20).

The coding of document-based data is the same process used in the coding of interview transcripts (which, in actuality, is another form of document). Merriam (1998) explained that coding is nothing more than assigning some sort of shorthand designation for various aspects of the data that allow for easy retrieval. The codes can be words or phrases, or letters or numbers that are shorthand for those words and phrases. Codes and their definitions are typically compiled into a codebook and the same codes and codebook used for interview transcript analysis can be used for documents. The codes and categories are then compared and contrasted, and relationships among them are identified. Coding and sorting codes into a classification system simplifies the complexity of reality and is a precursor to content analysis (Patton, 2002). When such taxonomy of analytic categories is expected to emerge from the data themselves, the method of constant comparison described by Glaser and Strauss (1967; Strauss & Corbin, 1998) is applicable for development of that taxonomy.

## Content Analysis

Content analysis presents even more powerful ways of analyzing textual data. It incorporates both categorizing and coding yet goes beyond them and is "a systematic procedure for describing the content of communications" (Merriam, 1998, p. 123). Content analysis was originally developed as a quantitative method where researchers established a set of categories and then words and phrases representing such categories were tallied and compared (Silverman, 2001). It is now recognized that the aim of content analysis should be to understand participants' categories. Subsequently, content analysis has developed into a variety of forms and encompasses such techniques and methodologies as discourse analysis, analysis of narrative structures, and ethnography (Silverman, 2001). Given necessary space limitations, qualitative content analysis and the other techniques are described briefly. Readers are invited to explore the specific methodologies through the further readings listed at the end of the chapter. A purpose of content analysis is to identify underlying themes, assumptions, beliefs, and the narrative, sense-making, and meaning-making structures of the document's author. Not unlike other aspects of qualitative methodology, "a good content analysis will answer some questions, but it is also expected to pose new ones, leading to revisions of the procedures for future applications, stimulating new research into the bases for drawing inferences, not to mention suggesting new hypotheses about the phenomena of interest" (Krippendorff, 1980, p.169).

An initial step in a discourse analysis is to delineate the target for inferences (Krippendorff, 1980). In a study of classroom instruction Tisdell (1993), for example, examined the syllabus and feedback on written assignments seeking evidence related to assumptions of the role of the instructor, the role and expectations of the students, the underlying purpose of the teaching–learning process, or the relative importance of various pedagogical methodologies. Just as categorization identifies a priori categories and coding identifies inductive categories, content analysis is driven both by specific inferential targets and questions, and by an open-ended search for symbolism and meaning being expressed by the author of the document.

Like analysis of interview and observation data, a content analyst must produce results that are trustworthy, authentic, confirmable, and auditable. Whatever results are generated through a content analysis, they must be open and accessible to scrutiny. Hodder (1998) recognized the limitations of drawing inferences and conclusions from "mute" documents and Krippendorff (1980, p. 172) cautioned, "inferences do not justify themselves." Just because something appears sensible to the researcher and internally consistent and coherent does not mean that it accurately reflects the symbolic content of a particular text or group of texts. Inferences must be made and held tentatively. Imputing meaning and symbolism into the text of a document without an avenue for confirmation (e.g., through interview) requires even greater tentativeness. For example, in an analysis of all incident reports of a college campus during a particular semester, references to female college students as "girls" may represent evidence of a lack of status on the part of women on campus or it may represent a particular cultural vocabulary on the part of security personnel that actually has no symbolic value. Krippendorff (1980) provided an example where opposing inferences could be made of the same evidence. Societal documents with a high frequency of symbols of love and sex may be indicative of a promiscuous society or it may infer repression. In the example about analyzing incident reports, researchers need to be tentative about the inference and not enter subsequent interviews with the conscious or subconscious goal of substantiating the meaning they have inferred from the incident reports. One suggested technique (Krippendorff, 1980) to increase confidence in inferences generated from textual analysis is to identify representative interpreters who are experts on the culture of the particular scene or informants of the symbolic qualities of the data.

## Discourse Analysis

One form of content analysis, discourse analysis refers to the process of analyzing the contents, themes, structures, and underlying messages and assumptions in the speaking and writing of people (Mills, 1997). Analysis can be either of dyads (e.g., analyzing correspondence between a mother and child) or of delimited groups of people. Love and Yousey (2001) analyzed the text-based discourse of student affairs professionals and compared that discourse to exhortative literature of the student affairs field. One of the values of conducting a discourse analysis is that it identifies issues of importance in a manner different than asking people what they believe to be important (Love & Yousey, 2001), and can be compared to what people are saying or asserting. A discourse analysis identifies on what issues people are spending their time and what they are putting into print.

## Analysis of Narrative Structures

An analysis of narrative structures focuses on the underlying structure of the text in question. For example, it may seek to discover the roles, functions, actions, plot devices, and relationships that exist in a text that may recur in other similar texts. A simple example is that of the fairy tale (Silverman, 2001), where the functions that recur across stories may include an evil force (e.g., dragon, witch, ogre), a ruler (e.g., king, chief), a loved one (e.g., daughter, wife, princess), a disappearance (e.g., kidnap, vanish, imprisoned), and a hero (e.g., knight, king). The point of such an analysis is to look for repeated structures across texts. Such an analysis conducted in a collegiate environment could focus on trying to discover the narrative structures contained in departmental annual reports or in letters to the editor in the school newspaper.

## Ethnography

An ethnographic content analysis is focused more on the processes through which texts depict the reality and culture of the group in question rather than whether such texts contain true or false statements, are accurate or inaccurate, or are true or biased (Silverman, 2001). Such a content analysis looks at the nature of the data and the symbolic meaning contained therein. Altheide (1987) indicated that "ethnographic content analysis is used to document and understand the communication of meaning, as well as to verify theoretical relationships" (p. 68). More than anything else, an ethnographic content analysis focuses on the symbolic manifestations of the material in question, that is, the assumptions, beliefs, values, and cultural artifacts being communicated by the author and how they are represented and communicated through the structure and content of the text. In an attempt to discover underlying assumptions, in a study of faculty interactions with and beliefs about college students one might look at how women students (girls?) or students (kids?) are referred to in the document.

Ethnographic content analysis involves "interrogating" the text. Such questions (adapted from Hammersley & Atkinson, 1983, pp. 142–143) could include:

What was the overt purpose of the text?
What may have been other underlying purposes?
How are texts written?
How are they read?
For what purposes?
On what occasions?
With what outcomes?
What is recorded?
What is omitted?
What is taken for granted?
What does the writer seem to take for granted about the reader(s)?
What do readers need to know in order to make sense of them?
What assumptions, beliefs, and values is the author communicating and
    how are they being communicated?

The preceding sections provide an overview to the topic of content analysis. The main point for readers is to recognize the various methods that can be used, depending on the focus of the research in question and on how deep an analysis is required to answer the research questions being explored.

## CONCLUSION

Written documents are a rich source of data from which much can be learned about the various populations on a college campus, the relationships among these populations, and the experiences, actions, and processes that are in evidence in the collegiate experience. In addition to its use in formal research, document analysis can also be helpful in institutional assessment processes as well. Document analysis requires intentionality, serendipity, organization, forethought, and openness. That is, one needs a clearly defined approach, but must be open to being surprised during the process of discovery. Although categorizing and coding data are important, document analysis goes beyond these processes and seeks to understand the relationships and structural interconnections among the various categories.

## FURTHER READINGS

Sources on content analysis include Altheide (1987) and Krippendorff (1980). An example of discourse analysis in student affairs is Love and Yousey (2001). Miles and Huberman (1994), Patton (2002), Silverman (2001), and Strauss and Corbin (1998) are sources on general methods of qualitative data collection and analysis, including document analysis.

## REFERENCES

Altheide, D. I.. (1987). Ethnographic content analysis. *Qualitative Sociology, 10*(1), 65–77.

Clark, G. K. (1967). *The critical historian.* Portsmouth, NH: Heinemann Educational Books.

Dey, I. (1993). *Qualitative data analysis.* London: Routledge.

Geertz, C. (1973). *The interpretation of cultures.* New York: Basic Books.

Glaser, B., & Strauss, A. (1967). *The discovery of grounded theory.* Chicago: Aldine.

Hammersley, M., & Atkinson, P. (1983). *Ethnography: Principles in practice.* London: Tavistock.

Hodder, I. (1998). The interpretation of documents and material culture. In N. K Denzin & Y. S. Lincoln (Eds.), *Collecting and interpreting qualitative materials* (pp. 110–129). Thousand Oaks, CA: Sage.

Krippendorff, K. (1980). *Content analysis: An introduction to its methodology.* Newbury Park, CA: Sage.

Lincoln, Y. S., & Guba, E. G. (1985). *Naturalistic inquiry.* Beverly Hills, CA: Sage.

Love, P., & Yousey, K. (2001). Gaps in the conversation: Missing issues in the discourse of the student affairs field. *Journal of College Student Development, 42*(5), 430–446.

Merriam, S. B. (1998). *Qualitative research and case study applications in education.* San Francisco: Jossey-Bass.

Miles, M. B., & Huberman, A. M. (1994). *Qualitative data analysis: An expanded sourcebook.* Thousand Oaks, CA: Sage.

Mills, S. (1997). *Discourse: The new critical idiom.* New York: Routledge.

Patton, M. Q. (2002). *Qualitative evaluation and research methods* (3rd ed.). Newbury Park, CA: Sage.

Silverman, D. (2001). *Interpreting qualitative data: Methods for analysing talk, text and interaction.* London: Sage.

Strauss, A., & Corbin, J. (1998). *Basics of qualitative research: Techniques and procedures for eveloping grounded theory* (2nd ed.). Newbury Park, CA: Sage.

Tisdell, E. J. (1993). Interlocking systems of power, privilege, and oppression inn adult higher education classes. *Adult Education Quarterly, 43*(4), 203–226.

Yin, R. K. (1994). *Case study research: Design and methods.* Thousand Oaks, CA: Sage.

## Chapter 7

# HISTORICAL METHODS

Robert A. Schwartz, *Florida State University*

Historian Charles Beard once categorized the work of historians as "we hold a damn dim candle over a damn dark abyss" (cited in Kaestle, 1989, p. 161). The difficulty in describing historical research as a method for inquiry is that there is no single methodological standard from which all historical research must flow. History is relativistic and changeable. However, Kuhn (1970) and others have shown that even the once permanent truths of physics and other "hard" sciences are mutable, so history is in good company.

As evidence of such changes, Donato and Lazerson (2000) argued that for more than 35 years, the history of higher education was defined by three books, Hofstader and Metzger's *The Development of Academic Freedom in the United States* (1955); Frederick Rudolph's *The American College* and University (1990); and Lawrence Veysey's *The Emergence of the American Research University* (1965). These books defined the historical role and nature of American colleges and universities. Each brought a different perspective to the interpretation of higher education, but overall, all three promoted a view of a system vigilant in the search for scientific truth in the face of political and religious challenges over a period of 300 years. As a system of higher education, American colleges and universities represented a noble system, infused with large sums of public and private money that worked best if left alone.

In the turmoil of the 1960s and 1970s, such a benign view of higher education seemed out of step and out of touch in a rapidly changing society (Donato & Lazerson, 2000). Slowly, new interpretations of educational history emerged. One of the first challenges to the status quo came in the form of revisionist histories on the role of women. By the late 1970s women were becoming the dominant gender on campuses. These new perspectives on educational history were soon followed by histories on people of color and ethnic minorities, and finally, studies of gay and lesbian faculty and students.

Educational history has changed considerably. Educational historians now take the view that there is no single truth but instead many strands of truth. Histories of education must recognize and appreciate that there are multiple perspectives. It is not the case that there were no women, people of color, or gays and lesbians in higher education before the 1970s, but the mainstream interpretations of higher educational history chose not to investigate or discuss them. Similarly, other revisions will surely arise in the future. What generalizations can and should be made in the future are not yet apparent, but past omissions are now quite clear.

In higher education, historical research can be a valuable tool for a variety of research purposes. Educational history can be used for policy evaluation and program assessment, as well as academic research. History is useful for the study of significant groups and individuals in higher education as well as those who have been excluded from higher education in the past (e.g., people of color, women, and ethnic populations).

There is no single historical method; nor are historical method appropriate in all situations. In that regard, historical methods are no "better or worse" than any other method described in this book. The defining question is, "What is it that you want to know?" This question should determine the viability and value of any research method.

If a historical approach will answer the research question pursued, the next step, to borrow from Kaestle (1992), is to ask, how do we know when we know? Or in other words, when do historical researchers know they are on to something? When can a historical generalization be accepted? What standards of evidence must be met to support a line of historical inquiry? Social truths are mutable and change over time. Therefore, any truth or generalization that comes from a historical study or piece of research is likely to be challenged at some point. This does not make historical generalizations impossible. On the contrary, it keeps historians busy because the "truth" must constantly be reexamined in the light of new discoveries and changing perspectives. "There is no single, definable method of inquiry [in history], and important historical generalizations are rarely beyond dispute. . . . History is a challenging and creative interaction, part science, part art" (Kaestle, 1988, p. 67).

Neustadt and May (1986) suggested that we see time "as a stream" and "imagine the future as it may be when it becomes the past" (p. 22). Historical analysis can bring an increased awareness of the past, generate fresh interpretations of the present, and, to a degree, give a glimpse of future trends. This chapter offers an overview of historical methods in research, evaluation, and assessment of higher education; specific reasons for a historical approach and concrete examples of the use of history are provided. Methodological references, sources of information, and examples of historical texts in higher education are identified.

## OVERVIEW OF HISTORICAL METHOD

A thorough literature review is critical to any research effort and history is no exception. A good literature review can involve considerable time, but the resulting richness of data collected, the perspectives gained, and the expanded knowledge of the researcher make this stage in the research process invaluable. In most cases, researchers will have at least a working knowledge of the history of education and, more specifically, higher education from prior reading and course work.

A quick review of one or all of the books listed earlier, Hofstader and Metzger's *The Development of Academic Freedom in the United States* (1955), Frederick Rudolph's *The American College and University* (1990, 1962); and Lawrence Veysey's *The Emergence of the American University* (1965) as well as Brubacher and Rudy's *Higher Education in Transition* (1997), may be a helpful starting point. Many readers may already be familiar with one or all of these books. Many texts used in courses in foundations of education courses also include discussions of educational history, including higher education.

A familiarity with historical trends, patterns, and general knowledge of education history makes research efforts much quicker and less labor intensive. As new sources of information are linked to prior learning, the researcher builds on previous connections and sources. The date of Harvard's founding (1636), the names of the nine colonial colleges founded before the Revolutionary War, and the purposes of the first and second Morrill Acts become a part of the historian's repertoire and create links to other historical facts. As these dates and events are recalled or become familiar, relational connections, locked away for future reference and contextual interpretation, are at the ready.

## READING HISTORY

Articles and books on a particular topic can serve as rich sources of information concerning historical method in education. *Reading* historical studies is excellent preparation for *doing* historical research in education. Good historical research in education helps to generate a good research question and develop avenues for further research. Current research in education history is a fertile training ground for the researcher new to the field (see Further Reading).

## Recent Histories of Higher Education

General histories of higher education include Geiger (1986), Graham and Diamond (1987), and Thelin (1982). Some recent anthologies, such as the *ASHE Reader on the Foundations of Higher Education* (1999) and the *ASHE Reader on the History of Higher Education* (1989, 1997), provide a rich array of articles on a variety of relevant topics. These recent histories update the earlier work on the history of higher education, as well as provide a framework for understanding events, activities, and people.

For example, if a study of collegiate athletics from a historical perspective is the focus of a study, it will be useful to become familiar with the topic from a broad perspective. Early reading might include Brubacher and Rudy (1997) and Rudolph (1990). More recent studies include Thelin's (1996) *Games Colleges Play: Scandal and Reform in Intercollegiate Athletics.*

If the study is a general review of college athletics growth over time, such reading will be very helpful. The broad background provided by these studies can be very helpful in understanding a particular region, group of institutions, or a specific institution. Should the study narrow to a single institution, institutional histories become a source of valuable information.

Understanding the context of higher education across several eras and then locating a specific institution within that context are critical to good historical research. Using the broad histories just cited as a framework is a means for checking the validity and reliability of the purported account of a particular institution. If an institutional saga asserts that women were admitted to a college at a time when other institutions were not admitting women, the reliability of the institutional assertions must be considered suspect.

## Institutional Histories

If the goal of a study is to examine a program, policy, or other activity or event at a specific institution, then knowledge of the college or university history is essential. Institutional histories are not, in general, held in high regard, as they are often written to celebrate the institution and expunged of controversy or unflattering events. Although the lack of a balanced or neutral perspective in many institutional histories diminishes them as critical works, they can still be valuable. They often contain a wealth of knowledge, anecdotal information, and folklore. A good understanding of an institution's history, the purposes of its founding, circumstance of its chartering, and historical examination of its rituals and traditions can be very revealing.

If the subject of a study is a specific event or action precipitated by an individual, there will be obvious value in reading a biography on that person if one exists. Similarly, journals, diaries, or other accounts written by or about an individual or groups of people may bring new information to light that will aid in developing a historical study. Although autobiographies are limited in number, it is possible to find accounts of life histories that include accounts of college life. If the event or activity is recent enough, there may be individuals who can provide primary, firsthand accounts of the event. In such cases, oral history is an excellent tool for research.

## METHODS

A research question can be generated in any number of ways. A question may arise from an event or action that is unanswered by existing information, a nagging discrepancy that remains unresolved, or a task assigned or assumed by occupations, such as policy planner, institutional researcher, or a student affairs staff person. Regardless of its origins, a good research question must be a topic that can be investigated and answered by data collection and analysis. Therefore, it is critical that the research question be well defined, feasible to study, and of genuine interest. For historical research, it will be important to consider: (a) What is the availability of primary, first hand information on this topic; (b) will the use of a historical method answer the research question(s) posed; (c) how urgent is the need for the information; and (d) will the audience/consumers of this information be receptive to the use of historical methods as a way to answer the question?

### Biography

Biography has become a very popular form of tracing history. Telling the life story of an individual who is famous for his or her contributions is one form of biography, which is familiar to most. Accounts of college or university presidents, significant educators, or creative individuals connected to a college or university are sources of historical value in higher education. Likewise, there are also recent biographies on individuals who were benefactors of higher education, such as Lyndon B. Johnson, who as President of the United States introduced sweeping legislation affecting education at all levels.

Reading biographies is an excellent source of information when conducting biographical research. In addition, specific information on writing biographical history can be found in a number of sources. *Writing Educational Biography: Explorations in Qualitative Research* (1998) by Kridel details the essential steps of biographical research and writing biographies in education. Other sources of support include professional associations, such as the Archival and Biographical Special Interest Group (SIG) of the American Educational Research Association, and regional and national associations formed around the study of history, such as the History of Education Society (HES) or the Southern History of Education Society (SHOES).

## Oral History

Oral histories, biographies, and autobiographies are significant arenas for historical data collection. These are sources of history created by or passed down from persons who experienced the events or activities of interest to the researcher. Tracking information through stories or personal accounts is an essential part of the human condition. The oral tradition is especially important in compiling histories for groups or cultures in which reading and writing were not common (e.g., African-American slaves or freedmen after the Civil War) or native peoples (e.g., Native American or Eskimo tribes) who did not have a common written form of expression, and others. Scholars have also made use of oral history in tracing events and activities in a variety of settings.

Wieder's (1988) article can be of value in understanding the power of oral history. He discussed a variety of oral histories, including his work on desegregation in New Orleans and the end of apartheid in South Africa as told by teachers in and around Capetown. Wieder also directed interested individuals to other oral historians, including Studs Terkel, whose popular books on American life are derived from oral histories. In discussing the specifics of oral histories, Wieder described the process of listening to and interpreting the stories of participants as they discuss historical events and actions.

## Local History

Another consideration is local history, exploring the world close at hand. Ronald Butchart offered methodological and source information on the process in *Local Schools: Exploring Their History* (1986). Although the focus was on schools, not colleges and universities, the ideas and concepts of local history, in conjunction with the previous discussion on institutional histories, should offer some significant insights into the process.

## TRADITIONAL TOPICS FOR STUDY

### Charters, First Entering Classes, and Founding Purposes

Many institutions use the date of their charter as the official starting date of the college or university. However, in many cases, although the charter may have been granted students may not have enrolled until months or even years later. As an example of such historical gaps, the University of South Carolina admitted African American men and women after the Civil War during Reconstruction. These events were occurring in the 1860s when the capital city, Columbia, was under marshal law enforced by federal troops in the 1860s. The forced integration did not last long once Reconstruction ended. When the federal troops withdrew, the institution quickly reverted to a student body that was all male and White. However, the university officially recognizes its first African American student as Henri Monteith, a young woman admitted in 1972 (Hollis, 1982).

Another example of historical research is to determine who founded an institution and for what purpose. Religious groups or churches founded many older, private, antebellum (pre–Civil War) institutions. These denominational institutions were often created to supply new ministers in support of the church. The religious origins often led to restrictions or limitations on student enrollments and curricular offerings. Over time, these religious goals expanded to include general and/or liberal arts education for young men and eventually for women, African Americans, and others with benefactors or the means to pay tuition.

### Rituals and Ceremonies

Rites, rituals, and ceremonies are an extant source of historical information that can provide a better understanding of and appreciation for an institution. Certain traditions and rituals often reflect an institution's culture and are a reflection of the past. Often, a chapel, erected for or by an earlier generation in celebration or in memory of a past event or person, is located in a central campus location. Founder's Days evoke the founding of the institution and are a rich source of history. Words etched into plaques and building edifices exude religious meaning (Manning, 2000). Trice and Beyer (1985) compiled a taxonomy of rites, rituals, ceremonies, and sagas that can be used to study campus life and history.

## SOURCES OF DATA

Historical data can be collected from a variety of "sources." As other chapters in this book have discussed, documents are prime sources for research and especially for historical inquiry. Documents may include letters, statistical records, books, photographs, notes, and minutes of meetings. The term can also be extended to include audio and videotape, and other recorded information. Newspapers, diaries, buildings and other structures are all sources of significant information for historical analysis and interpretation. Architectural histories can be quite useful, especially if directly related to issues such as student residences, union buildings, classroom facilities, and libraries. (See Duke [1996] for an example of architectural history and interpretation in higher education.)

A good historical analysis calls for a critical eye in interpreting and analyzing information and data, persistence, and a creative and imaginative approach to thinking about research. Just as a variety of statistical tests can be applied to different research problems, any number of historical approaches or applications can examine the universe of education history. The following section describes research terminology including *primary* and *secondary* sources, *internal* and *external* criticism, and oral histories of significance to any historical study.

### Primary and Secondary Sources

"Primary source" typically refers to an account of an event or activity told or related from the perspective of someone who witnessed the occurrence (Shafer, 1980). An example of a primary document would be a charter of an institution indicating the date, place, and name of the college. Another example is the Declaration of Independence. The minutes of a meeting or a photograph of a group of people with documentation of the time, place, and names of those present are other examples of primary sources.

Secondary sources, as the name implies, are accounts that are "secondhand" interpretations of an event, activity, or action. For example, a newspaper story is often a secondary account gathered from eyewitnesses. These accounts may be honest but it is an interpretation gained secondhand, not from an eyewitness or participant source; therefore, the strength of the data is less than that of a primary source, which can be verified more easily. As a nonhistorical example, accident investigations are notoriously difficult because they must rely on secondary information; even if there are eyewitness accounts of the accident, the information is often varied and conflicting. Just as passing information from one person to another can distort the original account, primary sources can be biased or distorted through this process, despite historians' reliance on them. A secondary source can be quite accurate and even improve on a primary source through the amalgamation of different perspectives.

## Authenticity

To authenticate a source and guard against an illegitimate piece of evidence is a valid caution in educational history. Any evidence is subject to error so care must be taken to ensure that the data is accurate and acquired from a reputable source (Shafer, 1980). A more likely problem is a flawed interpretation of the data by the researcher or others. Using internal criticism to ensure the validity of an interpretation made by a researcher analyzing a set of historical information is a critical step in the research process. In other words, to what degree does the analysis hold up given the sources of information used? Internal criticism takes into account the intent and purpose of the source or original recorder of the event, the context in which the information was reported or written, and supporting evidence or reports that add to or detract from the source. A variety of tests or challenges can minimize the chance of using inaccurate data to interpret an event, policy or activity. Comprehensive lists of the steps to be taken in internal criticism can be found in any number of books on historical research (see Barzun & Graff, 1985; Shafer, 1980).

In historical research, it is important to consider major areas of evaluation by asking the following questions. How does the source describe the event? Could the source be prejudiced toward one side or other? Was the source actually present during the event (primary) or is this a case of someone reporting on an event after the fact (secondary)? How much is the source's point of view corroborated by other witnesses or documentation? Does this description make sense, given other information uncovered? Asking these and similar questions as well as applying them to sources of information provide a solid beginning to internal criticism.

## HISTORY AS A MEANS OF INTERPRETATION AND ANALYSIS

Although historical methods are often used to trace historical events and occurrences, the same methods can be used to inform decision making and policy analysis. In a Harvard course for government policymakers, Neustadt and May teach their students how to use history to make better decisions. In their book *Thinking in Time* (1986), they suggested that policymakers use history to examine "likenesses and differences" between current and past events. Insights about policy can be gained by looking at "the known, the unclear and the presumed" (p. 91). Using a historical perspective, one asks, "What's the story?" to unravel the real from the perceived, the known from the unknown. Thinking in time (Neustadt & May, 1986) is really thinking historically. Through a greater awareness of history, we understand that the present and future are part of a stream of events rooted in the past. From this perspective, human endeavors can be understood more completely and clearly.

Using history to interpret and analyze patterns and policy decisions in higher education can be equally valuable. Learning more about events, policies, institutions, and people from a historical perspective expands the base of knowledge and information that researchers and decision makers need to analyze and interpret contemporary events. Instead of being disconnected from the past, we can acknowledge and appreciate that much of current American culture and society is based on actions and events in the past. Social institutions, including colleges and universities, mirror those cultural values and histories.

## HOW TO UNDERTAKE HISTORICAL RESEARCH

A necessary feature of conducting good historical research is access to a substantial amount of information or sources, both primary and secondary. For the researcher or practitioner concerned with research on students, the immediate campus can be a ready contributor of such information, especially as most campuses have a library, archives, and, as often as not, other less obvious repositories of information, such as student artifacts, institutional records concerning students and student life, and the collective memories of faculty and alumni, to name a few possibilities.

### The Early Search

For most historical researchers, note cards or a laptop are indispensable tools. Either can be used to record brief notes on bibliographic material during the literature search. Brief notations recorded on cards can be more physically appealing only because they can be sorted into different order quickly. Even in conducting research such as oral histories, note cards can be combined with tape-recorded data in an efficient process of organizing data. Whatever the choice, note taking is an invaluable tool in collecting the pieces of information needed for sound historical analysis

Using the college or university library, archives, or local museum or conducting exploratory interviews to frame the early search is typically the beginning point for most research efforts. The early stages should be used as a time for broad investigation of the research question. By scanning research collections (including electronic databases and government documents), a focus for further research emerges.

At the early stages, the process is often like detective work, locating clues or possibilities for more in-depth research by broadly scanning areas of interest. Even dead ends, research efforts that go nowhere, should be viewed as helpful because knowing there is nothing to be found narrows the search. However, some trails or inquiries emerge as possibilities.

As Shafer (1980) suggested, a regular and consistent format for the research process reaps huge dividends in the end. In examining bibliographic material from books, articles, or archival material, a researcher should include author, title, year, and the physical location of a source. In any written notes, it helps to make critical notations about collected data such as the topical area or relevance of the source, main theme of the article or research, and other pertinent information. A numerical rank (i.e., 1–10) or letter grade (i.e., A, B, C) can be used, where 10 or an A denotes higher quality or potential than 7 or a B.

The purpose for such careful tracking of data and data sources may only be appreciated later. Time invested noting sources and locations during the early investigation phase is invaluable later. When the information is reviewed during the analysis and integration process, choices can be made about use of material. Often a return visit to the same source can be problematic, especially when distance, financial resources, and impending deadlines enter in. Any data collected are subjected to some level of internal criticism as a check on reliability and validity. In particular, pay close attention to the circumstances under which the author of the source observed a particular incident, the author's ability to report, and his or her intent in reporting such information. Shafer (1980) called attention to concerns such as internal contradictions and the researcher's level of confidence after reading an account of an event. The quality of the final research report or essay is only as good as the accuracy and authenticity of the assembled pieces of historical evidence.

## Analysis and Synthesis

As information is collected and compiled, the research process reaches several stages of analysis and synthesis (Shafer, 1980). At this point, it is possible to combine, compare and select the most pertinent information in a meaningful manner. Certain information collected should corroborate other pieces as a more complete picture emerges. Note cards or computer entries may be arranged in chronological or thematic order. A rough outline or a time line of events, activities, and people is helpful. These visual aids allow for the arrangement and re-arrangement of data as new interpretations or associations emerge. It can also be helpful to describe the different arrangements or connections, which emerge for another person.

In writing an early draft of the findings, keep Kaestle's (1988)

> four fundamental methodological concerns in mind. These include (1) confusion between correlations and causes . . . causality is about how things work but correlations don't tell us much about how things work; (2) the distinction between evidence of ideas about how people *should* behave, and evidence of how ordinary people *in fact* behaved . . . ; (3) the distinction between intent and consequences . . . assuming that the historical actors could have foreseen the full consequences of their ideas and the institutions they shaped; and (4) defining key terms and avoiding both vagueness, using broad terms such as industrialization which defy specificity; presentism is applying present day interpretations or definitions to terms or events from the past. (pp. 68–70)

A careful researcher, regardless of methodology, needs to be cautious about generalizations and assumptions while simultaneously asserting some well-defined conclusions and interpretations. Unlike quantitative studies (which can and do have a significant place in historical research), there is no statistical level of significance that can be used to dismiss or confirm an historical interpretation. Rather, it is the responsibility of the researcher to critique the work for flaws or unfounded conclusions and later, the public viewing and critique of the historian's work.

To this end, it can be helpful, perhaps even essential, to have an outside person review work in progress or final drafts for omissions, errors or logical flaws. It will also be important to compare the findings to other interpretations in the same area. Although it is acceptable to have a conflicting or divergent interpretation, a new interpretation must withstand the rigor of scholarly criticism if it deviates from prevailing ideas.

As a clearer picture emerges in the initial drafts, it often helps to write in short bursts and focus on one area at a time. If there are natural breaks, such as decades, groups, or institutions, it may be easiest to concentrate on one at a time. More analysis and synthesis occur as the writing unfolds, so often the challenge is to "keep writing," to tell the story without immediate concern for revision.

As the investigation continues, the researcher may find that the original question changes or evolves. What was a clear, discernible research question can become murky and full of diverse, sometimes competing, possibilities. A common pitfall in any type of educational research but especially in historical research is the problem of too many interesting avenues that are tempting to pursue.

Researchers are advised to keep the original research question foremost and in focus. Does the original research question still make sense in light of all the accumulated research? Does the question need to be changed or can slight adjustments be made without losing sight of the original goal? Again, discussing the progress of the analysis with another person familiar with the study or intent of the research may be useful.

Another pleasant problem in doing historical research is that "You will probably know a lot more than you can write" (W. Reese, personal communication, December 1989). In one sense, the historical researcher must serve two roles: the investigator who uncovers the information, and the critic who examines and challenges the same data set. Once the research study is complete, the process is well worth the effort. But along the way, it can, at times, be overwhelming.

## Reporting Results

As drafts of the writing are produced, the researcher should make corrections in presentation, synthesis, and analysis of the data. Good writing is critical to good historical interpretation, so every effort must be made to ensure that the meaning of a piece is clear and that the work reads well. It is also not unusual to find that revisions enlarge an early work as it evolves over time. Additional efforts on the part of the author to be clear and coherent and yet rethink the interpretation may expand or condense the early drafts.

As the pieces fit together under the original or amended research question, the issue of how to present the research so that it is both informative and scholarly arises. In other words, how can the findings be presented to others so that they are interesting and valid? This is, in large part, a matter of good writing.

### Organization of the Findings

Several points about organization should be considered. Perhaps the most obvious means of organizing a historical study is chronological order. In essence, the researcher can discuss the data in the order in which the events

occurred and retell the story. In this way, the assembly is by date(s), starting
with the earliest and working forward to the present or latest. However, this
may not always tell the story accurately or provide the analytic interpretation that is appropriate or relevant. Other means include topical or even
geographical organization (Shafer, 1980). These are by no means conclusive;
the researcher must find the most appropriate means of broadly categorizing or organizing information themes.

## Voice In Historical Research

The erroneous assumption is often made that history speaks with a single
voice when, in fact, there are many historical voices. Consider how differently the history of the desegregation in the schools would be perceived from
the point of view of an African American student than a White student or
the parents of either child. Such alternative perspectives are ever present in
tracing the history of American higher education. It is well documented that
women students perceive, think, and feel differently about their collegiate
experience than do male college students (Belenky, Clinchy, Goldberger, &
Tarule, 1986; Gilligan, 1982). Consequently, women may have a much different history of reactions, perceptions and feelings about their collegiate
experience than do men (see Gordon, 1990; Graham, 1978; Horowitz, 1986,
1987; McCandless, 1999; Solomon, 1985). The same is true for other groups
whose experiences differ from the traditions of White, male, middle-class
America.

As a quick example, the myth of the deans of women as humorless spin-
sters who took delight in limiting the social freedoms of young women in
college persisted for years; they were characterized in campus myths as "snoop-
ing battleaxes" (Rhatigan, 1978). But recent studies (Nidiffer, 1999;
Schwartz, 1997a, 1997b) found quite the opposite to be true. Many deans of
women were members of a new generation of bright, educated women who
pursued college degrees with a passion and often held faculty positions prior
to becoming deans. They were instrumental in creating the first professional
associations in student affairs, as well as developing the first graduate programs in higher education administration. Deans of men, by contrast, were
much less interested in professional associations and shunned graduate study
in the field for a long time (Schwartz, 2002).

Without such revisions to historical myths and misconceptions, the
truth of past events, roles, and people is lost. Knowledge and use of historical
information, both in the discovery of new data and in the correction of erroneous assumptions or constructions, are ongoing tasks. New information
comes to light regularly as new data are found or released over time. History

is an organic process, not a fixed, concrete recitation of old information and inaccuracies.

## CONCLUSION

Historical research or reading historical studies can empower the researcher or the reader in ways that are difficult to replicate using other research methods. In higher education especially, the tendency of researchers is to focus on the present or to speculate on the future. Too often, researchers, administrators, and policymakers ignore or discount what happened in the past; old policies, events, or even people diminish in importance as they age (Rhatigan, 1978). However, those who can link past events, trends, behaviors, policies, and persons to patterns, cycles, and epochs are often respected, admired, and occasionally revered for their insight and wisdom. Awareness and knowledge of history make it easier to see forests where others may see only trees.

The most critical aspect of using historical research or assessment is to plunge in and do it. The historical method can be practical, useful, and enlightening, and it can be applied to almost any research or assessment issue. Individually, the greatest gain is to be able to see through an interpretive lens that connects events, actions, and people as a part of a continuum rather than as single, isolated bursts of activity. Historical analysis tells us that history is like viewing a movie, not just a single frame of the movie or a still photo.

The use of historical interpretation and analysis shows us similarities and analogies in the present and help us anticipate the future (Neustadt & May, 1986). Historical research methods can be a rich source of information and knowledge, and the data are often close at hand and accessible. The challenge is to tap into those sources and put this valuable research method to good use.

## FURTHER READING

Thelin (1982) and Neustadt and May (1986) provide some excellent examples for the use of history in their books. Urban and Waggoner's book (2000) is an excellent text on pre-Colonial education and religious sects, with the main epochs and developments. Other overviews of American education include those of Lawrence Cremin, Ellwood Cubberly, Joel Spring, Michael Katz, Robert Church, and Michael Sedlak. Journals (see the *History of Education Quarterly* and *History of Higher Education Annual*) are easily accessible and typically offer research articles, essays, and book reviews. An excellent guide to history of education topics and inquiry is *Historical Inquiry in Education: A Research Agenda* (Best, 1983). Shafer (1980) and Barzun and Graff's (1985) books are excellent sources of historical information and method. U.S. government records are a rich source of data, especially for a quantitative history (Angus, 1983). State and local government documents can be equally lucrative in terms of historical interpretation and analysis. Rudolph (1990), Graham and Diamond (1997), Veysey (1964), and Brubacher and Rudy (1997) remain essential guides to the 300-plus years of history in American higher education. Each of these books contains institutional histories as well as broad surveys of trends and patterns in higher education. In a similar vein but of more recent vintage is Geiger (1986). Tewksbury's book (1969) is an example of early quantitative historical research. A more contemporary work, Graham and Diamond (1997) is a creative interpretation and analysis of how research was and is conducted in universities and the impact of federal policy on higher education. McCandless (1999) and Horowitz (1987) are good overviews of student life from different perspectives. Fass (1977) concentrates on the student of the 1920s. Individual essays such as Graham's (1978) are informative as well.

## REFERENCES

Angus, D. (1983). The empirical mode: Quantitative history. In J. H. Best (Ed.), *Historical inquiry in education: A research agenda* (p. 7593). Washington, DC: American Educational Research Association.

Barzun, J., & Graff, H. F. (1985). *The modern researcher* (4th ed.). New York: Harcourt, Brace & World.

Belenky, M. F., Clinchy, B. M., Goldberger, N. R., & Tarule, J. M. (1986). *Women's ways of knowing: The development of self, voice, and mind.* New York: Basic Books.

Bess, J., & Webster, D. (Eds.). (1999). *ASHE Reader on the Foundation of Higher Education* (2nd ed.). New York: Simon and Schuster Publishing.

Best, J. H. (Ed.). (1983). *Historical inquiry in education: A research agenda.* Washington, DC: American Educational Research Association.

Butchart, R. (1986). *Local schools: Exploring their history.* Nashville, TN: American Association for State and Local History.

Brubacher, J. S., & Rudy, W. (1997). *Higher education in transition: A history of American colleges and universities* (3rd ed.). New York: Harper & Row.

Donato, R., & Lazerson, M. (2000). New directions in American educational history: Problems and prospects. *Educational Researcher, 29*(8), 4–15.

Duke, A. (1996) *Importing Oxbridge: English residential colleges and American universities.* New Haven, CT: Yale University Press.

Fass, P. (1977). *The damned and the beautiful: American youth in the 1920's.* New York: Oxford University Press.

Geiger, R. (1986). *To advance knowledge: The growth of American research universities, 1900–1940.* New York: Oxford University Press.

Gilligan, C. (1982). *In a different voice: Psychological theory and women's development.* Cambridge, MA: Harvard University Press.

Goodchild, L., & Wechsler, H. (Eds.). (1999). *ASHE Reader on the History of Higher Education.* New York: Simon and Schuster Publishing.

Gordon, L. (1990). *Gender and higher education in the Progressive Era.* New Haven, CT: Yale University Press.

Graham, H. D., & Diamond, N. (1997). *The rise of American research universities: Elites and challengers in the postwar era.* Baltimore: Johns Hopkins Press.

Graham, P. (1978). Expansion and exclusion: A history of women in American higher education. *Signs: Journal of Women in Culture and Society, 3*(4), 759–773.

Hofstrader, R., & Metzger, W. (1955). *The development of academic freedom in the United States.* New York: Columbia University Press.

Horowitz, H. L. (1986). *Alma mater: Design and experience in the women's colleges from their nineteenth century beginnings to the 1930's.* Boston: Beacon Press.

Horowitz, H. L. (1987). *Campus life: Undergraduate cultures from the end of the nineteenth century to the present.* Chicago: University of Chicago Press.

Kaestle, C. F. (1988). Recent methodological developments in the history of American education. In R. M. Jaeger (Ed.), *Complementary methods for research in education* (pp. 61–80). Washington, DC: American Educational Research Association.

Kaestle, C. F. (1992). Standards of evidence in historical research: How do we know when we know? *History of Education Quarterly, 32*(3), 360–366.

Kridel, C. K. (Ed.). (1998). *Writing educational biography: Explorations in qualitative research.* New York: Garland.

Kuhn, T. S. (1970). *The structure of scientific revolutions.* Chicago: University of Chicago Press.

Manning, K. (2000). *Rituals, ceremonies, and cultural meaning in higher education.* Westport, CT: Greenwood Press.

McCandless, A. (1999). *The past in the present: Women's higher education in the 20th century American South.* Baton Rouge, LA: University of Louisiana Press.

Neustadt, R. E., & May, N. R. (1986). *Thinking in time: The uses of history for decision-makers.* New York: Free Press.

Nidiffer, J. (2000). *Pioneering deans of women: More than wise and pious matrons.* New York: Teachers College Press, Athene Series.

Rhatigan, J. (1978). A corrective look back. In J. R. Appleton, C. M. Briggs, & J. J. Rhatigan (Eds.), *Pieces of eight: The rites, roles and styles of the dean by eight who have been there* (pp. 9–41). Portland, OR: NASPA Institute of Research and Development.

Rudolph, F. (1990). *The American college and university.* Athens, GA: University of Georgia Press.

Schwartz, R. A. (1997a). How deans of women became men. *Review of Higher Education, 20*(3), 419–438.

Schwartz, R. A. (1997b). Reconceptualizing the leadership roles of women in higher education: A brief history on the importance of the deans of women. *Journal of Higher Education, 68*(5), 502–522.

Schwartz, R. A. (2002). The rise and demise of deans of men in American higher education. *Review of Higher Education, 25*(4), 217–239.

Shafer, R. J. (1980). *A guide to the historical method* (3rd ed.). Chicago: Dorsey.

Solomon, B. M. (1985). *In the company of educated women.* New Haven, CT: Yale University Press.

Tewksbury, D. (1969). *The founding of American colleges and universities before the Civil War.* New York: Arno Press.

Thelin, J. R. (1982). *Higher education and its useful past: Applied history in research and planning.* Cambridge, MA: Schenkman.

Thelin, J. R. (1996). *Games colleges play: Scandal and reform in intercollegiate athletics.* Baltimore, MD: Johns Hopkins Press.

Trice, H. M., & Beyer, J. M. (1985). Studying organizational cultures through rites and ceremonials. *Academic Management Review, 9*(4), 653–669.

Urban, W., & Waggoner, J. (2000). *American education: A history* (2nd ed.). New York: McGraw-Hill.

Veysey, L. (1965). *The emergence of the American research university.* Chicago: University of Chicago Press.

Wieder, A. (1988). Oral history and questions of interaction for educational historians. *International Journal of Oral History, 9*(2), 131–138.

*Chapter 8*

# VISUAL METHODS

**Katie Branch,** *University of Rhode Island*

In recent decades technological developments that became accessible to many households shifted both the form and type of information available for popular consumption (e.g., home personal computer video games, video-recorded movies, Music Television). This explosion of information in the form of visual stimuli is, according to Denzin and Lincoln (1994), leading to augmentation of—if not the eventual replacement of—print literacy with visual literacy.

As a result of not only the proliferation of visually oriented cultural artifacts but also paradigmatic shifts in the underlying assumptions and approaches to ways of learning about phenomena of interest (see Kuhn, 1996), researchers, including master's and doctoral students, in several academic fields have turned their attention to how photographs and video recordings can be used as data sources (Branch Douglas, 1998a; Grady, 1996; Mann, 2002; Wang & Burris, 1994; Worth & Adair, 1972/1997). More specifically, qualitative researchers in academic disciplines such as anthropology, sociology, mass communications, and education have explored how visual methods grounded in photographic techniques can be used to enhance inquiry into complex human phenomena. Because of the economic and technical availability of cameras (i.e., minimal training is needed to use successfully) this chapter emphasizes the use of photographically produced still images.

## THEORETICAL FOUNDATIONS WITHIN VISUAL METHODS

Two conceptual foundations for the inclusion of photographic techniques as qualitative research methods include (a) alternative forms of representation and (b) semiotics.

## Representation

When discussing how sensory systems contribute to the process of how people gain knowledge or come to understand their lives, Eisner (1982) wrote:

> In order to achieve a social dimension in human experience, a means must be found to carry what is private forward into the public realm. This is achieved by employing . . . forms of representation. Forms of representation are the devices that humans use to make public conceptions that are privately held. They are the vehicles through which concepts that are visual, auditory, kinesthetic, olfactory, gustatory, and tactile are given public status. This public status might take the form of words, pictures, music, mathematics, dance, and the like. (p. 47)

Eisner described the relationship between forms of representation and perception as nonlinear and involving individuals situated in contexts, or environments. Because forms of representation influence perception, the employment of multiple forms of representation—such as visual (e.g., information gained through photographs or videos) and auditory (e.g., information gained through interviewing)—has epistemological justification: it has the potential to enhance what can be known.

## Semiotics

Another way of looking conceptually at photographs and video recordings is with a semiotic perspective. Those who take this perspective see such visual imagery as part of a broadly defined language system (Brecheen, 1982; Faccioli & Harper, 1996). Bruner (1990) noted that systems of signs (e.g., language) assist in providing symbolic meanings. Language systems help people make meaning by going beyond merely providing "information," or what may be commonly agreed on descriptions of tangible aspects of the physical world. When utilizing a semiotic perspective, photographs transcend a purely representational (i.e., documentation of concrete, physical "realities") nature and thereby become part of a communications paradigm. In other words, photographs and video recordings have meanings that transcend the physical nature of the image.

### VISUAL METHODS TECHNIQUES

Harper (1987, 1988) organized ways that photographs can be used in research processes into the following classifications: scientific, narrative, phenomenological, and reflexive. This typology also can be used to label video recordings.

## Scientific Images

Photographs categorized as "scientific" are ones that are taken and analyzed by researchers for the purpose of categorizing parts of wholes (Harper, 1988). In practice, this use of photographs is called the "cataloging approach." Examples of photographs being used in this manner are studies on time and space (i.e., proxemics), architectural change, and the physical layouts of college and university campuses.

## Narrative Images

Photographs used in a "narrative" fashion also are those taken by researchers. The purpose of these photographs, however, is to "show social life as a process made up of social interactions" (Harper, 1988, p. 63). These photographs illustrate or tell a story. Narrative photos utilize what Harper calls "familiar narrative conventions," which follow a "character" and/or show events over time. Although not viewed as research per se, photo essays, such as those published in *Life* or *Look* magazines during the 1960s and 1970s, used photographs in this narrative fashion.

## Phenomenological Images

Researchers who take "phenomenological" photographs "use their own subjective experience as a source of data" (Harper, 1988, p. 61). This style of research often combines visual images with other forms of representation—such as music. The result is a sensory evocative presentation of the insights gained during the inquiry process. By using photographs and other nontextual forms of representation in a phenomenological manner, the researcher evokes questions about the taken-for-granted aspects of people's daily lives (Harper, 1987).

## Reflexive Images

When people involved in the study take photographs, they are considered "reflexive." Such images create opportunities in which "the subject shares in the definition of meaning; thus, the definitions are said to 'reflect back' from the subject" (Harper, 1988, pp. 64–65). Reflexive photographs are sometimes taken as the result of the initiation of a research project. In other circumstances, previously taken photographs are utilized. The key is that study participants take the photographs and are the primary interpreters of these images. Ziller (1990) noted that this approach "may be the preferred representational system for subjects with communication difficulties or across cultures" (p. 35).

## DATA COLLECTION LOGISTICS

Because of the ease of use and availability of still cameras, most research employing visual methods concentrates on this medium. Photographs produced by researchers for the purposes of cataloging information or telling a story visually (i.e., scientific and narrative) are more common than those photographs produced by study participants (i.e., reflexive). In the instances of researcher-produced images, those who have technical competence in using their cameras typically possess the ability to generate rich, meaning-laden data or visual documents for study. Although there are ethical considerations about the use of researcher-produced photographs, the next sections of this chapter discuss the more complicated logistical and ethical concerns of using participant-produced photographs as data sources. Many of the principles outlined next also can be applied to video-produced images, but for ease of discussion, emphasis is on still photographic images.

### Obtaining Photographs

Among the most inexpensive ways of having study participants produce reflexive photographs is to provide them with disposable, or sometimes referred to as "single-use," cameras. Typically, these cameras have a built-in flash unit. In order to track who produced what photographs, it is helpful if the first exposure on each camera is of a number, letter, or other symbol associated consistently with the specific study participant who receives that camera. The researcher should take this photograph before giving the camera to the study participant; thus, the symbol–participant match can be recorded and the researcher can ensure that the camera is working properly. Before taking photographs, participants need to be oriented to the task (see the section Research Questions Addressed via Visual Methods) as well as the proper operation of the camera, especially the flash feature. Although the flash on single-use cameras typically fires automatically, participants often need to be shown physically the spatial range that the flash will illuminate. Because of the potential for errors when using the flash as well as possible problems in film development, participants can be given a notebook in which to record comments about the image they were trying to capture in that particular photograph. Participants also can be prompted to write additional thoughts in their notebooks, such as why they took that particular image and what meaning that image has for them.

An ethical consideration to discuss with participants before they begin taking photographs relates to their personal safety and the privacy of others. Participants should be made aware that if they attempt to take a photograph that includes images of others and those people object, they should not proceed with taking that photo. Rather, they can take another photograph that illustrates the same intended message or write in their notebook about what image they wanted to capture.

## Sharing Images with Others

An ethical concern with participant-produced photos is acquiring informed consent from anyone whose identity may be discernable to use that photograph in publications or presentations. Although photographs containing identifiable images of people can be used during data analysis, they cannot be shared beyond the researcher without first obtaining written consent. If being able to show these images to others is crucial, study participants/photographers must distribute and collect consent forms for others to sign as they take the photographs. If this is not a concern, study participants can be asked if they have access to (which they likely may not) and are willing to approach identifiable people in specific images about obtaining permission to show those photographs to a wider audience. Because this request to show publicly the image did not occur at the time the photo was taken, the aspect of choice without penalty should be emphasized to both the participant/photographer and the person in the image.

## Photo Elicitation Interviews

After study participants have finished using their cameras and the film has been developed (utilizing a service where the film is developed and images are printed "in house" helps to prevent loss and to protect privacy), the images serve as touchstones for interpretive interviews. Such interviews are conducted with the respondents who took the images and are discussions about what those photographs mean to those people. This style of interviewing is called "photo elicitation interviews" or "photo-interviewing" (Blinn-Pike & Eyring, 1993; Dempsey & Tucker, 1994). Dempsey and Tucker wrote:

> Photo-interviews yield different and often "richer" data than that obtained from verbal interviewing procedures alone. Because the concrete

nature of the photographs coexists with the interview queries, informants tend to respond in a more mindful fashion. (p. 61)

Because such interviews provide a forum in which participants describe and interpret each photograph, it is crucial that the focus is on the meanings participants sought to convey via their images. Previously written notebook comments can serve as question prompts and participants can be asked if they have ideas that could not be expressed visually that they would like to share verbally.

## Data Analysis

Knowing and understanding participants' interpretations of their reflexive photographs is crucial for inductive data analysis. Keeping the images in context with interview data and comments from participant notebooks allows meaning to emerge from these multiple sources of data.

For in-depth data analysis, verbatim transcripts of the audiotapes from photo elicitation interviews are helpful. Comments recorded in participants' notebooks as well as their photographs can be embedded in these transcripts. Having the images digitized onto a compact disc or having multiple hard copy prints of photographs so the photographs can be merged with interview and notebook data keeps the images "in context" during data analysis.

## Coding and Categorizing

After the preparation of the visual and textual materials, the researcher can undertake a process often referred to as "unitizing." A unit is a small piece of information (a phrase, sentence, paragraph, image) that can provide some type of relevant information to the researcher while remaining autonomous of additional data (Bogdan & Biklen, 1997; Lincoln & Guba, 1985). Following the unitizing process, each data chunk is given a code or codes by the researcher that describes its meaning and relevance to the research questions. After all identified data units are coded the categorization process, which is the clustering of these units into broader constructs, begins. Computer software programs can assist with the mechanical tasks of applying multiple codes to single units of data and sorting coded data units into categories. Although various programs are available, currently software known as ATLAS.ti (see www.atlasti.de) focuses on assisting with analysis of visual-based data. Depending on the research goals, the broader constructs that emerge during categorization can be used to develop themes or serve as foundations in theory building.

## STRENGTHS AND LIMITATIONS OF VISUAL METHODS

As an additional form of data, photographs provide an alternative to as well as an augmentation of the "traditional" or most widely utilized forms of representation in research that are grounded in written and spoken language. By including photographs in qualitative studies, researchers can seek to gain deeper, richer, more complex understandings of people's lives. As Eisner (1994) wrote:

> Pictures portray what words may never be able to reveal. Hence, to limit one's expressive options to words, particularly to propositional language [(i.e., primarily text-based assertions related to truth "testing")], is to limit what can be conveyed about the world in which we are interested. (pp. 190–191)

Many people's early experiences of formal schooling include the practice of "Show and Tell." Think back to the excitement of not only being able to hear about something significant to another person but also being able to *see* something that went along with that verbal explanation. As Detenber and Reeves (1996) noted, "emotional responses are affected by the form a message takes, as well as by its content" (p. 80). When images are incorporated into research findings, the visual sensory mode is again utilized to expand understandings of complex phenomena. In a keynote address at the 1996 Conference on Qualitative Research in Education, Eisner (1997) stated, "One of the basic questions scholars are now raising is how we perform the magical feat of transforming the contents of our consciousness into a public form that others can understand" (p. 4). Incorporating visual imagery into publicly shared presentations and publications is one of these ways.

Another strength of incorporating photographically produced visual imagery into the inquiry process and research findings is the enhancement of authenticity. Authenticity, one of the broad criteria employed when making judgments about the rigor and value of qualitative research (Lincoln & Guba, 1986; Manning, 1997), emphasizes the importance of context to qualitative inquiry. In particular, providing a balanced presentation of viewpoints (i.e., fairness) and raising awareness about the experiences of study participants (i.e., ontological authentication) are enhanced through the use of visual methods.

Finally, in research conducted by Branch Douglas (1998b), reflexive photographs and photo elicitation interviews were used in such a way that participants demonstrated high levels of investment in the project. Respondents attributed the deep level of reflection expressed to the reflexive photograph activity. This reflection appeared to be directly linked to two factors: (a) employing a method for data collection that directly involved the visual sensory mode, and (b) utilizing a method that prompted a greater amount of "time on task." Time on task, or the focused commitment of time and physical or psychological energy to the accomplishment of a certain goal, is a concept prevalent in the learning theory literature (Alexander & Murphy, 1998). In higher education settings, Astin (1984) called for the use of the time-on-task concept—or involvement—to increase student learning and personal development.

## Altering Images

A perceived limitation related to using visual methods can be doubt among audience members about who produced the images. Given that photographs and video recordings can be manipulated readily through computer software, the researcher must specifically point out to viewers if any alterations to the original images were made and, if so, what and why these alterations occurred. Sometimes it is necessary to make alterations to images to preserve confidentiality (e.g., blurring words on signs that identify fraternities, sororities, residence halls; removing frames from video that contain identifiable images for which consent was not obtained); however, such alterations should be clearly noted.

## RESEARCH QUESTIONS ADDRESSED VIA VISUAL METHODS

Most research questions can be reframed to include a visual component. To promote the use of the visual sensory mode, however, specific prompts need to be created. For example, the purpose of a doctoral study conducted by Branch Douglas (1998a) was to describe first-year, African American students' impressions of the campus environment at a predominantly White public university as well as explore the meanings of these perceptions. To begin to achieve this purpose, Branch Douglas asked students to "take pictures that will illustrate your impressions of [this university] or that will help you to describe your impressions" (p. 419). The study's research questions could be explored more fully by augmenting the research methods with photography, which assisted the researcher in understanding how these students perceived and made meaning of the campus environment. An example that demonstrates how videotaping enhanced the ways that research questions were explored is Stage's (2001) study of discourse in a mathematics classroom. Stage used videotapes of classes to prompt college students to describe their understandings of material that had been presented earlier.

## Examples for Higher Education Settings

Within higher education research, James Banning used a camera to document and promote discussions about campus climate and culture. Banning used photography to examine the campus environment for sexist messages (1992); to explore messages that pedestrians receive about safety, functionality, pleasure, and informal learning on campus (1993); and to look at how Hispanic/Latino culture is portrayed in a campus environment (Banning & Luna, 1992). He also recommended using photography as a tool in assessing the ethical climate on campus via documentation of tangible cultural artifacts (1997). Banning (1997) wrote:

> Qualitative data-gathering methods typically fall into three classes: observations, analysis of documents, and interviews. Obtaining photographs of campus artifacts captures all three methods. A photograph captures an observation and becomes a document for analysis, and if the notion that a picture is worth a thousand words has merit, then the photograph is a brief interview as well. (p. 99)

### Greek-Letter Affiliation

To assess campus climate and culture, students Perka, Matherly, Fishman, and Ridge (1992) used reflexive photographs and photo elicitation interviews to examine what a particular university meant to students involved with selected Greek-letter organizations. Three African American undergraduate students affiliated with historically Black Greek-letter organizations and three White undergraduate students affiliated with predominantly White Greek-letter organizations were asked to take photos of what the predominantly White university they were attending meant to them. Although both groups of students took photos showing the importance of academic experiences, affiliation with Greek-letter organizations, and involvement in cocurricular activities, the African American students took more photos that represented personal frustrations or challenges and culturally significant events or locations than the White students. The White students used a less personalized frame of reference: "the assumed frame of reference of the general student population" (p. 12). Consequently, the White students took more photographs of buildings and locations that were a part of campus history and traditions than the African American study participants.

### Initial Impressions

Branch Douglas (1998a) used the Perka et al. (1992) study to inform her research on first-year, African American college students' perceptions of the environment at a predominantly White university. Six overall impressions of the campus environment emerged in that study: campus beauty, large campus size, consciousness of being black, influence of Greek-letter organizations, prevalence of voluntary racial and cultural separation, and preparation for the future. Harrington and Lindy (1999) used the framework provided by Branch Douglas's study to investigate how first-year students' impressions of their university impacted institutional commitment.

## First-Year Student Seminars

Oliver and Oliver (2000) incorporated reflexive photographs and narrative notebook entries into a research project that was part of a first-year experience course taught at Florida State University. They gave their students the following prompt: "Your job is to take photographs chronicling your life as a first-year student at Florida State University. You have 12 days to take photographs that are descriptive of your experiences as first-year students just embarking on his or her college career" (p. 1). Oliver and Oliver (2000) used the student-produced photographs and accompanying narratives (i.e., description of the photo, where and when taken, and comments about the significance of the subject matter) to generate themes about these students' experiences. The "top five" themes were living experiences (on- and off-campus), class-related homework, parking and transportation issues, meeting people/friends, and buildings and places on campus.

In ongoing research examining the campus climate for lesbian, gay, bisexual, and transgender (LGBT) students, N. J. Evans (personal communication, 13 April 2002) asked freshman honors students to collect data via cameras and journal entries. Evans met weekly with each student to discuss what the students learned. When students completed the picture-taking process she engaged them in dialogue about what each of their photos meant and why they took those particular images. While discovering more about indicators related to the campus climate for LGBT students, Evans also explored the impact of project participation on each student (e.g., how, if at all, attitudes changes; if there are differences in what students see based upon their sexual orientations).

## Enhancing Inquiry Skills

In addition to use in first-year student seminars, visual methods also have been incorporated into courses designed to enhance students' skills as researchers. For example, in a course for undergraduate architecture students, Ahrentzen (1997) assigned a project in which she wanted to accomplish the following:

I have them see how photography can also be a valuable tool to better understand how clients and users experience places. It also is a technique that enables these students to interview users who are different from themselves, and who may see the world with different eyes, or different lens, from these architecture students. (p. 8)

To meet these goals, she asked students to go on walk-throughs of a setting of their choice with two setting users who differ from them on social demographic characteristics. The users try to describe their perceptions and experiences of that setting via a camera. Then, after the film is developed, each architecture student uses the photographs to further talk with the users about how the physical or social aspects of that setting impact them. In another example, Margolis (1998) used photographs in an assignment for a graduate-level course in education. The goal of this assignment was to use photographs to explore and expose the hidden curricula in an institution of higher education.

## CONCLUSION

The use of visual methods, particularly in research exploring questions of meaning making and understanding underlying processes, can enhance both how data are uncovered and how findings are conveyed. Broadening how study participants can explain and illustrate their lived experiences allows more holistic portraits of complex human phenomena. Augmenting written and spoken words with visual imagery during research presentations (e.g., journal articles, conference presentations) can increase the depth of understanding about these same phenomena.

Within higher education research, the use of visual methods has been limited. Keller (1998) wrote, "Too much of today's 'empirical' higher education research consists of abstracted arm-chair and computer findings. Actual observation of campus, practices, norms, and behavior needs to increase, as does the use of the senses in research" (pp. 275–276). By incorporating photographically produced images into the research process, the visual sensory mode is drawn upon in the inquiry process. Because many of today's students rely on visual stimuli as a critical sensory modality for learning, it is imperative that the use of visual methods in inquiry processes be expanded.

## FURTHER READINGS

For a qualitative study using photographs made by children and follow-up with interviews that provided rich understandings of their lives, see Ewald

(1985). Collier and Collier (1986) provide numerous recommendations and examples about using still, movie, and video cameras in field research. Worth and Adair (1972/1997) is "a classic" about using moving images. Harper (1994) is another helpful methodological resource. For a listing of visual methods books available through Sage Publications, visit their Web site at http://www.sagepub.com; type the word visual in the "Search Products" box, and click on the "Go" button.

## REFERENCES

Ahrentzen, S. (1997). Class notes: The photo-interview method. *Design Research News, 28*(2), 8–9.

Alexander, P. A., & Murphy, P. K. (1998). The research base for APA's learner-centered psychological principles. In N. M. Lambert & B. L. McCombs (Eds.), *How students learn: Reforming schools through learner-centered education* (pp. 25–60). Washington, DC: American Psychological Association.

Astin, A. W. (1984). Student involvement: A developmental theory for higher education. *Journal of College Student Personnel, 25,* 297–308.

Banning, J. H. (1992). Visual anthropology: Viewing the campus ecology for messages of sexism. *Campus Ecologist, 10*(1), 1–4.

Banning, J. H. (1993). The pedestrian's visual experience on campus: Informal learning of cultural messages. *Campus Ecologist, 11*(1). Retrieved 8 April 2002 <http://wbarratt.indstate.edu/ce/v11n1.htm>.

Banning, J. H. (1997). Assessing the campus' ethical climate: A multidimensional approach. In J. Fried (Ed.), *Ethics for today's campus: New perspectives on education, student development, and institutional management* (New Directions for Student Services, No. 77, pp. 95–105). San Francisco: Jossey-Bass.

Banning, J. H., & Luna, F. C. (1992). Viewing the campus ecology for messages about Hispanic/Latino culture. *Campus Ecologist, 10*(4), 1–4.

Blinn-Pike, L. M., & Eyring, M. (1993). A model for teaching about photographic research methods: Presentation, critique and revision. In R. M. Boonzajer Flaes & D. Harper (Eds.), *Eyes across the water two: Essays on visual anthropology and sociology* (pp. 105–117). Amsterdam: Het Spinhuis.

Bogdan, R. C., & Biklen, S. K. (1997). *Qualitative research for education: An introduction to theory and method* (3rd ed.). Boston: Allyn & Bacon.

Branch Douglas, K. (1998a). Impressions: African American first-year students' perceptions of a predominantly white university. *Journal of Negro Education, 67,* 416–431.

Branch Douglas, K. (1998b, November). *Seeing as well as hearing: Responses to the use of an alternative form of data representation in a study of students' environmental perceptions.* Paper presented at the annual meeting of the Association for the Study of Higher Education, Miami, FL.

Brecheen, K. (1982, July). *Towards the conceptualization of the photographic image.* Paper presented at the Annual Meeting of the Association for Education in Journalism, Athens, OH.

Bruner, J. (1990). *Acts of meaning.* Cambridge, MA: Harvard University Press.

Collier, J., Jr., & Collier, M. (1986). *Visual anthropology: Photography as a research method* (rev. ed.). Albuquerque, NM: University of New Mexico Press.

Dempsey, J. V., & Tucker, S. A. (1994). Using photo-interviewing as a tool for research and evaluation. *Educational Technology, 34*(4), 55–62.

Denzin, N., & Lincoln, Y. (1994). Methods of collecting and analyzing empirical materials. In N. Denzin & Y. Lincoln (Eds.), *Handbook of qualitative research* (pp. 353–360). Thousand Oaks, CA: Sage.

Detenber, B., & Reeves, B. (1996). A bio-informational theory of emotion: Motion and image size effects on viewers. *Journal of Communication, 46*(3), 66–84.

Eisner, E. W. (1982). *Cognition and curriculum: A basis for deciding what to teach.* New York: Longman.

Eisner, E. W. (1994). *The educational imagination: On the design and evaluation of school programs* (3rd ed.). New York: Macmillan.

Eisner, E. W. (1997). The promise and perils of alternative forms of data representation. *Educational Researcher, 26,* 4–10.

Ewald, W. (1985). *Portraits and dreams: Photographs and stories by children of the Appalachians.* New York: Writers and Readers.

Faccioli, P., & Harper, D. (1996). IVSA 96: Echos of Eco. *Visual Sociology, 11*(2), 3–7.

Grady, J. (1996). The scope of visual sociology. *Visual Sociology, 11*(2), 10–24.

Harper, D. (1987). The visual ethnographic narrative. *Visual Anthropology, 1,* 1–19.

Harper, D. (1988, Spring). Visual sociology: Expanding sociological vision. *American Sociologist,* 54–70.

Harper, D. (1994). On the authority of the image: Visual methods at the crossroads. In N. Denzin & Y. Lincoln (Eds.), *Handbook of qualitative research* (pp. 403–412). Thousand Oaks, CA: Sage.

Harrington, C. F., & Lindy, I. E. (1999). The use of reflexive photography in the study of the freshman year experience. *Journal of College Student Retention, 1*(1), 13–22.

Keller, G. (1998). Does higher education research need revisions? *Review of Higher Education, 21,* 267–278.

Kuhn, T. S. (1996). *The structure of scientific revolutions* (3rd ed.). Chicago: University of Chicago Press.

Lincoln, Y., & Guba, E. (1985). *Naturalistic inquiry.* Beverly Hills, CA: Sage.

Lincoln, Y. S., & Guba, E. G. (1986). But is it rigorous? Trustworthiness and authenticity in naturalistic evaluation. In D. Williams (Ed.), *Naturalistic evaluation* (New Directions for Program Evaluation, No. 30, pp. 73–84). San Francisco: Jossey-Bass.

Mann, E. (2002). *Latino college students' experiences at a predominantly white university.* Unpublished master's thesis, University of Rhode Island, Kingston.

Manning, K. (1997). Authenticity in constructivist inquiry: Methodological consideration without prescription. *Qualitative Inquiry, 3,* 93–115.

Margolis, E. (1998, Autumn). Making the invisible visible: Photographing the hidden curricula in higher education. *IVSA* [International Visual Sociology Association] *Newsletter,* pp. 5–8.

Oliver, R., & Oliver, T. (2000, April). *Photos 2000: Utilizing reflexive photography to chronicle early freshmen experiences.* Presentation at the annual convention of the American College Personnel Association, Washington, DC.

Perka, P., Matherly, C., Fishman, D., & Ridge, R. (1992). Using photographs to examine environmental perceptions of African-American and White Greek members: A qualitative study. *College Student Affairs Journal, 12*(1), 7–16.

Stage, F. K. (2001). Symbolic discourse and understanding in a college mathematics classroom. *Journal of General Education, 50*(3), 202–229.

Wang, C., & Burris, M. A. (1994). Empowerment through photo novella: Portraits of participation. *Health Education Quarterly, 21,* 171–186.

Worth, S., & Adair, J. (1997). *Through Navajo eyes: An exploration in film communication and anthropology.* Albuquerque, NM: University of New Mexico Press. (Original work published 1972 by Indiana University Press, Bloomington)

Ziller, R. C. (1990). *Photographing the self: Methods of observing personal orientations.* Newbury Park, CA: Sage.

*Chapter 9*
# LEGAL RESEARCH METHODS

**Michelle Thompson,** *New York University*

Legal research is frequently used in higher education. It can form a background for analysts of policy, be the subject of a journal article designed to inform administrators about an issue, or be the beginning of fact-finding for an administration preparing to develop campus rules and regulations. This chapter is designed as a "how to" guide to legal research for higher education professionals and students.

The following are some of the conditions in higher education that could prompt legal analysis:

- To formulate background for a dissertation or other research project such as analysis of admissions policy or on identity-based scholarship policy.
- To explore the legality of existing policy, for example, campus promotion and tenure policies.
- To address a problem/event/crisis that requires the development of new policy—for example, an increase in violent crimes around the campus or low graduation rates among female students in a specific field of study.
- To address research questions such as the relationship of legal decisions to admissions for women or the relationship of religious higher education institutions to the state.
- To address education-related regulatory concerns—for example, adjusting school registration systems for international students to be in compliance with the Bureau of Citizenship and Immigration Services (BCIS).

Virtually all aspects of education can be the subjects of legal actions and an institution should be clear about its vulnerability on these issues.

However, understanding legal research is not only about avoiding liability; it can be a way of building relationships among students, among faculty, among administrators, and between students, faculty, and administrators. Awareness of legal boundaries can be the basis of creating expectations and developing a more harmonious learning environment. Furthermore, legal research can be incorporated into academic research and writing. For many reasons, policy in and of itself makes for interesting academic study, and the law provides a means of better understanding higher educational policy. Knowledge of the current state of the law and a focus on persuasive sources are useful for developing policy. A researcher can also use law to identify legal trends and how they are informed by current and past societal debates, politics, science, and other relevant factors.

A caution, having extolled the virtues of an ability to conduct legal research: This chapter is about legal research, not about the practice of law. Only those licensed to practice law, by taking and passing the bar examination in their state of practice, may represent themselves as lawyers. Only those individuals licensed to practice law may dispense legal advice. Learning how to do legal research is useful; however, the work should be discussed and checked with an institution's legal counsel, particularly if the research is designed to provide advice on taking a particular course of action. This is one of the important components of avoiding liability—a member of an academic community should not take inappropriate or, of greater concern, illegal action because someone has the ability to find legal opinions that lack sound legal analysis. This chapter examines a case study based on a hypothetical campus situation to demonstrate relevant legal issues. The details of the case, called a "fact pattern," provide the framework for legal research. The chapter shows how to identify legal sources, find the law, read a legal case, and finally determine if the found cases are current.

## THE FACT PATTERN AND HOW TO ANALYZE IT

This chapter demonstrates the tools of legal research through a hypothetical situation called a *fact pattern*. The legal question for research is dictated before beginning a search. In contrast, a student of history does not necessarily know the conclusion historical research will yield. Therefore, the historical researcher searches for everything related to the history of Harvard University and its relationship with the city of Cambridge, Massachusetts, for example. While this is an expansive topic for research, the conclusion is open ended. Even if the researcher has a sense of the sorts of conclusions she or he wants to draw, only after examining the sources can the conclusion be determined. In comparison, legal research is more limited. The legal researcher knows the position he or she would like to pursue and uses cases to support an argument on either side, whether or not it is ultimately the winning argument.

Furthermore, if a researcher tried to find every case that applies to, for example, "free speech cases," research would be eternal. The researcher begins by generating a summary of the facts that lead to a particular situation. Those facts could stem from campus incidents. Those facts are used to limit research. With legal research, the law does not identify the facts. The facts identify the law.

Consider this hypothetical fact pattern: A vice president at State University is charged with coordinating the annual commencement exercises. The faculty committee in charge of graduation designed the program in the fall and invited the off-campus speaker. After 11 September 2001, they decided that the student speaker should be Muslim to provide information about cultural differences between Muslim and non-Muslim peoples. In February, they extended an invitation to a summa cum laude senior named Abdul Sayed, an involved and integral member of the campus community. Abdul was eager to have the opportunity to speak at graduation about his religious background because it is so important to him. The committee asked Abdul to provide them with a copy and the title of his speech by 1 May, one month before graduation, so that they could print programs. Abdul busily worked on the speech in his dorm room and, as requested, Abdul turned in a copy of his speech entitled "Jihad in the West" on 1 May. The committee became alarmed when they saw the title and sent the vice president a copy of the speech. In their alarm about the title, no one had read the speech and, given the mounting tasks to be completed, neither had the vice president. Someone in the vice president's office leaked a copy of the speech to the press. The phone started ringing incessantly and the vice president now had to take calls from reporters representing the major networks and cable news providers about the speech. Angry parents and students sent the vice president's office e-mail and left telephone messages demanding that the student speaker be removed. The vice president believed firmly in open discussion of all issues in an academic setting and was loathe to remove Abdul from the program. Abdul should give his speech. However, given the war on terrorism, the vice president feared that the university would be placed in an impolitic position. State University is subject to federal law as well as to the laws of the State of New York. What are the vice president's options in this situation?

Although this situation is hypothetical, it is the type of conflict that frequently occurs in a campus situation. Whenever one is pulled to do legal research, there is an underlying situation prompting the research. The first question to ask is, what are the facts of a particular occasion or series of occasions that trigger the research question? The same sorts of questions should arise for the academic researcher. This fact pattern presents a daunting set of issues to tackle, but by following a sequence of considerations one can dissect them to provide the legal research questions and then proceed to do research.

Consider the following when analyzing fact patterns:

- Parties or persons in the case.
- Objects and things involved.
- Locations/places involved.
- Basis of the case.
- Defense to the action (how the party potentially being sued would defend themselves in the case).
- Relief sought.

Although the novice legal researcher may not have answers to all of these questions, the more cases are read, analyzed, and examined, the more readily answers can be developed. Each question is addressed in turn.

## Parties or Persons in the Case

The researcher begins by identifying the parties and persons in the case and their relationships to each other (Wren & Wren, 1986). Whether the parties involved are members of particular classes of people or groups is a component of this question (e.g. women). The parties in this case are the Muslim student delivering the speech, the faculty committee making the decisions about who will participate in commencement, the vice president of the university, and State University. Other potential parties are students at State University, their parents, and alumni of State University. The list of potential parties should be as broad as possible.

## Objects and Things Involved in the Case

Next, the objects or things involved in this case should be identified. In this case the answer is simple because a speech is the only thing involved.

## Places Involved

One can then identify the places involved in this set of facts. The location of the graduation ceremony is involved, because that is where the speech would be delivered. Remember that at this point the vice president has not decided to allow or disallow Abdul to speak. The University itself is also involved as this is where the decision about the speakers was made, and in this case, where the speech was written. The place also includes the state where this case occurs. The researcher knows that the potential defendant is State University, but additionally, for legal research purposes the state in which State University is located is important; the case follows the laws of New York. That this university is in the United States should not be taken for granted because this case will also involve federal law.

## Basis of the Case

One then analyzes the legal basis of the case. This means "the legal theory on which the plaintiff's case is based" (Wren & Wren, 1986, p. 35). Once the parties in the case are identified, the legal bases for their actions can be better understood. The vice-president has only two options in this set of facts: Let Abdul speak, or remove him from the program. It is assumed that if Abdul does not speak, he would file suit against State University claiming that the university denied his right to speak. The question becomes why he would sue. He would sue because he did not get to present his speech—his free-speech rights under the first amendment of the U.S. Constitution were abridged. Therefore, the basis of this case would be the unlawful denial by the university of his freedom of speech. Other potential bases of the case exist as well, and a lawyer would identify as many bases on which to sue for as many parties as possible. The researcher's goal is similar, to develop many bases to consider the impact of legal issues on higher education. For example, the researcher could examine the extent to which the university denies religious freedom on campus, uses federal money to establish a particular religion on campus, and is liable for harboring potential terrorists. All these issues could be considered bases for civil and criminal actions. For the purpose of this chapter, only the free-speech issue will be discussed.

## Defense to the Action

Once the claims that the individual could bring are determined, developing a defendant's (the party being sued) defense is the next task. The researcher wants to determine the claims the defendant may bring to defeat the plaintiff's claim (Wren & Wren, 1986, p. 35). For this purpose, the university might claim that Abdul's speech is unprotected speech—meaning that the right to free speech is not absolute and that people cannot say anything anywhere.

## Relief Sought

Finally, one must understand what relief is being sought, meaning, "what the plaintiff is seeking" (Wren & Wren, 1986, p. 36). Abdul might seek an injunction to prohibit the University from barring his speech. Defendants also seek relief, and one should examine what the defendant could seek.

In reading the fact pattern and identifying the necessary questions to begin legal research, the laws we are looking for can be determined. Now that this sharper guide for beginning legal research has been developed. The next step is to find the law connected with these issues.

## SOURCES OF LAW

First, it is important to discuss the variety of legal sources available to the researcher. This discussion is the same whether researching state or federal law (Figure 9.1). Conventional legal sources include: common law—cases that are decided by judges; legislation—law that is passed by legislatures; constitutions—documents composed to lay out the structure of governments and to describe individual rights under a given jurisdiction; regulations—laws passed by governmental agencies; and finally, executive orders—laws issued outside a legislative body, by the president or state governor. Other sources can be used, such as scientific studies, journal articles (legal and other types of journals), and newspaper articles, to try to affect the law; however, these are not legal sources. More is said about these sources later. Nevertheless, the common law interprets all sources of law.

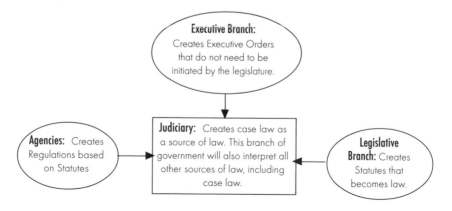

**FIGURE 9.1.** State and federal sources of law.

Each of these important sources of law rises to differing levels of legal significance. Judges have to give more weight to some sources of law than to others (Figure 9.2). Using the wrong source of law can undermine policy recommendations and/or higher education academic research. Therefore, research should be based in primary sources, sources binding upon judges unless there is a constitutional or plain statutory reason why one would pay no attention to it. Secondary sources are legal sources that appear outside the jurisdiction of the court hearing a case. In this case, the source of law is merely recommended. For the federal appellate level, this can mean outside the circuit in which the court is located. For the Supreme Court, all sources of federal (including statutory) law are secondary sources of law, unless the source of law is a decision issued by the Supreme Court (and then it is primary law) (Figure 9.3).

Anything based on state law, at this level, is a secondary source. Frequently, a specific statute or state court decision is the primary issue in the case. Facts triggered by issues that arise under state law should be researched, analyzed, and examined on the level of state law, many criminal law cases for example. If the legal analysis is based on state law, anything from the federal

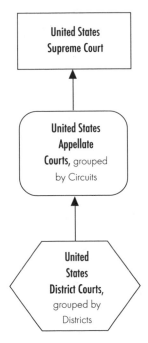

**FIGURE 9.2.** Hierarchy of federal courts.

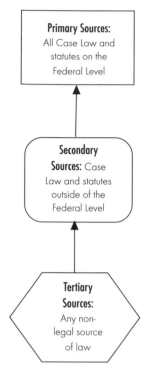

**FIGURE 9.3.** Levels of legal sources.

government is binding on the states and therefore is not a secondary source of law. The only exception to this rule is if a particular area of law has been relegated to the states through the Ninth Amendment of the Constitution. However, any law from outside of the state in question that is not federal case law or statute is a secondary source of law. Finally, federal issues can easily be raised, even if the facts initially arise out of state legal analysis.

The next level of legal sources is the tertiary set of sources. One could regard tertiary sources of law as any other piece of information one may bring to bear on a case. These sources range from law review articles to social science/scientific studies. Often these sources are used to clarify the facts in a particular case. These are often not strictly legal sources but are additional resources brought to bear on a given situation. It is important to remember that these are tertiary in legal research, although they are probably not tertiary sources of law in other disciplines. For the academic researcher, tertiary sources of law may fuel the legal research question. Ultimately, the level of sources is less critical for this research.

## FURTHER IDENTIFYING THE LEGAL ISSUES

That Abdul may sue the university because he was denied the right to give his speech has been identified as a legal claim. He might argue that the university denied his right to free speech. That the university would defend its decision on the basis that his intended speech was not protected speech, as defined by the First Amendment, has also been identified as the opposing claim. These claims are the basis for doing legal research with this particular set of facts. The first source one examines is the First Amendment of the U.S. Constitution. It states, "Congress shall make no law respecting an establishment of religion, or prohibiting the free exercise thereof; or abridging the freedom of speech, or of the press; or the right of the people peaceably to assemble, and to petition the Government for a redress of grievances" (Cover & Resnick, 1991, p. 8). The task then becomes parsing every word presented in this primary source of law. One attributes different meanings to these words to create legal claims for each side represented in a case. Congress did not tell Abdul that he could not speak; the university did. This provides a concrete legal issue to research. Return to the language of the First Amendment. It states that Congress shall make no law prohibiting the free exercise of religion. In this case, it is not Congress that prohibits Abdul's speech, but the university. Therefore, the legal question is whether the university is liable because it is not Congress that is prohibiting the exercise of free speech. This question can be further refined: Because this university is a public institution, one run by the state, for the purpose of this chapter it will be assumed that it is liable as a state. The research question will be altered to address "whether a state is bound by the First Amendment."

The university's defense should next be examined. The university defends itself by saying that Abdul's speech is not protected speech under the First Amendment. An interesting question arises here: The Constitution says nothing about unprotected speech, just that there are no limits on free speech. So then another legal question is "whether there is something called protected and/or unprotected speech and whether Abdul's speech is permissible speech." This second question is one focus of this chapter. Questions concerning the free exercise of religion can also be framed; however, this issue is not examined here. After reading this chapter, the religion-related issues can be researched to gain experience in conducting legal research.

## FINDING THE LAW

Clearly, answers to the two legal questions just delineated will be found in places aside from the U.S. Constitution. Therefore, the Supreme Court cases that bear on these issues should be found. For the purpose of describing how to do the legal research, the focus will be on the legal issues of (1) whether a state is bound by the First Amendment and (2) whether the speech written by the student is permissible speech under the U.S. Constitution's First Amendment.

As discussed earlier, there are many sources of law, but the focus here is on the U.S. Supreme Court issues, so the task becomes finding the Supreme Court cases. Most of the Supreme Court cases are published and are compiled in books called *reporters*. West is one company that publishes these reporters, using a system that provides summaries of decisions with headnotes that summarize the rules of law in each case. The headnotes are classified by a topic and key number system that makes it easier to find cases both by rule of law and factual situation (McFadden, 1997, p. 3). The problem becomes determining which heading to look under to find the two issues listed above.

Within the West digest indices, those that explicitly discuss constitutional law are readily apparent. Under the constitutional law headings, there are many cases that address the issue of whether states, in general, are covered by the First Amendment. These cases should be carefully examined. One example of an important case is key number 925: "Constitutional Law—freedom of speech and press—protection by Fourteenth Amendment," which states "The freedom of speech and of the press secured by the First Amendment against abridgement by the United States is similarly secured to all persons by the Fourteenth Amendment against abridgement by a state" (*Schneider v. State [Town of Irvington]*, 1939, p. 147). This directly addresses the fact pattern and the related research issue because it directly states that the First Amendment is explicitly applicable to the states.

Another heading in the same Supreme Court reporter, "Constitutional law—freedom of speech—scope —," states that "the freedom of speech which is secured by the Constitution does not confer an absolute right to speak, without responsibility, whatever one may choose, or an unrestricted and unbridled license giving immunity to every possible use of language and preventing the punishment of those who abuse their freedom" (*Whitney v. California*, 1927, p. 357). This suggests that there could be some limits on the type of speech that someone may use and that unprotected speech may exist.

The headings and the cases cited under the headings are reviewed until one begins to gain a perspective on the cases that would be useful for research, rather than reading the entirety of cases. Case reporters cite cases first by the case name and then the citing numbers. Legal cites are organized by the volume number, the reporter, and then the page number. Therefore, *Whitney v. California*, one of the cases referred to later, is cited this way: *Whitney v. California*, 274 U.S. 357, indicating reporter volume number 274, *U.S. Reports* as the reporter, and 357 as the first page of the case in the reporter. Your local library will have a list of the reporters, some which will be common to virtually all research libraries and others that are specific to the state and legal jurisdiction of your particular locale.

## Reading Legal Cases

*Schneider v. State (Town of Irvington)* and *Whitney v. California* are two previously identified cases useful for researching these legal issues. How are they read to glean what is needed to provide policy recommendations or for academic research? It is often useful to "brief the case," meaning to summarize the case. Many cases are well over 50 pages long, and one does not want to have to repeatedly read the entire case to elicit information. The researcher wants to be able to quickly refer to it. In this way, legal research is not unlike other sorts of research. There is a set of items that should be easily identified with each case:

- *The parties in the case and their arguments.* Although the parties in a case may begin as plaintiff and defendant, the appellant and appellee are the names of the parties at the Supreme Court level. The plaintiff may have lost at the Court of Appeals level and decided to file an appeal with the Supreme Court. Because the plaintiff is the moving party in the Supreme Court, he or she is the appellant at this level. Nevertheless, for the sake of ease in case briefs, the parties can be refered to as plaintiff and defendant based on the way the parties appear in the case title of the Supreme Court decision.
- One then wants to have a sense of *the facts that created the case.* Understanding the facts is critical because that allows one to identify similarities or differences in the case to the situation being researched.
- *The procedure of a given case,* meaning the way a case moved from the lower court level to the Supreme Court (in this case). The appellant may have appealed directly from the trial court. It would be unusual for the Supreme Court to take a case like this; however, be aware of this as the decision will explicitly discuss the reasons why the case was taken and may provide additional information for a particular set of circumstances. Furthermore, many legal issues are created simply out of these procedural facts, such as whether a case should be dismissed because it was filed in the wrong circuit.
- *The legal issues raised in the case.* These are the legal questions posed to the court for a solution. The advantage of using the West reporters is that at the beginning of the cases, they have a section of headnotes that state the rules of law from which one can directly derive the issues. An example, is whether the Fourteenth Amendment makes the First Amendment of the constitution binding on the states.

- *The rules of law, or holdings, in the case.* The West reporters list these in the headnotes portion of the case and they are restated throughout the decisions, verbatim. Holdings are the legal conclusions by which future cases will be determined. Our legal system is based on legal precedent and these holdings are the precedents for future decisions.
- *The legal reasoning* is why the court drew its legal conclusions based on the language of the decision.
- *Note any concurrences or dissents.* These are interesting parts of cases. The concurrences are agreements with the outcome of the majority of the court. However, the basis on which a justice agrees often differs and provides some variation in the legal reasoning. Dissents are outright disagreements with the majority on the outcome and reasoning of a case, and again, these are accompanied by altogether different legal reasoning. Sometimes concurrences and dissents become the basis for majority opinions in later cases and are useful in formulating a future set of policies or future legal arguments. Concurrences and dissents are secondary sources of law as they are not the rule of law themselves.

Once the cases are briefed, whether the facts address a situation similar to the fact pattern and the state of the law in a particular situation becomes clearer. Keep in mind that although cases seem factually dissimilar, they may raise identical issues that may warrant closer examination. Furthermore, at first glance, an argument may seem unsupported by the law; however, concurrences and dissents could provide supportive angles. Two examples of briefed cases are printed at the end of the chapter. For the academic researcher, the concurrences or dissents may drive the argument.

Two cases speak directly to the fact pattern described at the beginning of this chapter, *Schneider v. State,* 308 U.S. 147, and *Whitney v. California,* 274 U.S. 357. The researcher then briefs the cases as described above and discusses how they are applicable to State University. *Schneider v. State* addresses state statutory prohibitions on handbill distributions about seemingly unpopular issues. The case speaks directly to the issue of whether freedom of speech and press are applicable to the states through the Fourteenth Amendment. One of the primary issues in this case was whether a municipality overreached in protecting its health and welfare by limiting the distribution of handbills. Another issue is whether the city too broadly limited speech. The final issue is whether the First Amendment applies to the state. On its face, the facts might seem remote from State University's case. However, given that *Schneider* discusses unpopular speech and a state's attempt to limit that speech, the researcher would want to take note of this case. It does suggest that because the Supreme Court held that "[t]he freedom of speech and of the press secured by the First Amendment against abridgment by the United States is similarly secured to all persons by the Fourteenth against abridgment by a state," this would be a case to pay attention to (*Schneider v. State [Town of Irvington]*, 1939, p. 147). The University could not prohibit Abdul's speech with a defense that the First amendment does not apply to the states.

Additionally, *Whitney v. California* should be examined for additional guidance. This case defines protected speech and the limits a state may place on such speech. It is interesting because it deals with the participation of U.S. citizens in the Communist Party and related organizations. The manifestos of these organizations call for the violent overthrow of the United States and state governments, even while their members participate in the U.S. political system. In State University's fact pattern, the question becomes whether Abdul's speech possibly calling for the violent overthrow of the U.S. government is protected speech. In *Whitney v. California,* an act called the Syndicalism Act prevented such activity. The officials at State University fear that any apparent support for Islamic Jihad is akin to one's joining the Communist Party and advocating the violent overthrow of the U.S. government. The court ruled in *Whitney* that the Syndicalism Act is not "repugnant to the Due Process Clause as a restraint of the rights of free speech, assembly, and association" (*Whitney v. California,* 1927). The court states that unless the statute is arbitrary and capricious, it must stand (*Whitney v. California,* 1927), and that the court will leave it to the judgment of the legislature to judge what acts involve danger to the public peace and security of the state. Although in this case a statute is involved, it ultimately concerns a state's restriction of someone's freedom of speech and association. The university could provide some defense if it prohibits Abdul from speaking because supporting Islamic Jihad apparently (remember, no one actually read his speech and all were distracted by the title) is akin to supporting the Communist Party in that Jihad can be interpreted as advocating a violent attack on the state in the way that organizing people for the violent overthrow of the government is in the context of the Community Party.

Only two cases were examined that addressed these two issues. The West headnotes will suggest several additional cases to review. The reviewer should be familiar with as many cases addressing the legal issue as possible. Notice that all cases tend to refer to the same core of cases. The researcher should gain familiarity with that core of cases. Finally, notice in the preceding analysis that the fact pattern is often referred to. The analysis may refer to facts that are not remembered by the reviewer. It is important while doing research to continually revisit the original fact pattern so that the law applicable to the case is fully evaluated. The next section discusses other ways of finding cases to ensure the law is current.

## UPDATING THE LAW

It seems that the university would have a legal basis for making sure that Abdul does not speak. After all, his speech is arguably not protected by the First Amendment. However, before making these final judgments, there is one other task: making sure that the law is still valid. This is a useful mechanism that can be conducted more easily than in other disciplines because the researcher can turn to *one* source to determine whether something is valid. This is "shepardizing a case" because updating the law requires one to turn to the Shepard's Citators.

Wren and Wren, in their text *The Legal Research Manual* (1986), describe shepardizing this way:

> It involves tracing the subsequent treatment of cases, statutes, and some other legal authorities by using reference works called Shepard's Citations (often referred to as "citators"). Although citators at first appear to be formidable and impenetrable, you'll feel comfortable using them after a little practice. (p. 96)

This process can be conducted both through written volumes and on the computer at most academic institutions. Once the citation for a given entry is obtained, go to Shepard's for that citing authority. For *Schneider* and *Whitney*, turn to the Shepard's for the U.S. Reports as that is the publication that distributed these cases. While shepardizing a case, the researcher should make sure the volumes and the paperback supplement located in the back of the hardcover volume are examined; the paperback contains the most recent citations. If there is a consequential citing for a given case, it will indicate with a letter before the case that refers to the case to be updated (all of the citings are consequential; however, some suggest treatments that may alter arguments). There is a History and Treatment Abbreviations guide at the front of the Shepard's volume. The researcher is most concerned if a case has been criticized, limited, or, perhaps most importantly, overruled. If a case has been overruled, there is no basis for referring to it in a policy or legal discussion as the case no longer bears merit and would not be convincing authority, except for, perhaps, historical purposes. If a case has been criticized it means that the court does not agree with the reasoning in that particular case although it has not been overruled. A limited case means that the case only applies to the facts and issues raised in the case that the court considered.

Referring to Shepard's for the two cases being examined, interesting information emerges. Both cases are rather old: *Schneider v. State* was decided in 1939 and *Whitney v. California* in 1927. Starting with *Schneider v. State*, the case that establishes that the First Amendment is directly applicable to the states through the Fourteenth Amendment, one sees that it is sometimes distinguished and sometimes explained (the case is interpreted in a significant way). However, there are no treatments of this case that would be immediately alarming and it could be relied on as good law. It would also be useful to examine the cases where it was distinguished and explained for further understanding of the application of it to this case. Nonetheless, the case is still good authority.

In examining *Whitney v. California*, notice the number of times that this case has been questioned in other Supreme Court decisions. This could indicate that the court is prepared to overturn their decision in this case. Actually, after reading and beginning to brief this case, the court's position appears to be rather odd. Upon further examination, the decision has been overturned in *Brandenburg v. Ohio*, 395 U.S. 444. At this point, it would be useful to examine what was said in this decision. Just examining the headnotes of this case, one immediately notices the holding of *Whitney v. California* that is being overturned: "The constitutional guaranties of free speech and free press do not permit a state to forbid or proscribe advocacy of the use of force or of law violation, except where such advocacy is directed to inciting or producing imminent lawless action and is likely to incite or produce such action" (*Brandenburg v. Ohio*, 1969, p. 444). The facts in this case revolve around participants in the Ku Klux Klan, a group whose views are equally as controversial as those of the Communist Party or those who believe in Islamic Jihad. Nevertheless, the vce-president of the university cannot prohibit Abdul from speaking based on the title and potential content of his speech; that position is legally remiss. Only through shepardizing the case do we learn that unless his speech is likely to produce imminent lawless action, Abdul cannot be prohibited from speaking. Such is the value of making sure the cases are current. Again, notice that shepardizing cases can point the researcher in the direction of many other cases that could bear on the question being researched.

## CONCLUSION

This chapter described the process of reading and determining what is a relevant fact pattern, the basis of asking questions for legal research. After determining the parties and the issues, cases were identified that spoke to this particular set of facts. There are many more issues and cases, statutes, constitutions, and regulations that could bear on this question that went unexamined in this chapter. More thorough research would have examined the breadth of these legal options. Continue legal research on this question for additional practice to see what else can be found that would bear on this question. It is exciting to use the cases found to make policy arguments and recommendations to other circumstances. However, before making recommendations based on your research, please be cautious, as the business of providing legal advice is reserved for those who are licensed attorneys. Rely on the general counsel of a university for such advice. Other sources can reveal the sorts of cases that immediately impact on the college and university environment. These sources will be listed at the end of this chapter. The latitude in using cases for academic research is bound only by one's creativity.

Through an understanding of how to conduct legal research, the relationships between current students, administration, and the families of students are understood. In this example, all parties involved could use information discovered to try to bring the seemingly irreconcilable parties together and to identify a solution that truly upholds the notions of academic freedom and free speech that colleges and universities try to nurture. Many events that occur on college and university campuses would test these relationships. The ability to develop an institution's policy on the basis of sound legal research can actually prevent situations from developing into conflicts. These tools, used as a basis for academic articles as well as legal research methods, are valuable research tools for researchers and administrators.

## FURTHER INFORMATION

For more information on how to conduct legal research, see Kaplin (1995), Lewis (1976), and McFadden (1997). For examples in the higher education literature that employ legal research technique, see Pavela (1997), Stage and Downey (1999), and Tucker (1998).

## SAMPLE CASE BRIEFS

### Schneider v. State (Town of Irvington) 308 U.S. 147

*Plaintiff:* The plaintiffs are the people who were arrested and convicted in state court. They argue that the laws prohibiting the distribution of handbills and literature restrict freedom of speech and freedom of the press.

*Defendant:* The defendants are the cities that passed the ordinances. They argue that the ordinances are valid on their face; therefore, failing to seek a permit under the statutes does not allow the plaintiffs to contest the validity of the statutes. The ordinances represent the proper uses of the state's police power, and free speech and press are subject to the state's police power.

Examine these statutes under the due process clause and the only test is reasonableness. The intent of the ordinances is not to suppress speech but to ensure the public welfare.

*Facts:* The basis for the facts arose from three different cities. Los Angeles had an ordinance stating that people may not distribute handbills. The appellant was charged with distributing handbills for the "Friends of Lincoln" brigade that would discuss the war in Spain. The ordinance in Milwaukee is similar. This appellant's flyers concerned a labor dispute. Police arrested him and not anyone who threw the leaflet away. In Worcester, Massachusetts, the ordinance prohibited the distribution of any handbill, flyer, etc. The appellants' papers announced a protest meeting. No papers were thrown on sidewalks. In Irvington, New Jersey, one could not canvass, distribute circulars, or go from house to house without a written permit from the chief of police. Applicants had to state specific items that had to be noted in the request. The last appellant was a member of the Jehovah's Witnesses and canvassed door to door. Her materials could be bought for a small sum. She was convicted under the statute.

*Procedure:* In Los Angeles, the plaintiff was convicted; the plantiff appealed and the conviction was affirmed, and then the California Supreme Court declined to rehear the questions. In Milwaukee, the plaintiff was convicted and the Wisconsin Supreme Court affirmed the conviction. In Worcester, the plaintiff was convicted and the Supreme Court of Massachusetts overruled challenges and the convictions remained intact. Finally, in Irvington, New Jersey, the defendant was convicted and two appellate courts affirmed. All of these cases were then appealed to the U.S. Supreme Court.

*Issues:*
1. Whether the First Amendment is secured to the states by the Fourteenth Amendment.
2. Whether a municipality acting in the interest of public safety and welfare can limit the liberties in the Constitution.
3. Whether municipalities may regulate the use of their streets.
4. Whether free speech and free press deprive a municipality of prohibiting people from throwing literature in the streets.
5. Whether freedom of speech is a fundamental right.
6. Whether the courts should pay attention to the effects of legislation on the freedom of speech or press.
7. Whether an ordinance preventing the distribution of literature to prevent littering, even if only enforced against those who litter, is unconstitutional.
8. Whether an ordinance prohibiting the distribution of literature, unless one obtains a police permit, is an abridgement of freedom of speech and the press.

*Holdings:*
1. The first amendment is secured to the states by the Fourteenth Amendment.
2. A municipality may not pass legislation limiting fundamental liberties, even if aimed at protecting the public health and welfare.
3. Municipalities may regulate the use of their streets to keep them open to moving people and property if they do not limit a Constitutional right.
4. The Constitutional guarantee of free speech and press does not deprive a municipality of the power of preventing literature from being thrown in the streets.
5. Freedom of speech is a fundamental right.
6. Courts should examine the effect of legislation that is charged to abridge freedom of speech and of the press.
7. Legislation prohibiting the distribution of handbills in public streets, even if the purpose is to prevent littering, is unconstitutional.
8. Legislation requiring that an individual register with the police, where the police have the discretion of rejecting a candidate for not being of good character or free of fraud, is unconstitutional for abridging free speech and a free press.

*Reasoning:* The court provided examples of behavior that would not be protected speech: (a) standing in the middle of the street against traffic laws and stopping traffic; (b) prohibiting someone from passing because they did not take a piece of literature; (c) throwing literature in the streets.

Free speech is what the Founders intended and the court wants to ensure this right remains in place. Courts have to weigh the circumstances and the substantiality of reasons for abridging free speech. The legal test the court applies for an evaluation of these circumstances is whether the legislation imposed penalties for handing out pamphlets.

Keeping the streets clean is an insufficient justification for the ordinance. The burden the state assumes for keeping the streets clean flows from the Constitutional protections of free speech and press. The state can punish those who litter. Clean streets do not justify the police power used to prevent the distribution of handbills, etc.

When the police are allowed to censor materials through the process of issuing permits, it is a breach of the First Amendment. This is the case even if there is a charge for the materials the individual(s) is distributing.

## Whitney v. California 274 U.S. 357

*Plaintiff:* The plaintiff is an Oakland resident involved in the Communist Party. The plaintiff argued that the Syndicalism Act (the legislation being challenged in this case) runs afoul of the due process and equal protection clauses of the Fourteenth Amendment. The act also restrains the right of free speech, assembly, and association.

*Defendant:* The defendant is the State of California. The act does not violate the due process and equal protection clauses of the Fourteenth Amendment, nor does it violate the equal protection clause because the states are using their rightful police power to maintain the public welfare and safety.

*Facts:* The plaintiff had been a member of the Oakland Socialist Party. They broke off and formed the Communist Labor Party of America and she went to the convention to participate in the founding of the local branch. The party agreed to have capitalism overthrown and to establish a Communist state, partly both through violent overthrow of the government and through regular political action. She said she never intended for the organization to be an instrument of terror.

*Procedure:* Plaintiff was charged in violation of the Criminal Syndicalism Act in the Superior Court of Alameda County. The District Court of Appeals affirmed this decision. The Supreme Court of California refused to hear her appeal. She filed a writ of error to the U.S. Supreme Court and it decided to hear the case.

*Issues:*

1. Whether the Supreme Court can hear a writ of error from a state court if federal issues are present.
2. Whether the Supreme Court should give weight to a statement the highest court in the state made on a federal question.
3. Whether the Supreme Court can pass on (disregard) a federal question not explicitly raised in the pleadings, etc.
4. Whether the question of one's participation in the building of the Communist Party can be reviewed by the Supreme Court, as it is a question of fact.
5. Whether the way this California statute defined syndicalism was vague and violated the due process clause.
6. Whether the syndicalism act violates the equal protection clause because it only punishes those who advocate violent means to achieve their goals.
7. Whether arbitrary and capricious is the standard by which the equal protection clause voids a state's police laws.
8. Whether the party challenging a state law has the burden of showing the law is unreasonable and arbitrary.
9. Whether a state may ban what it finds evil without going after all such evils.
10. Whether freedom of speech is an absolute right.
11. Whether speech advocating the unlawful use of force and violence, can be infringed upon.
12. Whether presumptions are in favor of a statute.

*Holdings:*

1. The Supreme Court of the United States has no jurisdiction to review a judgment of a state court of last resort on a writ of error unless a federal question exists.
2. The Supreme Court will review the decision of a state's highest court if a Constitutional, and therefore a federal, question exists.
3. The Supreme Court cannot pass on a federal question, even if it is buried in the record.
4. Whether someone is a member of the Communist Party and builds the party is a question of fact not to be reviewed by the Supreme Court.
5. This statute defining criminal syndicalism is not vague.
6. There is no equal protection violation because this statue punishes those who advocate violent means of changing industrial and political conditions.
7. The equal protection clause does not prevent the state from adopting police laws unless the laws are arbitrary and capricious.
8. The party challenging legislation has the burden to show that the law is arbitrary and capricious.
9. A state may properly direct its legislation against what it deems an existing evil without covering the whole field of possible abuses.
10. There is no absolute right to free speech.
11. Statutes don't infringe upon speech that advocates violence, acts of force, or terrorism to achieve industrial or political change.
12. Every presumption is to be indulged in favor of the statute.

*Reasoning:* The Court defines the primary issue as whether "the Syndicalism Act and its appreciation in this case is repugnant to the due process and equal protection clauses of the Fourteenth Amendment" (*Whitney v. California,* 1927). The plaintiff argues that this act violates the due process clause because it is vague. The test for vagueness is, can a reasonable person guess at a statute's meaning and differ about its application? The Court has upheld acts that are more vague than the one before the Court. The test for whether a statute is valid under the equal protection clause is whether it has a reasonable basis and is not arbitrary. This act is not based on a classification and affects everybody the same way and is therefore reasonable and not a violation of the due process clause.

*Concurrence:* The opinion is concerned that with the court's ruling, a step in preparation that threatens public order will be punished. However, free speech and expression are not absolute rights. Enacting a statute does not make it valid. The Court must examine when the interest is the right of free speech and assembly. The test the judge would apply to this case is how remote is the danger. He states that the courts have not set a standard for this. "To justify suppression of free speech there must be reasonable ground to fear that serious evil will result if free speech is practiced" (*Whitney v. California*, 1927). There is a big difference between advocacy and incitement, and that has to be remembered. This means immediate serious violence is expected. Only emergencies can justify the suppression of free speech. Imminent danger is not enough if the evil was not serious. Police measures can be invalidated because they were unduly harsh or oppressive. They remain valid if there is a serious probability of injury to the state. In this case, he sees evidence of a conspiracy with these facts to commit serious crimes. This is why he would leave the judgment intact.

## REFERENCES

*Brandenburg v. Ohio.* (1969). 395 444 (Supreme Court 1969).

Cover, R. M., & Resnik, J. (1991). *The federal procedural system: A rule and statutory source book.* Westbury, CT: Foundation Press.

Kaplin, W. A. (1995). *The law of higher education: Legal implications of administrative decision making.* San Francisco: Jossey-Bass.

Lewis, M. R. (1976). Social policy research: A guide to legal and government documents. *Social Services Review, 50*(4), 647–654.

McFadden, D. L. (1997). Legal research for historians. *Western Legal History, 10*(1 & 2), 3–30.

Pavela, G. (1997). Disciplinary and academic decisions pertaining to students: A review of the 1995 judicial decisions. *Journal of College and University Law, 23*(3), 391–401.

*Schneider v. State (Town of Irvington).* (1939). 308 147 (Supreme Court 1939).

Stage, F. K., & Downey, J. P. (1999). Hate crimes and violence on college and university campuses. *Journal of College Student Development, 40*(1), 3–9.

Tucker, B. P. (1998). Disability discrimination in higher education: A review of the 1997 judical decisions. *Journal of College and University Law, 25*(2), 349–359.

*Whitney v. California.* (1927). 274 357 (Supreme Court 1927).

Wren, C. G., & Wren, J. R. (1986). *The legal research manual: A game plan for legal research and analysis* (2nd ed.). Madison, WI: Adams & Ambrose.

*Part 4*

# USING PREEXISTING DATA
# AND RESOURCES

*Chapter 10*

# SECONDARY ANALYSIS
# OF DATA

**Deborah Faye Carter,** *Indiana University*

Primary research involves data collection and analysis, whereas secondary data analysis is the use of data that have already been collected for another purpose (Fortune & McBee, 1984; Kiecolt & Nathan, 1985). Most of the chapters in this volume refer to specific research techniques. However, secondary analysis does not refer to a specific statistical technique; it simply refers to the kind of data used (Kiecolt & Nathan, 1985). Secondary analysis can be useful for researchers, practitioners, and/or doctoral candidates writing dissertations who are interested in studying higher education settings. Collecting primary data on college students can be an expensive and time-consuming activity. Given the myriad ways in which many institutions collect data on students, it may be possible to use data collected for another purpose, to analyze for a particular unit's goals and aims (this is discussed extensively in chapter 12).

This chapter discusses the strengths and weaknesses of secondary data analysis as it relates to survey data and the kinds of databases that may be useful in higher education settings. The chapter also offers practical suggestions and recommendations for conducting secondary data analyses.

## POSSIBILITIES AND LIMITATIONS OF SECONDARY ANALYSIS

The strengths of secondary analysis are several. First, this kind of analysis can save personnel, money, and time. The main resources associated with secondary data analysis involve "obtaining the data, preparing them for analysis . . . and conducting the analysis" (Kiecolt & Nathan, 1985, p. 11). The time it takes to obtain secondary data is significantly shorter than the time it takes to develop a survey, administer it, and create a database. Also, it is possible to complete a secondary data analysis project individually, whereas a large primary data collection project may necessitate a team of researchers and/or research assistants.

Depending on the kind of data used for secondary data analysis, many of the national databases have representative samples and strong data collection techniques. These databases contain information on thousands of students. Typically, institutional research offices (or federal/state governments) have already manipulated the data, so that many problems with the data have been identified and perhaps addressed. For instance, often in the federal databases, some sampling issues or coding problems are typically resolved before the data are available to the general public. In fact, the National Center for Educational Statistics (NCES, 2002) includes an advisory for all researchers using the data sets to perform analyses using certain sample weights so as to correct for sample bias.

The limitations of secondary data analysis include the lack of availability of data, the inappropriateness of databases for certain research questions, and the difficulty obtaining accurate documentation on the databases. It may be difficult to gain access to some databases that may be useful for the research project at hand. Several federal databases through the National Center of Educational Statistics (NCES, 2002) are committed to wide distribution of some forms of the data. In addition, there are restricted-use versions of the NCES databases that are more difficult to obtain. Other national databases of surveys of college students have restrictive data use policies and involve paying a fee for use of the database for a certain period of time, or paying on-site research assistants to analyze the data and sending the results to the person requesting the analyses.

A second limitation is the potential inappropriateness of databases for addressing certain research questions. Unlike primary research, where a researcher can design a survey to meet his or her needs, in secondary data analysis, a researcher must find the database(s) that can address the research questions. Typically such databases do not address the questions as completely as one might like, and there may be variables, unexamined in the database, that may have contributed to additional understanding of the core problem. Thus, secondary data analysis is a technique where researchers have to do their best with the database(s) that are available.

Finally, obtaining good documentation on the databases can be challenging. It is critical to know several key things about the database: how the databases were constructed, when the data were gathered, how many people were surveyed initially, what the actual survey questions were, and if and how any variables in the database were constructed or altered. This documentation can help researchers develop proper understanding of how to treat variables in the database and how to interpret the results of the analyses. Documentation such as this exists for federal databases; however, such detail is sometimes difficult to come by for other national and local surveys.

## TYPES OF DATABASES

This section provides a more extensive description of three main types of databases that can be used for secondary data analysis in higher education settings. Other types of databases may be appropriate for secondary data analyses, but are not covered here.

### Federal Databases

Federal efforts at data collection mostly aim to develop databases that are representative of the nation at large. Therefore, the federal databases can be useful for examining national trends for faculty, high school students, or college students at the particular points in time that the federal studies were done. Some widely used databases include the National Education Longitudinal Study (NELS), which is a longitudinal study of eighth-grade students that continued after high school graduation, and the Beginning Postsecondary Student Longitudinal Study (BPS), which is a longitudinal study of 1992 first-year students.

In addition to the databases that survey students over several years, other federal databases may be of interest to higher education researchers and practitioners. The National Postsecondary Student Aid Study (NPSAS) examines how postsecondary students fund their college experiences. The National Study of Postsecondary Faculty (NSOPF) is a comprehensive study of faculty in 1987 and 1992.

NCES runs training workshops on the federal databases in the summer. These workshops are advertised at various national meetings of professional organizations and typically individuals can attend for free (by applying for a small grant) or for a small fee. Many institutions also have summer statistics workshops where individuals can use their own databases to learn how to do analyses.

Institutional researchers frequently utilize the Integrated Postsecondary Education Data System (IPEDS)—a database that reports various statistics about all of the postsecondary institutions in this country. Statistics reported to IPEDS include average tuition, percent of students receiving financial aid, demographic information on students and faculty, and additional institutional information. What is unique about IPEDS is that people can develop institutional comparisons of similar institutions based on the various statistics reported to IPEDS. Therefore, if a researcher were thinking broadly about comparing his or her home institution with other institutions nationwide that have similar enrollments, public/private affiliation, and faculty/student ratios, the researcher could develop a database of this information using IPEDS (IPEDS, 2002).

One main limitation of the federal databases is that they often cannot address institutional interventions in an appropriate manner. If researchers were interested in the specific impact of a set of programs or policies on a particular college campus, it would be better to utilize campus-specific databases rather than the federal databases. In short, the federal databases are best for addressing national trends and are appropriate for research questions that may involve broad institutional comparisons (e.g., students attending two-year vs. four-year institutions).

## Institutional/National Databases

A second type of data is the institutional/national surveys. Two popular examples of this type of survey are the Cooperative Institutional Research Project (CIRP, 2002) and the College Student Experiences Questionnaire (CSEQ, 2002). Many institutions pay to use these surveys every year and receive the results in a database format to use and reanalyze for secondary analysis purposes. Institutions may allow for offices other than the institutional research (IR) office (which often distributes and analyzes the data) to use the data. CSEQ and CIRP typically can add questions to the standard survey instruments that are institution specific in the event there are certain issues or programs—not represented on the standard survey—that the institution is interested in exploring. Also, the CSEQ and CIRP instruments may provide data comparisons between the survey results for one campus and the whole population of survey participants or to similar institutions.

## Single-Institution Data

A final kind of secondary data is that which a single institution collects. Some institutions invest in major data collection themselves, and this may be used subsequently for secondary analyses. The advantage of institutions collecting their own data is that they can construct their own survey that may better suit their needs. Another advantage is that the survey data may be merged with registrar records and/or other databases to add additional demographic and outcome variables. The disadvantage is that the survey results might not be easily comparable to other institutions. Once a major data collection has been undertaken, those data can be reanalyzed year after year and may suit the needs of various units on campus, and results may be interesting to faculty and practitioners/administrators alike.

## SECONDARY DATA ANALYSIS IN ACTION

The previous sections provided a definition of secondary analysis, discussed strengths and weaknesses of the technique, and described the main types of databases. The remaining sections of this chapter provide a case study of a higher education administrator who wants to use secondary data analysis and describes the main steps in performing such analyses. This example is for illustrative purposes. Any member of the higher education community (faculty, doctoral students and dissertation researchers, administrators, etc.), with proper training, can perform secondary data analyses.

## The Case of Karen Cordova

Karen Cordova is the Director of Orientation and First-Year Programs at State University. The university, one of the two largest public institutions in the state, has a total undergraduate enrollment of about 25,000 students. Karen has held her position for two years and feels comfortable enough in her role to think about more complex ways that her office can improve programs and program delivery to students.

The Orientation and First-Year Programs Office oversees several programs for first-year students. The office organizes and delivers three orientation programs: a 6 week program in the summer for students who are low-income and academically at risk, and two programs that are conducted a few days before the first day of classes—one for reentry students and one for the undergraduate population at large. In addition, the First-Year Programs Office conducts an orientation for Freshman Interest Groups (FIGs) that involves about 50% of that population.

Karen wants to research the impact her office has on student retention on campus (particularly first-year retention). She is also interested in investigating how orientation programs affect student satisfaction with the university, and whether the programs help students learn more about the campus, campus procedures, and how to solve problems (e.g., billing problems, financial aid problems) more effectively.

In addition, State University is going through a bit of a budget crisis. State appropriations are down and concern exists that campus budget cuts may affect various student affairs divisions. Karen knows anecdotally that students really enjoy the program and feels her office contributes to student success, but she would like to do research to see if her beliefs are supported. Given the budget cuts and the fact that her office staff is very small, Karen has decided that she does not have the resources nor the time to design a primary study, distribute surveys, enter the data, analyze the data, and report findings. She is interested in utilizing secondary data analysis, which she understands may be a cost- and resource-effective way of addressing some of her research questions.

## Seeking Assistance

Before Karen begins the analyses, she decides to seek assistance in how to do secondary analysis. Seeking assistance is an activity that may last the entire time a person is working on a secondary analysis project. If analyzing secondary data is not a task that individuals do very often, it may be appropriate for them to take advantage of research assistants or IR staff members or to audit their campus statistics courses. Even if individuals have considerable expertise in working with secondary data, they still need to ensure they have appropriate documentation on the databases and will probably want to consult with individuals who have developed the database(s) to confirm their understanding of the survey design and the main variables.

## Secondary Analysis Steps

The following six steps, modified from Fortune and McBee's (1984) nine, are required for secondary research analysis: (1) identifying the research problem, (2) gaining access to appropriate data bases, (3) constructing the research design for the problem and specific database(s), (4) preparing the data and examining key variables, (5) analyzing the data, and (6) reporting the results. Using Table 10.1, the following sections of the chapter discuss each of these six steps.

### Identifying the Research Problem

As with any study, the first question that should be asked is, "What and who are you studying?" Individuals completing primary analyses would proceed to constructing the survey, focusing on distributing the survey to a particular sample of students and then planning how to enter the survey data before

**TABLE 10.1**
**Karen Cordova's Steps in Performing Secondary Data Analyses**

| Step | Description | Karen Cordova's actions |
|------|-------------|--------------------------|
| 1. | **Identifying the research problem** | Given the databases available to Karen, she could only focus on one of her two proposed research questions: the effect of orientation and first-year programs on student retention. |
| 2. | **Gaining access to appropriate databases** | She spoke to the Dean of Student Affairs and the Institutional Research Office to gain access to the annual university survey data. |
| 3. | **Constructing the research design** | Karen requested that the survey data be linked with institutional retention information. She also decided to focus on some key variables for her study: orientation program attendance, transition to college variables, demographic information, GPA, and academic experiences, in addition to retention information. She decided that logistic regression would be her major statistical method of choice. |
| 4. | **Preparing data** | |
| 4a. | Generate a list of variables | She performed a Descriptives command using SPSS. Karen checked data for correct coding, looked at the mean averages and standard deviations of all variables, and verified sample sizes. |
| 4b. | Identify key variables | Since the institutional research office cleaned the database before giving access to Karen, for this step, she only had to verify that the data were present for most students. |
| 4c. | Perform any data transformations | Karen recoded some variables and checked their distribution through histograms. |
| 4d. | Select the target sample | She wanted to focus on first-year, full-time undergraduate students only, so she selected those students for statistical analyses. |
| 5. | **Analyzing data** | |
| 5a. | Examine methodological design | Karen checked her design with the actual data set, and her plans fit well with the actual data. |
| 5b. | Statistical analyses may need replication | Karen determined demographic information for the students in the orientation programs. She also examined general trends of students who attended the orientation programs. Karen performed logistic regression to see if the orientation programs had an effect on students' retention. |
| 5c. | Reporting results | Karen composed a report for the Dean of Student Affairs. |

the data analyses could begin. However, for secondary analyses, the construction of the research problem is then directly linked with the content of databases. In previous sections, I discussed the types of databases that may be available to researchers. It is important for individuals thinking about secondary analysis to have a good idea of the research problem, and to have a good idea of what can be studied in various databases. Therefore, individuals need to know not only what kinds of questions can be addressed in secondary analyses (generally), but also what kinds of questions can be addressed using data from each specific database to which they have access.

Recall the main research questions that Karen Cordova had: (1) the effect orientation and first-year programs have on student retention and satisfaction with the university; and (2) whether her office's programs helped students learn more about the campus and campus procedures. Karen researches various databases at the federal and national level and concludes that the annual survey that State University handed out to first-year students would be the database that would best suit her needs. She realizes that given the databases available to her, she can focus only on the first research question. No database at State University contains variables that allow her to address student satisfaction.

## Gaining Access to Appropriate Databases

Gaining access to various databases is one of the key issues in conducting secondary data analyses. Research plans have changed when certain databases were not available for use. One way to gain access to databases is to contact individuals on campus who have the responsibility for maintaining the database or who have used the databases in the past. Karen's first task to formally gain access to the database is to speak to the Dean of Student Affairs to discuss what she needs to do to obtain the data. Often the IR office on a campus is a good place to start for institutional database needs. Given the campus, IR offices may have differing guidelines with regard to providing data. Some offices may ask that the researcher work with an IR staff person while performing analyses, particularly if a merge of registrar's data with another data source is needed. If individuals are interested in using federal databases for their analyses, the NCES web site is a good place to look for the guidelines and procedures for obtaining access.

## Constructing the Research Design for the Problem and Specific Databases

Once researchers have access, they need to examine the databases carefully to design their data analysis. When undertaking this examination of the databases, it is important to have the actual survey instrument that was administered. It is crucial to know the exact wording of the survey questions when designing the analysis and in interpreting results. Also, researchers should ensure they have clear documentation regarding how the survey was administered and the time points represented by the data in the database. Is the database longitudinal (multiple time points are represented) or cross-sectional (data gathered at one point in time)? A final issue that should be clear in the documentation of the database is whether any variable transformations were performed in the database or whether there were alterations to the sample.

Researchers also should begin to start thinking about the statistical techniques they want to use in analyses and which variables may need to be further investigated, recoded, or grouped with other variables into a scale. In Karen Cordova's example, she may find that the particular institutional database asks questions she wants, but that the database does not provide information about retention rates. Karen decides to ask her contact person in the IR office whether it is possible to link the survey database with retention information. She discovers that because the survey information can be linked with student ID numbers, such a merge can be done. The IR staff person merges the databases for Karen and gives her access to the new database.

Not everyone can obtain a database that may so easily address their needs, but it is presented it here as a possibility. Given increases in technology and the ways that various campus offices are linked by similar software, it is more likely in the future that several institutional databases can be linked with surveys to provide necessary background information on students.

There are two final main parts to constructing a research design: making preliminary decisions on which statistical packages to use and completing human subjects forms. Different statistical packages have specific capabilities regarding the kinds of analysis that can be done. Sometimes choosing a statistical package is a personal preference issue (e.g., using SAS or SPSS for multiple regression), whereas at other times the statistical package selected is the only one that may be available for performing an advanced statistical function. Utilizing resources on campus for statistical training may be necessary when deciding on appropriate software to use for analyses.

A final issue is human subjects approval. Human subjects approval varies from campus to campus. Some campuses do not require that human subjects approval be granted if secondary analysis is performed or if campus administrators perform the research as opposed to faculty or graduate students. Other campuses do require such approval. Therefore, researchers need to become acquainted with the human subjects policies on their campuses to determine whether approval is necessary. Human subjects approval, if necessary, must be granted before the analyses can begin, so once the research design is adequately developed, the application should be submitted to the appropriate committee.

## Preparing the Data and Examining Key Variables

After researchers complete a research design (in the third step) for analyzing the data, they put this plan into place for the fourth step. Typically, preparing the data for analysis is a time-consuming task and involves several substeps.

   *a. Generate a list of all the variables in the database* that shows the high and low values, the number of cases, and the mean average and standard deviation. For example, the "Descriptives" command in SPSS provides this information. Completing this first substep is critical because researchers can determine whether the design they constructed matches the actual data, and they can determine whether additional data manipulation, previously unanticipated, needs to be done.

   When examining the Descriptives output in Karen Cordova's study, the researcher looks for several things. Usually when data are completed, placeholders are entered for missing responses. For instance, assume a survey question asks respondents to indicate on a scale of 1 to 5 "the degree to which orientation programs helped them adjust to college." Frequently, a "9" is entered for all missing responses to this question. Analyzing the data without indicating that "9" responses are missing can artificially skew the means of items. It is important to identify particular responses as missing where necessary. Various statistical software packages handle the identification of missing values differently. Therefore, the researcher, perhaps in consultation with experts and others on campus, must appropriately use the software to handle those cases with missing data.

   A second thing to look for in the Descriptives output is whether there are any data entry or data merge problems. Karen receives documentation on the database that the college adjustment variable is supposed to be scaled from 1 to 5, but the descriptive output shows that the low value is $-1$ and the high value is 60. Therefore, Karen must investigate this variable in detail to determine the problem. Possibly the difference in the ranges may be due to the coding of missing data, but on her own or with the help of her IR office or other experts, Karen still needs to track down the problem.

   Third, researchers should examine the means and the standard deviations of the main variables in the research design. Most statistical procedures work best on sets of variables where there is a fair amount of deviation in the responses. In Karen's study, if all the students responded to a similar degree that orientation programs helped them adjust to college (with the standard deviation being quite small), this indicates that perhaps the satisfaction variable may not be a good one to use in certain statistical functions. It may be helpful to look through statistics books to see what the common assumptions are behind various procedures, or it may be useful to consult with experienced researchers who can help interpret the findings and can suggest appropriate statistical procedures.

Fourth, looking at the N—the number of valid responses—can help researchers discover whether there are problems with missing data and sample sizes. It is particularly important to examine how the number of valid responses may change throughout the database—especially if the database is comprised of data from different sources. Examining the valid N is particularly important when databases are merged because a smaller percentage of individuals may have responded to survey data than are on the institutional databases.

*b. Identify the key variables that are of interest to the research problem.* The key variables are those that are the focus of the research design developed in the third step. Often, because these variables are the focus, they necessitate more rigorous investigation before analysis begins. A first step toward further investigation of key variables is confirming the kind of numeric variables that are being used. Numerical variables can be classified as ordinal, categorical, or continuous. Statistical techniques vary depending on what kind of variables will be used. In developing a research design, a statistical analysis plan was formulated, but such plans may need to be changed if the variables have a different classification than previously assumed.

For instance, if your dependent variable is whether a student left or stayed—this is typically a dichotomous variable (a type of categorical variable) and researchers often must use logistic regression to address this research question. If your dependent variable is GPA or credits earned, this is typically a continuous variable, and a range of techniques such as multiple regression or analysis of variance may be used to address the research question.

Another component of more rigorous investigation is the examination of the scatter plots or histograms of (continuous) dependent variables to see how the variable is distributed. Some statistical techniques assume that variables need to be normally distributed, whereas other techniques allow for more skewed distributions. Also, researchers may want to do more rigorous investigation of variables in preparation for data transformations. If the database contains multiple measures of similar items, Karen may decide to add the variables together to make a scale. Before a scale can be constructed, Karen needs to perform factor analyses and reliability analyses.

*c. Perform any necessary data transformations.* This step involves creating variable scales, determining how missing data will be dealt with, and recoding variables. Variables that include a numerical value for missing cases need to be recoded prior to analysis.

After all data transformation is completed, researchers should save the data with a new name to separate the new file from the original files. Also, it is important to keep documentation that describes the kinds of transformations made to the file so that if there are data problems in the future, they can be tracked down. After the file is saved, researchers need to run a Descriptives list of the key variables in the database again (see preceding substep) and compare this to the previous Descriptives list to make sure the data transformations were completed correctly.

   *d. Select the target sample of the analyses.* After the data transformations are completed, the researcher needs to focus on the sample. Going back to Karen's scenario, she will be most interested in focusing on first-year, full-time undergraduate students. She knows that students could utilize three different orientation programs and that some students can attend more than one. Her first step in selecting a sample will be to select only those individuals who were first-year, full-time students over the previous five years. Because variables in the data set represent the date of students' first semester at State University and number of credits enrolled, she can select only the students who were first-year students in the last five years and attended full-time. Karen is also primarily interested in the students whose first semester was the fall semester because the orientation programs are most fully developed for fall-semester students. Karen decides to run Descriptives on the data again after she has narrowed down her sample.

## Analyzing the Data

Once the data are obtained, the two most time-consuming aspects of secondary analyses are data transformations and data analyses. The previous steps covered data transformation possibilities, and this step describes analyses. There are two main elements to this step: constructing the design, and performing the analyses.

   *a. It is important to look over the proposed methodological design* to determine whether the design developed in the third step fits the database after data transformations are performed and the sample is selected. One key element of checking the design again before analyses is that variables may have changed in the recoding process (gone from ordinal to dichotomous; ordinal to continuous) and therefore the statistical procedures previously chosen may not fit the new database. This again may be an area where individuals may want to consult with individuals experienced in performing statistical analyses.

   *b. Typically, statistical analyses that involve more than one variable need to be replicated* several times to account for different variables that may be included in the model. Karen decides to start her analyses by trying to determine the demographic information for students in each of the three orientation programs. She decides to choose 10 to 15 key variables and run mean averages and frequencies on each the variables. She thinks it would be important to see the general trends of students who were in each orientation program. She also wants to see which students took advantage of more than one orientation.

After Karen completes the descriptive statistics of the model, she decides to perform logistic regression to see if the orientation programs had an effect on students' first-year retention. She uses items from the survey of first-year students and combines that information with end of first semester GPA to see which variables might have affected students' retention. Karen has little experience with logistic regression, but a graduate assistant completing a practicum in her office for the year has recently taken advanced statistical courses. This student assists Karen with the methodology and the refining of the statistical models.

## Reporting Results

After Karen and Janice work to complete all the analyses, she decides to present the information to the Dean of Student Affairs and uses charts and a 20-page report to outline her main findings. When reporting results, an important consideration for Karen is her audience. Karen knows that other administrators on campus may not have familiarity with advanced statistical techniques, so she feels it is important for her to have tables and graphs that are simple to explain. Karen relies on several statistics resources and published articles that seemed to explain advanced techniques in a clear fashion. These resources help her develop a clear report, whose implications are not buried in a sea of statistical jargon.

If the primary purpose for doing secondary analysis is not for publication in an academic journal, the presentation of the results should be easily understood and the use of jargon should be limited. It is also helpful to go to the library and look up published articles using similar statistical techniques so it is clear what the standards are for displaying information in table format. Many social science fields use the *Publication Manual of the American Psychological Association* (APA) as standard reporting format. In an administrative setting, the reports may not need to be as formal, but APA style still has useful guidelines for appropriate ways to discuss research, research methods, and how to display data in tables.

## CONCLUSION

Secondary data analysis can be a cost-effective means to study the impact of higher education on various populations. It requires fewer resources than primary data, and given the amount of data collected on the college student population specifically, learning how to merge data and analyze them for the purpose of assessing effective delivery of programs and services is a critical need. This chapter highlighted some of the main issues with regard to secondary data analyses and discussed practical database issues in performing secondary analyses.

## FURTHER READING

To read more about specific techniques using secondary data analyses, see Ewell (1995), Lenth (1991), and Staman (1987). See Pedhazur (1997) for information on multiple regression techniques. For examples of secondary data analyses, see Carter (1999, 2001), St. John, Paulsen, and Starkey (1996), and Hurtado, Inkelas, Briggs, and Rhee (1997).

## REFERENCES

Carter, D. F. (1999). The impact of institutional choice and environments on African American and White students' degree expectations. *Research in Higher Education, 40*(1), 17–41.

Carter, D. F. (2001). *A dream deferred? Examining the degree aspirations of African American and White college students.* New York: Routledge.

College Student Experiences Questionnaire. (2002). *College student experiences questionnaire research project.* Retrieved 1 May 2002. <http://www.indiana.edu/~cseq>.

Cooperative Institutional Research Program (2002). Retrieved 1 May 2002. <http://www.gseis.ucla.edu/heri/cirp.htm>.

Ewell, P. T. (1995). *Student tracking: New techniques, new demands* (New Directions for Institutional Research, no. 87). San Francisco: Jossey-Bass.

Fortune, J. C., & McBee, J. K. (1984). Considerations and methodology for the preparation of data files. In D. J. Bowering (Ed.), *Secondary analysis of available data bases* (New Directions for Program Evaluation, no. 22, pp. 27–49). San Francisco: Jossey-Bass.

Hurtado, S., Inkelas, K. K., Briggs, C., & Rhee, B. (1997). Differences in college access and choice among racial/ethnic groups: Identifying continuing barriers. *Research in Higher Education, 38*(1), 43–75.

Integrated Postsecondary Data System. (2002). *The Integrated Postsecondary Education Data System.* Retrieved 11 December 2002. <http://nces.ed.gov/ipeds>.

Kiecolt, K. J., & Nathan, L. E. (1985). *Secondary analysis of survey data.* Newbury Park, CA: Sage.

Lenth, C. S. (1991). *Using national data bases* (New Directions for Institutional Research, no. 69). San Francisco: Jossey-Bass.

National Center for Education Statistics. (2002). *Survey and program areas.* Retrieved 1 May 2002. <http://nces.ed.gov/surveys>.

Pedhazur, E. J. (1997). *Multiple regression in behavioral research* (3rd ed.). Orlando, FL: Harcourt, Brace.

Staman, E. M. (1987). *Managing information in higher education* (New Directions for Institutional Research, no. 55). San Francisco: Jossey-Bass.

St. John, E. P., Paulsen, M. B., & Starkey, J. B. (1996). The nexus between college choice and persistence. *Research in Higher Education, 37,* 175–220.

*Chapter 11*
# POLICY ANALYSIS

**Teboho Moja,** *New York University*

Policy analysis refers to one or several stages in the policy process. The absence of a single clear definition of what policy refers to adds to the complexity of what is often referred to as policy analysis. Green (1994) argued that the definition of policy "would have to capture the difference between basic and procedural policy, between prescriptive and permissive policies, and policies simply expressing the bare application of standard requirements in administration" (p. 2). The definition ranges from policy as a combination of rules to policy as a strategic choice.

Policy analysis could consist of a study of choices made in a particular setting to address a particular problem or problems by the state, an agency, or an institution. The study could be designed to focus on a course of action taken, that is, policies adopted, and to conduct a comprehensive analysis of the outcomes of those choices. Policy analysis could focus on an analysis of changes that have taken place within a specified period to assess whether the changes were a result of policy or whether other factors played a role in the success or failure of policy to address specific problems. Policy could also be used as a variable in an attempt to explain organizational processes or procedures for decision making or factors that could influence policy.

Policy analysis research, within a democratic environment, is possibly the most participatory of all research in higher education. Without broad involvement of everyone concerned with an issue, at every level, the analysis is doomed to failure or, at best, has serious limitation. The participatory nature makes each analysis a negotiation, with competing contributions, needs, and observations all playing a role in this dynamic process. Coleman (1991) argued that it is not necessary to involve stakeholders in all stages of research but only in the research design and analysis of data. However, most policy formulation studies involve stakeholders in most stages.

The participatory nature of this process can be illustrated through a scenario where the director of a residence hall needs to develop new policy. For example, there might be a need to develop a policy to address the problem of increasing levels of incivility based on race, ethnicity, sexual orientation, and gender. A whole range of constituencies can be involved in the policy analysis process. Representatives of different groups affected directly or indirectly can be involved in discussions over the issues at hand or even present written submissions on how the issues can be addressed. In turn, those representatives can have discussions with their constituents and develop policy positions to be submitted for consideration. Administrators of residence halls can also present their input through reports and recommendations. Court documents analysis can provide data of cases dealing with hate speech, and all inputs and information can be used to develop a policy document for discussion by the administrative council before final policy is adopted. For information on conducting legal research, see chapter 9.

The current envisioning project of the California Master Plan is an example of policy analysis within a democratic environment. The process includes broad consultations within the state and beyond, as well as input from international experts around choices to be made as a way of building consensus. It is important to remember that policy analysis includes a study of choices made or to be made to address a problem by a state or institution.

It is also important to make a distinction between policy analysis from a researcher's perspective and policy analysis for policy formulation purposes. The policy analysis process by a researcher may be more focused on understanding the debates informing policy, the potential outcomes of policy, and the policy instruments chosen. One conducting policy analysis research could focus on analyzing trends in the debates and in documents on policy discussions to address the issue of race-based admissions. The researcher could also conduct policy outcome analysis of case studies of institutions that have implemented similar policies to assess their successes, failures, or unanticipated outcomes. There could also be an analysis of policy instruments used such as funding mechanisms or incentives to encourage implementation of policy. The outcome of such research would not be new policy but generation of knowledge, offering insights into what could possibly work or an understanding of success and failure. The outcome for an experienced researcher could be advice or recommendations on action to be taken.

The focus of this chapter is on the policy analysis process that involves taking action to address a problem or stimulate change. In a scenario where the faculty of a small liberal arts college is troubled by the seeming disconnection of its commuting and part-time students and declining enrollments, a policy analysis dissertation project could study the trend, whereas policy research by an experienced researcher might focus on the development of new policies to reverse the trend. The research outcome of the former will inform other scholars in the field and the faculty senate on these students and the ways the college can serve them. The latter would lead to the actual development of new policy on how to serve those students and other policy options such as recruiting local students to fill the gap.

## REASONS FOR EMBARKING ON A POLICY ANALYSIS PROCESS

Higher education administrators are often involved in policy analysis for the sake of providing research findings that are of immediate use within their own work environment. The administrative units within which they operate serve as sources of information for policy analysis. The action required often includes setting goals to be achieved. Such goals are influenced by the values and principles adopted by an organization, institution, or government. For example, a commitment to ensure that there is equal access to opportunities provided by an institution, commitment to improving quality, or commitment to promoting efficiency within an institution would shape the type of action taken by an institution. In policy formulation the values underpinning new policies need to be prioritized because it is difficult to achieve all of them on an equal basis.

Various reasons trigger a need to embark on a policy analysis process. The following are some of the conditions that could lead to the development of new policy.

- To examine the effectiveness of existing policy—for example, the effectiveness of policies in addressing diversity issues among students, staff, and faculty.
- To address a problem/event/crisis that requires the development of new policy—for example, an increase in violent crimes around the campus or a problem of low graduation rates among female students in a specific field of study.
- To create public policy for a new need that has arisen—for example, the use of the Internet in residences or on campus. At the state level it could be policy for schools on the use of computer networks.
- To address requirements to comply with guidelines put forward by funding agencies or government—for example, the need to report on the registration status of international students on campuses.

The information needed to guide policy analysis may be acquired from various sources within institutions. Policy analysis may make use of existing data such as the evaluation records of existing programs or throughput rates of groups under investigation. Institutions are a good source of information needed in the policy analysis processes. Data that are readily available are in most cases quantitative in nature. For example, in addressing the problem of low graduation rates, there are likely to be data on the number of students entering the program under investigation, data on graduation figures, drop-out figures, and duration of study before graduation. Quantitative data are useful for mapping out trends, establishing patterns, and tracking performance of a selected sample. Quantitative data provide essential information but have limitations in the sense that they do not always provide explanations for observed trends.

In contrast to readily available quantitative data, qualitative data—fundamental to policy analysis—are often not readily available. In addressing the issue of graduation rates of female students in a science program, it is unlikely that there would be data on record pertaining to the experience of female students in the program or their perceptions of the program. Undertaking a range of studies and organizing policy debates in which representatives of various campus constituencies discuss solutions to problems could generate new data where such data are not readily available. The advantage of using or supplementing qualitative data with quantitative data is that the latter provide in-depth understanding and offer explanations for changes or observed trends. Cloete et al. (2002) studied changes in a higher education system as a result of new policies and used quantitative data to track changes that took place and qualitative data collected through interviews and reflections by key players to interpret and understand factors that contributed to change in that system, as well as reasons for choices that were made in the implementation of policy.

In making a case for the likelihood that local resources are directly relevant, Hite (2001) included interviews as a key local resource or subjective human knowledge resource in policy processes. A wide range of people involved in a program under review could provide perspectives on information needed in the policy analysis processes. These could include students, faculty, staff, and alumni of the program. The department of chemistry described in chapter 1 could use data collected through interviews with alumni and students who have participated in the web-based chemistry class offered or used the web labs in their own classes to develop department-wide policy on web-based chemistry lab modules. Additional data could be collected through interviews conducted with faculty and graduate assistants involved.

Additional important resources in policymaking are records and reports of past experience within the institution or lessons from the experience of others in addressing similar issues. Past experiences provide data on records of successes, failures, and perhaps unintended outcomes in policy implementation. Policy discourses in the form of criticism or proposals in higher education, which are not generally regarded as research, may also provide valuable information (Kaneko, 2000). A literature review of the area and issue under scrutiny can also serve as a valuable resource. Hite (2001) suggested that literature review in policy analysis serves the purpose of informing the design of new policy and that it is useful for the comparison with other settings similar to the one under investigation.

## POLICY PROCESSES

The process of policy analysis includes the identification of a problem as well as the development of a solution to the problem. The problem must be identified in terms of policy, that is the need to state the problem as a policy problem; then determine the policy objectives; and finally make policy decisions. The provost could identify a policy problem from a study conducted by a sociology professor, curious about hierarchy and social support in the academy, particularly for untenured professors, who has published a report on the lack administrative support within the institution. The provost can identify the problem as a policy problem, and can then ask the associate provost to write a discussion document for consultation with the broader constituencies within the institution, stating policy objectives that would address the problem. Finally, policy decisions can be made and new policies put in place to provide more support to faculty, particularly untenured faculty. The process of making policy is sometimes as complex as the problem it seeks to resolve. If the problem is clearly stated, it becomes easier to focus on the problem or a set of problems related to the issues being addressed. Later in the chapter I return to the issue of defining a problem.

The process followed in policy analysis is as critical as the actual outcome of that process. In some instances good policies have failed simply because the process was not inclusive. Those affected by the new policy ultimately rejected it or even intentionally sabotaged its implementation process. The role players in policy processes include a range of actors such as the decision makers and those who are affected directly or indirectly by the decisions made. Consultation with a wide range of players is sometimes critical, depending on the impact of the policies to be adopted. The benefit of consultations is that it provides an opportunity for those affected by a new policy to be informed before the process is completed and for them to make a contribution to the process. Consultations also contribute to consensus building among those affected by policy and to its effective implementation at a later stage (Moja & Hayward, 2000). It is important to remember that consultations play a dual role in listening to the actor's views as well as building consensus around strategies that should be adopted in addressing problems.

Policy processes are often messy and unstructured (Evans, Sack, & Shaw 1995). Successful policy analysis could be considered an art, with the researcher carefully orchestrating several kinds of events and data collections to engender as broad participation as possible, as well as the widest range of possible, solutions in the analysis. The sequence of stages and the number of stages depend on conditions existing within an institution. The time it takes to complete a process also varies widely, depending on the issue to be addressed and the resources available.

The process could involve an analysis of existing policies, data collection, the conducting of studies, promoting debates, scenario-building exercises, consultations with various constituencies, and other activities. In analyzing existing policies, there is a need to determine the effectiveness of those policies and to understand what has and what has not worked and the reasons for that. For data collection, the use of local resources has an advantage of immediate and direct relevance to the problem under investigation. If data are not readily available, it might be necessary to conduct a study to generate the data needed. Data could be generated through debates on an issue, and that could serve the purpose of incorporating different perspectives under discussion. Scenario building exercises are helpful in projecting possible impact of policy under consideration.

Policy processes are informed by policy research and require some understanding of both qualitative and quantitative research methods. There are advantages and limitations in the use of either qualitative or quantitative approaches to policy research. Both approaches could be used to collect different kinds of data. To be useful in making policy recommendations, data collected using both approaches need to be linked during the analysis stages. Lack of technical training and expertise should not be perceived as an obstacle to acquiring and applying research data in policy analysis processes. Handbooks such as those by Stephen Hite (2001) provide guidance to educational policymakers in accessing relevant data and evaluating research results, specifically for policy formulation. There are also courses that teach research methods, specifically for policy formulation purposes in specific disciplines.

## POLICY STAGES

Policy stages are sometimes referred to as policy cycles or steps. In this chapter, reference is made to *stages*, as the use of the terms *cycles* or *steps* creates the impression that the process is orderly. The use of *steps* or *cycle* creates the expectation that one step neatly follows the other to complete the cycle. Policy processes are not linear, even though there are identifiable stages that will be discussed in the next section. Evans et al. (1995), in studying educational policy formulation processes in a number of countries in Africa, concluded that the process is "complex, less clearly ordered, and seldom reflects a simple application of technical rationality in decision making" (p. 2).

The literature on policy analysis is often presented in handbooks or how-to books (Bardach, 1995; Fogler & LeBlanc, 1994; Stockdye & Zeckhauser, 1978), with stages, ranging in number from about four to eight, that sometimes include substeps (Weimar & Vining, 1992). The California Department of Finance has developed a matrix of the steps for policy analysis, making use of 17 sources that identify a total of 10 steps, which are used in different combinations, by different authors. Presenting policy stages "helps to make sense of the challenge, even though it does not provide fully applicable guidelines for policymakers working in real world settings" (Evans et al., 1995, p. 4).

In this chapter, I have clustered the stages into the following categories:

- Policy research.
- Policy options.
- Policy recommendation and adoption.
- Policy implementation, assessment, and adjustment.

The number of stages and the emphasis on some of the stages are often influenced by the nature of the problem, the resources available, the political environment, or the analyst's background.

## Policy Research

Policy research is a critical stage in policy analysis processes. Policy research is conducted to inform the policy process and to specify what kind of data is needed at the different stages. A review of research literature is critical and needs to be done in the early stages of defining the problem to be addressed or in formulating research questions. It is important to remember that the research questions in policy analysis processes are more practical in nature and are aimed at providing practical answers. The questions differ from theoretical questions aimed at generating knowledge for knowledge's sake, that is, seeking the truth and contributing to knowledge production processes.

Successful policy analysis processes rely on the availability of educational research. However, there is recognition that there is a shortage of high-quality educational research (Hite, 2001). Part of the problem is that higher education research, in particular, is perceived as not being scholarly, because it is more theme driven than discipline driven. It has, however, the advantage of providing information that has been generated by researchers and highly sophisticated practitioners (Teichler, 2000).

Policy research aims at drawing conclusions or generating data that have policy implications. Research methods are used to develop research, but the nature of issues under investigation and the scale of the project often determine the process to be followed. If extensive research methods are used in policy formulation processes, they should include a research question, literature review, data collection, qualitative and quantitative analysis, policy formulation, and evaluation. The results need to be presented in such a way that they meet the needs of the decision makers for policy adoption purposes. A challenge in policy research is the need to raise the quality of policy research and to increase the impact of that research on new policies.

### Defining a Problem

There is need for a systematic study of the problem in order to make recommendations for policy. It is important to understand the reasons why policy is needed in a specified area and what purpose it will ultimately serve. Good policy choices depend on an understanding of the existing conditions within an institution. An assessment of the situation is likely to clarify the problem and to assist in formulating the research questions. The processes of clarifying the problem or formulating research questions need to include other role players, to ensure that alternate perspectives of the problem are taken into consideration. An example might be the need to diversify the student population at a higher education institution.

Using this example, it would be important to start by analyzing existing policies and programs on diversity, to assess how effective or ineffective they are. The process would entail an analysis of institutional records to collect data that indicate directly the effectiveness of the relevant policy. Quantitative data could indicate the representation of different groups within an institution. Information that may not be readily available, through institutional records, might be the data that refer to "feelings" that there are discriminatory practices that work against achieving diversity on campus. In this instance, climate surveys, although expensive and time-consuming, could be a useful aspect of problem definition.

### Information Sources

Various sources could be used in the literature review process and for collecting data necessary for policy analysis. Higher education as a field of study has the advantage of having a mixture of practitioners, researchers from various disciplines, as well as higher education researchers contributing to the understanding of the field (Hite, 2001). Some of the sources identified include the following:

- Higher education commission reports for reform.
- Higher education regional symposia reports.
- Research produced at institutions of higher education.
- Research produced by small or large higher education research units.
- Government policy documents.

These can be added to existing local information to provide a broader context or to provide suggested solutions to specific issues.

## Policy Options

Data analysis should lead to the drawing of conclusions that would be recommended as policy options. Policy options are choices made from a set of alternative actions to address a specific issue. Policy options can be presented as the outcomes or results of policy research. The outcomes need to be presented as a synthesized research report to be useful for policy formulation purposes. There is need to put emphasis on applicability of the results, taking into consideration institutional applications and sensitivity to existing constraints, particularly resource constraints.

Different solutions can be explored as options and the anticipated outcomes of each option can be weighed. This would entail a combination or comparison of options, to assist in making policy choices. Factors to take into consideration when comparing the options include costs, that is, the affordability of implementing the proposed policy/solutions, and the acceptability of those policies to those affected. Another criterion for weighing options is to consider the efficiency and effectiveness of the options outlined, to addressing the problem identified.

The process could include a scenario-building exercise to "predict" outcomes. In scenario building, quantitative and qualitative data analysis may be used to understand possible outcomes within a specific institutional environment. The advantage of predicting an outcome is that it provides analysts with a base for assessing the effectiveness and efficiency of the policy options that address the problem identified in the previous stage. There might be a need at this point to revisit the problem identified and to redefine it. The original definition could be extended to include unanticipated outcomes predicted through scenario building as well as anticipated outcomes. Through this process, the advantages of the option chosen can be compared with the cost involved in implementing it. The acceptability of the preferred option may also be assessed, as well as the potential impact of the new policies. It is important for policy analysts to spell out the advantages and disadvantages of the different options proposed, and they should even indicate their preferred options.

## Policy Recommendations and Adoption

Policy recommendations and adoption are part of the policy analysis process and could include further consultations. Policy recommendations are proposed solutions to the problem, and policy adoption requires decision making. Those charged with the task of addressing an identified issue could present policy recommendations in a report that could then serve as a discussion document. Such reports often reflect collectively shared values, areas of consensus, and sometimes include areas where there are differences that have not been resolved. In most cases, issues that are difficult to resolve are highly sensitive in nature and require political decisions. The report could then be widely circulated for consultations, responses, and general feedback. It is at this stage that those actors who have not been directly involved in the process can be informed about the issues under discussion and make their input in the process of formulating new policy. Depending on the nature of the problem, there might be a need to reach consensus through consultations, debates, and perhaps even focus groups. This stage also contributes in ensuring that there is support for new polices before their implementation.

Adoption of policy entails the production of a policy document that has taken into consideration the feedback received. It is up to the decision makers to use their discretion as to what should be included in the final document and what should be left out, in order to reflect their own stance on the issues.

## Policy Implementation, Assessment, and Adjustments

Policy implementation is another stage in the policy formulation process. Implementation is part of the process, as there is need to monitor the implementation process for success or failure, so that adjustments may be made to the new policies. Policy formulation processes are in themselves challenging and each stage seems to be more difficult than the preceding stage. It is often at the implementation stage that good policies fail. There are different opinions as to why good policies sometimes fail at this point. Some suggest a combination of factors, such as lack of implementation capacity, lack of resources, and external factors that have an impact on institutional policies (Cloete et al., 2002)

Policy implementation requires the development of an implementation strategy and a plan to carry out action, "spelled out" in the policy. The action plan might outline target objectives and in some instances completion dates. The development of an implementation plan makes monitoring of the policy implementation process, as well as the assessment of the impact of policy, much easier.

During the implementation stage, various players and actors involved in translating policy into action, continue to influence policy. The influence could be either positive or negative, particularly if there is no consensus on the strategy or action to be taken to address an identified issue.

The monitoring of implementation processes is critical for assessing impact of the new policies, as well as for making the necessary adjustments to achieve the set objectives. Assessment and monitoring of policy implementation would provide feedback on what the following steps should be. There might be a need to make adjustments to adopted policies or even to start the process all over again by developing new policies. Making adjustments by means of democratic processes is sometimes confusing to certain actors, because the activity might be perceived as proposing new policies while excluding the input of the other actors.

## CONCLUSION

The policy analysis stages could seem confusing, but what is important is to remember that for either a student or an experienced researcher, the five basic steps are first, problem definition or identification; second, data collection (both are referred to as the policy research stage earlier in this chapter); third, analysis; fourth, development of options (both referred to as policy option stage); and finally, recommendations or advice (referred to as policy recommendation and adoption stage). A complete policy cycle would include the final stage referred to as implementation, assessment, and adjustment for practitioners.

Policy analysis entails two broad challenges. One is that of democratizing the processes through broad participation by actors who would be affected by new policies and by actors who are likely to be the implementers of the new policies. Coleman (1991) suggested that interests could be represented in the design of the research and data analysis stages only. Others, however, argue for broad participation at all stages. The process is time-consuming but essential if there is need to build consensus around choices to be made and successful implementation of policy.

The other challenge is that the policy stages are not clearly demarcated and therefore overlap with each other. There could be overall policy adopted, and in implementing it, a strategy or action plan could be perceived as new policy and could be contested by those affected. In highly democratized situations, decision makers are often frustrated by the actors' demand for continued participation so that they feel that democratic processes constrain their activities and delay implementation processes. Once sufficient consensus is reached, it is important to conclude the consultation process and not be caught in an infinite loop of consultations.

## FURTHER READING

For more information regarding techniques used in policy analysis, see Hite (2001), Coleman (1991), and Birkland (2001). For examples of policy analysis in the literature, see Pillay and Cloete (2002) and the National Commission on Higher Education (1996).

## REFERENCES

Bardach, E. (1995). *Policy analysis: A handbook for practice.* Washington, DC: Library of Congress, Department of Finance Training Library.

Birkland, T. A. (2001). *An introduction to the policy process: Theories, concepts, and models of public policy making.* Armonk, NY: M. E. Sharpe.

California Department of Finance. (1997). *Policy stages matrix.* <http://www.dof.ca.gov/fisa/bag/matrix.pdf> (15 March 2002).

Cloete, N., Fehnel, R., Maassen, P., Moja, T., Perold, H., & Cibbon, T. (Eds.). (2002). Transformation in higher education—Global pressures and local realities in South Africa. Cape Town, South Africa: Juta and Company.

Coleman, J. S. (1991). Social policy research and societal decision making. In D. S. Anderson & B. J. Biddle (Eds.), *Knowledge for policy: Improving education through research.* New York: Falmer Press.

Evans, D. R., Sack, R., & Shaw, C. P. (1995), *Formulating education policy: Lessons and experiences from Sub-Saharan Africa.* Association for the Development of African Education. Paris, France.

Fogler, S. H., & LeBlanc, S. E. (1994). *Strategies for creative problem solving: Six steps to problem solving.* New York: Pearson Education.

Green, T. F. (1994). Policy questions: A conceptual study. *Education Policy Analysis Archives, 2*(7).

Hite, S. J. (2001). *Reviewing quantitative research to inform educational policy processes.* Paris: UNESCO—International Institute for Educational Planning.

Kaneko, M. (2000). Higher education research, policy, practice: Contexts, conflicts and the new horizon. In U. Teichler & J. Sadlak (Eds.), *Higher education research—Its relationship to policy and practice.* Paris: International Association of Universities.

Moja, T., & Hayward, F. M. (2000). Higher education policy development in contemporary South Africa. *Higher Education Policy, 13,* 335–359.

National Commission on Higher Education. (1996). *Report—A framework for transformation.* Parow, South Africa: CTP Printers. <www.gov.za/education>.

Pillay, P., & Cloete, N. (2002). *Strategic co-operation Sscenarios: Post-school education in the Eastern Cape.* Report produced by compress. <www.compress.co.za>.

Teichler, U. (2000). The relationship between higher education research and higher education policy and practice: The researcher's perspective. In U. Teichler & J. Sadlak

(Eds.), *Higher education research–Its relationship to policy and practice*. Paris: International Association of Universities.

Stokdye, E., & Zeckhauser, R. (1978). *A primer for policy snalysis*. New York: W. W. Norton.

Weimar, D. L., & Vining, A. R. (1992). *Policy analysis: Concepts and practice* (2nd ed.). Englewood Cliffs, NJ: Prentice Hall.

## Chapter 12

# USING AND ENHANCING EXISTING DATA TO RESPOND TO CAMPUS CHALLENGES

**J. Fredericks Volkwein,** *Pennsylvania State University*

Despite their apparent popularity among those seeking degrees and credentials, today's colleges and universities face several interrelated public criticisms and concerns. First, many students are not successful and few campuses can explain why: Some students are highly successful, others struggle and take longer to graduate, and still other students seem to disappear after a few semesters. A second concern regards organizational productivity and inefficiency. Virtually every sector of the economy except education has made substantial gains in productivity over the years. Considerable resources are devoted to the processes of recruiting, educating, and graduating diverse populations of students in a competitive environment. Student dropouts and delays in college completion produce costly inefficiencies in the educational system. A third concern pertains to the high cost of higher education—a concern expressed by parents, college students, and taxpayers alike. Since 1970, tuition and fees on public and private campuses have risen on average at a rate that is double the increases in the Consumer Price Index. The fourth concern focuses on effectiveness. Most customers are willing to pay more for higher quality and better service, but it is not clear that our higher tuition prices translate into higher quality. There is ample evidence from employers and researchers alike that many college graduates are not as well educated, nor as employable, as they were in the past and as they need to be in the future.

When these competing concerns about student success, productivity, cost, and educational effectiveness all collide at the campus level, they create an array of campus tensions for campus leaders, planners, institutional researchers, and student affairs administrators at all levels (Volkwein, 1999). This chapter describes how universities can use, and have used, systems of local data gathering to respond to these concerns with facts and evidence to better inform internal and external stakeholders, as well as to take corrective action.

## SUGGESTIONS FOR USING EXISTING LOCAL DATA

Some very practical steps can be taken locally by the campus to address these problems and alleviate these concerns—start with a model or a framework, conduct an inventory of existing information, avoid the paralysis of the grand plan, and use the results for constructive organizational change.

### The Value of a Model

Start with a model that shapes research and data collection activities so that they provide information about institutional goal attainment, effectiveness, and improvement. Whether derived from the research literature, adapted from another college, or developed locally, a model encourages thought clarity, serves as a guide for designing data collection and analysis, and makes campus decision support efforts more efficient. A model-driven system of periodic data collection avoids the expensive trap, sometimes stimulated by accountability pressures, of the need to measure everything all the time.

Higher education scholarship has produced an array of theories and models that explain the relationship between students and their colleges (Pascarella & Terenzini, 1991). Drawing from this pool of available models, at least four major assertions regarding the interactions between students and their colleges and the influences of collegiate experiences on student outcomes can be cited. The most traditional view is that precollege characteristics such as student backgrounds, academic preparedness for college, and clear goals are the main factors accounting for differences in academic performance, persistence behavior, and other educational outcomes (Astin, 1991; Feldman & Newcomb, 1969; Stark, Shaw, & Lowther, 1989).

A second group of perspectives falls under the general description of studen–institution fit models (Pascarella & Terenzini, 1991). Perhaps the most widely researched of these models claims that student persistence and growth depends on the degree of successful integration into the academic and social structures of the institution (Spady, 1970, 1971; Tinto, 1987, 1993). Other student–institution fit models focus on the importance of student involvement and effort (Astin, 1984; Pace, 1984), on the importance of support from friends and family in college adjustment (Bean, 1980; Bean & Metzner, 1985; Cabrera, Castaneda, Nora, & Hengstler, 1992; Nora, 1987), and on financial variables and the student's ability to pay (Cabrera, Nora, & Castenada, 1992, 1993; Cabrera, Stampen, & Hansen, 1990; St. John, 1992). Although the majority of these models have been constructed to explain one outcome, student persistence, several researchers have successfully used these and similar models to explain other outcomes including student growth and satisfaction (Pascarella & Lorang, 1982; Stage, 1989a, 1989b; Strauss & Volkwein, 2002; Terenzini, Springer, Pascarella, & Nora, 1995a, 1995b; Terenzini, Theophilides, & Lorang, 1984a; Terenzini & Wright 1987a; Volkwein 1991; Volkwein, King, & Terenzini, 1986; Volkwein & Lorang, 1996; Volkwein, Valle, Blose, & Zhou, 2000). More recently, one model has been presented to explain the educational outcomes of community college students (Voorhees, 1997). More than others, the Voorhees model emphasizes the competing demands of family, work, and community.

A third set of assertions emphasizes the importance of campus climate in student adjustment (Bauer, 1998). Perceptions of prejudice, discrimination, racial harmony, and tolerance of diversity have gained increased attention as factors accounting for the differences in persistence rates between minorities and nonminorities (e.g., Cabrera, Nora, Terenzini, Pascarella, & Hagedorn, 1999; Fleming, 1984; Hurtado, 1992, 1994; Hurtado, Carter, & Spuler, 1996; Loo & Rolison, 1986; Nora & Cabrera, 1996; Smedley, Myers, & Harrel, 1993). All students need to be able to function in a safe environment, without fear of oppression, stigma, or violence, in order to maximize their chances of success (Reynolds, 1999). Creating a campus climate for all students that allows for optimal development is a major factor in successful student outcomes (Upcraft & Schuh, 1996).

Fourth, structural/functional perspectives, drawing from the literature on organizations, encourage researchers to give greater attention to those variables that reflect the influence of organizational characteristics (Hall, 1992; Strauss & Volkwein, 2002; Volkwein & Szelest, 1995). Studies of colleges and universities, as particular types of organizations, have shown that campus mission, size, expenditures, complexity, and selectivity exert small but significant influences on a variety of internal transactions and outcomes including student learning and skills, values, aspirations, and educational and career attainment (Pascarella & Terenzini, 1991; Toutkoushian & Smart, 2001; Volkwein, Szelest, Cabrera, & Napierski-Prancl, 1998). In their recent synthesis of the literature, Berger and Milem (2000) concluded that an array of organizational features and behaviors influences student experiences and outcomes. The Berger and Milem conceptual model extends the Pascarella model (1985) and the Weidman model (1989). These are the only models that give prominence to campus organizational behaviors and structural characteristics as influences on student outcomes.

These four perspectives—precollege characteristics, student–institution fit, campus climate, and organizational characteristics—provide complementary theories regarding the influences on educational outcomes. In order to capture a holistic perspective of educational outcomes, and to respond sensibly to campus environmental problems, it is useful to start with a model to guide the development of measures and data collection. The most straightforward approach is to start with a simple input–process–output, or IPO, model. Two such models are shown here and they have served as organizers for research conducted at Pennsylvania State University and the State University of New York at Albany. Both models assume that a variety of outcomes (outputs) are the products first of characteristics and experiences that students bring with them (inputs), and second of their various college experiences inside and outside the classroom (processes).

The Penn State Model (Figure 12.1), developed by Patrick Terenzini for the National Study of Student Learning, serves as a good organizer for gathering categories of information related to learning outcomes (Terenzini et al., 1995a, 1995b). The Albany Model (Figure 12.2), developed by Volkwein (1991, 1992) suggests in greater detail some of the information items and

### Student Learning Model
Terenzini et al. (1995, 1996)

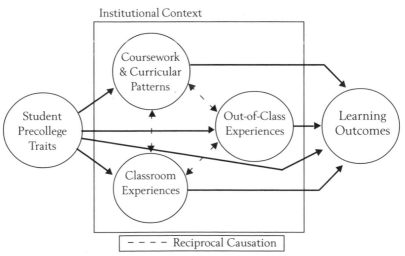

FIGURE 12.1. Penn State's student learning model.

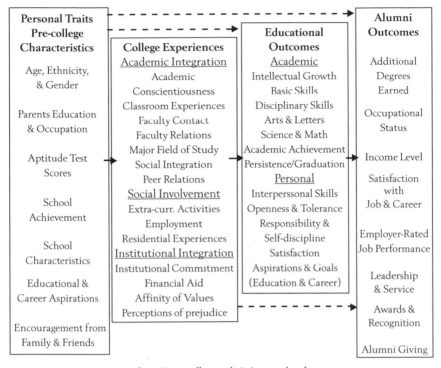

<http://www.albany.edu/ir/reports.html>

**FIGURE 12.2.** Albany outcomes model.

scales that reflect the four perspectives and concepts from the literature discussed above. The educational outcomes in the Albany Model are products of a multiyear strategic planning and mission development process that identified particular goals and outcomes for undergraduate education at the institution. Each outcome can be examined in relation to the precollege and college experiences that produced it.

## Avoid the Paralysis of the Grand Plan

Although models are beneficial organizers and guides for data collection and analysis, campuses should avoid the paralysis of the grand plan. The "grand plan" is the attitude, typical in academic organizations, that there must be a comprehensive, long-range research plan for data collection and analysis, and that you can't do anything until there is administrative, faculty, and governance agreement. In the real world outside academe, successful research and analysis often starts simply with existing evaluative efforts and data and then builds upon them. Rather than the scholarly strategy of starting with a research question and then designing a scientifically controlled data collection, it is often advantageous to work backward from existing data and examine what questions can be answered from it, before collecting new data. Getting started in this way can produce early findings that not only influence campus decisions and policy, but also enhance subsequent, more formal data collection.

## Conduct an Inventory of Existing Sources of Information.

Many campus offices store information that is potentially useful once it is examined for its relevance to a particular model or to mission goal attainment. Academic departments and administrative offices alike sometimes collect information that they do not have the time nor resources to examine thoroughly. Offices engaged in student advisement and services and support activities frequently survey students and collect information that has value beyond their particular operation. Campuses should launch new data collection activities only after reviewing and learning from what's already available. Sources of information can include:

- Admissions and student recruitment data.
- Surveys of prospective and entering students.
- Financial need/aid data.
- Student ratings of instruction.
- Retention and graduation rates for different student subgroups.
- Frequency of use data for services and facilities.
- Academic program reviews.
- Reviews/evaluations of offices, services, facilities.
- Academic testing and course placement exams.
- Surveys by various offices of particular student or faculty populations.
- Career placement, alumni reunion, and alumni survey information.
- Exit interview/survey information from departing students and faculty.
- Student transcript request data.
- Fund-raising data.
- Student transcripts with enrollments and grades in courses and majors, academic standing, and credits earned elsewhere.

This inventory can be a particularly useful exercise if it is taken to the next step—matching the data and information against an outcomes model. Table 12.1 illustrates how this is accomplished, at a particular university. Arraying the data in this way sets the stage for analytical studies that examine the connections among all these variables.

**TABLE 12.1**
**Local Variables That Are Consistent With the Albany and Penn State Models**

| | | |
|---|---|---|
| Precollege variables | Total SAT score | Class rank |
| | Ethnicity/diversity | Graduate school aspirations |
| | Male/female | Science and math oriented |
| | Age | Goals for major and career |
| | Financial need | Service/activities/leadership |
| | Parent's education | Entry status (transfer credit, |
| | Marital status | advanced placement) |
| | Dependent children | Special abilities/interests |
| | High school average | (athletics, art, music, theatre) |
| College experiences | Classroom experiences | Faculty relations/advisement |
| Academic integration | Study habits | Faculty contact–social |
| | Remediation | Faculty contact–academic |
| College experiences | Peer relations | Hours employed on/off campus |
| Social integration | Perceptions of climate | Support from friends/family |
| | Financial aid mix | Use of, and satisfaction with, |
| | Social/activities | services/facilities |
| | Involvement | |
| General outcomes | Cummulative GPA | Would attend "all over again" |
| | Goal clarity | Additional degree aspirations |
| | Retention/graduation | Loan repayment/default |
| | Time to degree | Overall satisfaction |
| Outcomes | General education skills | Arts, letters, and humanities |
| Intellectual growth | Social and behavioral | Science and engineering |
| | sciences | |
| Outcomes | Interpersonal skills | Responsibility/self-control |
| Personal growth | Openness/Tolerance | Leadership/team building |

## EXAMPLES OF STUDIES USING EXISTING DATA

Presented next are several examples of the ways campuses have used local data to address important policy problems and to shape decisions. Each example begins with a set of local data that reflects an array of measures about student precollege characteristics, college experiences, and outcomes. Every campus has a strategic self-interest in periodically collecting such data and maintaining data sets. The examples described here are entirely transportable to other campuses. The first example (A) uses simple descriptive statistics on registration data, nothing more complicated than tests of significant difference between means, to examine the similarities and differences between populations of transfer and native students. The second example (B) compares students who graduate on-time with "extenders" who take longer. This example begins with descriptive analysis of transcripts and finishes with multivariate analysis. The third example (C) uses an accreditation self-study as a stimulus to aggregate the results from several multivariate outcomes studies. This exercise draws a powerful conclusion about the impact the university has on its students and what matters most.

## Example A: Comparing Freshmen and Transfers—Responding to Faculty and Community College Concerns

At one university, a small group of faculty complained to the provost and to members of the faculty senate about the poor quality of transfer students in their classes. These faculty members believed that the university was lowering the quality of undergraduate education by favoring transfer students over freshmen who were better qualified. They argued for stiffer admissions standards in general, but especially for more rigorous screening of community college transfer students. These complaints were aired in several meetings of the university senate and its committees, eventually made it into the student newspaper, and got back to some of the university's most prominent community college transfer sending institutions.

   This is a hot-button issue for many universities, but especially at this campus where the enrollment management and budget targets are heavily dependent on a steady flow of upper division community college transfers. The university had a number of formal transfer credit agreements with community colleges in the state, and the faculty criticism placed these agreements at risk. Moreover, the open campus debate did little to make community college transfer students feel welcome at the university. The problem required analysis.

   There are both educational and economic reasons for being interested in the collegiate experiences and outcomes of transfer students. They constitute a significant and growing population, ranging from around 30% to 40% of bachelor's degree recipients at the majority of four-year colleges and universities, including the one discussed here. The economic stability of many colleges depends on successfully attracting those who begin their first years at some other institution. Only a scant handful of studies examine the transfer experience and its impact on the growth and development of this population. How do transfer students and native freshman compare in terms of their university experiences, academic performance, intellectual growth, and other outcomes?

   Having assembled an inventory of existing information along the lines just summarized, the institutional research staff at this particular university began an immediate comparison of juniors and seniors who entered the university via different routes. Quickly available information included the annual retention and graduation rates for various student groups, the advisement center data on academic probation and dismissal, survey data from entering freshmen and transfers collected every two to four years, and responses to the latest senior outcomes survey (collected every four years). This information was used to identify a group of several hundred recent survey respondents; transcripts were examined for these students.

The resulting descriptive analysis of the two populations showed the following:

- Retention and graduation rates for new community college transfer students exceeded those for new freshmen.
- Rates of academic probation and dismissal were almost identical in the two populations.
- The transcript analysis suggested that about half the transfer students made an easy academic adjustment and exhibited a solid academic performance in the first two semesters after transfer. The other half performed poorly in the first one or two semesters, and about half of these recovered (25% of the total population) and half did not. In the two semesters before graduation, the academic records of the seniors who entered as freshmen and those who began their college education at a community college were indistinguishable.
- The native seniors reported superior experiences in areas related to social integration, friendships, activities involvement, and personal growth, while the transfer students tended to be more oriented toward gaining career skills, and less involved socially.
- In sum, there were over four dozen measures of campus experiences and outcomes showing trivial differences between the two populations. The satisfaction survey data for the two groups revealed no significant differences on those items reflecting their academic integration, faculty contact, and intellectual growth. The two groups exhibited similar profiles of overall satisfaction, general education values, feeling that they made the right decision, and plans for graduate school and additional degrees.

Thus, the differences between community college transfers and native frosh at this university appeared mostly outside the classroom. The two groups exhibited similar rates of academic success and failure, and they reported similar academic experiences, satisfaction, and intellectual growth. Transfer seniors were more career oriented and less socially connected to their peers, but in most other important respects there were no statistically reliable differences between the two groups.

Once these findings were shared with various internal and external audiences, they had a calming effect on the debate and gave the president and provost valuable messages to carry. Internally, the discussion turned its focus toward creating a more engaged social climate for transfers, and on overcoming the rocky first two semesters that some transfer students experienced academically. Externally, the report stimulated a series of university meetings with community-college presidents and provosts. Eventually, reports were developed to provide community colleges with annual feedback about the academic performance of the students sent from their settings to the university.

## Example B: A Study of Extenders—Students Who Take Longer Than Normal to Graduate

There appears to be a rising tendency for many full-time undergraduate students to take more than 4 years to graduate. Large numbers of students who enter college as full-time freshmen take 5 and 6 years to complete a bachelor's degree—so many, in fact, that national databases and college guidebooks no longer report 4-year graduation rates. The Federal Student Right to Know Act requires 2-year campuses to report a 3-year graduation rate and 4-year campuses to report a 6-year rate. Does the longer time to graduation reflect a flexible system or a flawed one?

These students, called "extenders" have attracted much attention over the last decade. Several states, California, Florida, Oregon, and Texas among them, have taken action against students characterized as staying in college too long and accumulating excessive credits. Policies aimed at charging students a higher tuition when they take more courses than needed to graduate have been introduced. Particularly striking was the apparent absence of any research evidence about why students were lingering. Indeed, each of the separate state plans hypothesized a different behavioral impact from a tuition surcharge on targeted students, further suggesting that legislators had no research on which to base their policy assumptions.

Although there is a good deal of research on persisters and dropouts, little empirical investigation exists on extenders. What are the reasons that some students take longer than normal to complete a bachelor's degree? Are students who extend their programs more like those who take only 4 years to graduate, or are they more like those who drop out? We know from the vast retention research that various academic, social, and financial factors influence student persistence, but do these same factors contribute to the longer time-to-degree by some students? What factors are the most strongly associated with these behaviors among students at the university? In this case, a university used the various concepts and measures from the student retention literature and examined their relevance to the outcomes of taking longer to graduate

### Phase I—Descriptive Transcript Analysis

Phase I, the descriptive aspect of this research, reviewed representative transcripts of traditionally admitted, first-time, full-time freshmen who had completed one of the institution's student opinion surveys in the past decade. These were divided into three groups: those graduating in 4 years, those graduating in more than 4 years, and those not graduating. The transcripts contained a variety of information about course enrollments each semester, grades, academic standing, and credits earned elsewhere. The transcript information was merged with survey data that included questions about their satisfaction with college, plans to graduate, their employment during the academic year, and their reasons for taking fewer than 15 credits. The university used bivariate descriptive statistics to summarize the findings of the transcript analysis and found the following:

1. The percentage of students taking longer than 4 years to graduate grew from less than 10% of the entering cohorts in the 1980s to over 20% in the 1990s.
2. The most apparent reason for students to take longer than 4 years to graduate was that they completed fewer than 15 credits a semester, usually due to a mid-semester drop, rather than a course failure. However, a growing number of students registered for fewer than 15 credits at the beginning of the semester.
3. Attempting fewer than 15 credits a semester was not restricted to students taking longer to graduate. Indeed, a large number of students adapted to college by using a combination of advanced placement and summer-session credit to enable a lighter credit load during the regular academic year.
4. One in five extenders took longer to graduate because they withdrew for one or two semesters and returned. One in four of these students had been placed on academic probation, whereas the remaining students left for a time, indicating that the reason was financial, medical, personal, death in family, or transfer.
5. Telephone interviews with a sample of those who left without a degree indicated in significantly greater proportions that they were not satisfied with their academic grades and that they had problems with courses that were too difficult or did not fit their expectations. These students had more academic difficulties than other students, and in large numbers were later academically dismissed.

Thus, the first descriptive phase of this research was a transcript analysis, finding that students who take longer to graduate had some of the same characteristics as those students who graduated in 4 years. Both groups came to the university with advanced placement credit (but four-year completers had more). Both completed fewer than 15 credits in some semesters (but extenders did it more often). Both groups expressed some problems with course and faculty availability (but 4-year completers adjusted). Both reported similar college work experiences, but extenders had higher financial need and tended to work more often.

The transcript studies and selected telephone interviews did not suggest that precollege characteristics such as age, sex, race, and high school grades were factors in extender behavior. Four-year graduates and extenders also employed roughly similar strategies in earning additional credits to supplement regular semester credits. Students taking longer to graduate were generally as satisfied with this outcome as those who graduated on time. Those students who did not graduate tended to experience more academic adversity and financial need. Unlike 4-year completers and extenders, some of whom also experienced academic problems, dropouts were not able to rebound from difficulty and to complete a degree.

## Phase II—Multivariate Analysis

The multivariate analysis for this study was conducted on several hundred representative juniors and seniors who entered the university as first-time, full-time freshmen and who responded to an outcomes survey by completing at least 90% of the questions. The student survey was administered every three or four years on the campus and contained items that were drawn directly from the student–institution fit literature. The respondents were representative with respect to age, gender, and race. Although not all majors were present in the sample, the 15 largest majors were represented in approximate proportion to their numbers in the undergraduate student body.

Since the transcript analysis suggested that the major cause of extender behavior was the habit of taking fewer than 15 credits per semester, the multivariate analysis focused on this behavior as the dependent variable (using OLS regression). The university survey contained specific measures for academic integration, social integration, encouragement, finances, and goal commitment, borrowed not only from Cabrera's work (1992, 1993) but also from studies by Pascarella and Terenzini (1983), Terenzini et al. (1982, 1984), Nora (1987, 1990), Volkwein et al. (1986), Volkwein (1991), and Volkwein and Carbone (1994). The student survey also contained various measures of campus life and campus climate (course availability, perceptions of prejudice, racial harmony, and student satisfaction with campus responsiveness, rules and regulations, facilities, and student voice in decisions). The alpha reliabilities for the various multi-item scales were recalculated for this population and many exceeded .80, and all but one were above .70.

What measures were most strongly associated with taking longer than normal to graduate and with registering for fewer than 15 credits per semester? Using the number of semesters with fewer than 15 credits as the dependent variable in an OLS regression model, and with 30 academic, social, financial, campus life, and other variables included in the analysis, only three variables exerted a significant influence on extended graduation, and in a model removing growth and satisfaction outcomes measures the same three were significant—protecting a high GPA, having heavy work and family responsibilities, and active social involvement on the campus. A scale of items reflecting student desires to protect a high GPA and have more free time was twice as influential as the scale reflecting work and family responsibilities, and three times as influential as a scale reflecting campus social involvement.

The existing enrollment management and student–institution fit literature generally concentrates on two student populations: persisters and dropouts. This study investigated a third population that we called extenders—those ostensibly full-time students who take longer than 4 years to complete the B.A. This university addressed the topic by applying a transcript analysis to one student population and a multivariate analysis to a second. Both the transcript analysis and the multivariate analysis suggested that students become extenders by completing too many semesters with fewer than 15 credits. The largest population of those who did this more often than others were academically talented students protecting a high GPA for admission to graduate schools such as law, medicine, and business. Another significant group of students who engaged in extender behavior were those with high financial need and heavy work and family obligations. The other measures of precollege characteristics, academic integration, social integration, campus climate, encouragement by family and friends, and goal clarity were not significantly related to extender behavior. Thus, students who take longer to graduate or who tend to register for fewer than 15 credits were not significantly different from students who graduate in four years on most variables that measure academic, social, and administrative aspects of the campus. Even the measures of self-reported growth and overall satisfaction appeared to be unrelated to delayed graduation. Extenders appeared to have neither more nor less academic and social integration and goal clarity than nonextenders. These students appeared not to be negatively impacted by taking longer to graduate and were generally satisfied with their experiences.

The combined findings of the study had an unexpected impact on the university. First, it was decided that these three separate groups presented difficult policy problems and further discussion of new policy and legislation for the campus and the system was discontinued. For one thing, the largest group was composed of relatively satisfied, grade-conscious extenders, and the university was reluctant to interfere with the ambitions of its most academically talented graduate-school-bound students (especially because most were full-tuition-paying customers). For another thing, the large group of financial need extenders were apparently doing their best to balance the academic demands of college with the financial demands of their personal and family circumstances. Any attempt to shorten the time to degree for either of these two largest groups of extenders seemed unwise, both managerially and educationally. The third relatively small group of special-situation students who withdrew temporarily to take care of unpredictable family, health, or personal circumstances were not captured by the regression model, nor otherwise identifiable in advance, but the university needed to construct appropriate policies and support services to assist them.

A second unexpected development occurred when the faculty senate and the undergraduate council used the findings of the study to justify a reassessment of the structure of the undergraduate curriculum. If so many students, especially talented ones, were progressing through the university by taking four courses per semester, perhaps that would be a desirable standard for all. A few departments and programs already had in place a four-course/four-credit system on the educational grounds that more concentrated attention to fewer subjects constituted sound educational practice. The strengths and weaknesses of such a curricular conversion are still being explored.

### Example C: Using the Accreditation Self-Study to Stimulate Organizational Change

Colleges and universities undergo regular scrutiny by both regional and specialized accrediting bodies. Historically, the purpose of accreditation has been summative, for quality assurance. However, campus officials strain at the workload associated with multiple self-studies and accreditation visits, and sometimes see few benefits. Administrators and faculty alike dread forthcoming reaccreditation reviews because of the human resource and other costs of the self-study process.

This negative view of accreditation has gradually forced accrediting bodies, especially regional ones, to implement three important changes over the past few decades. First, they have shifted away from a summative focus on meeting explicit standards toward a formative focus on self-improvement. Second, they have shifted away from the earlier overconcentration on resources and other inputs toward a concentration on outcomes in the belief that results matter most. The North Central and Southern accrediting bodies were early leaders in this trend toward outcomes assessment, which now is prominently embedded in the Middles States and Western regional accrediting standards as well (c.f. Middle States, 1996). Third, they have encouraged campuses to base their accreditation self-study on existing campus processes, like strategic planning or program evaluation, rather than to generate a one-time, stand-alone self-study document. In fact, several campus leaders have used the accreditation self-study as a "chariot for change" with the blessing of the regional accrediting body (Ratcliff, Lubinescu, & Gaffney, 2001). Although many academic leaders still consider the accreditation process burdensome, they welcome these changes.

The university president, in this example, wanted to use the upcoming regional reaccreditation process to build on and learn from the assessment and evaluation resources of the campus, rather than to invest the institution's energy and resources in a one-time process that would evaporate as soon as the site-visit team left the campus. In this particular case, the university prepared for the accreditation self-study by conducting a meta-analysis of all available campus assessment information. The results of this exercise stimulated a host of changes in undergraduate education, and in some respects served as a catalyst for organizational transformation.

After discussions with the provost and the regional accreditation staff, the president appointed the self-study steering committee and charged it with the task of assembling and summarizing all the assessment and evaluation information on the campus. The offices of academic affairs, student affairs, and institutional research were asked to cooperate with the chair of the steering committee because each of these offices housed analytical expertise. Student affairs periodically collected survey data from entering students, as well as campus climate and satisfaction surveys, especially from students in the residence halls. Academic affairs regularly monitored and analyzed student admissions, enrollment, retention, and academic performance statistics, as well as academic program reviews. The office of institutional research was responsible for conducting outcomes studies every 3 to 4 years, as well as responding annually to guidebook requests for summary data about students and faculty. Analysts from each of these three offices formed a working group to assemble and integrate the information from these separate sources.

After conducting an inventory of relevant information and studies, the group used an IPO model to classify existing campus data along the lines suggested in Table 12.1 earlier in this chapter. In an exercise that lasted almost a year, the group both summarized the results of existing studies and undertook the analysis of data that had been collected but not systematically studied. Each of the three offices had collected and stored student-level data that had never been linked to existing data in the other offices. The self-study provided the stimulus to examine more thoroughly than before the linkages among precollege characteristics, campus experiences, and subsequent student outcomes.

Figure 12.3 and Table 12.2 show the some of the results from this collective effort. Each bar in Figure 12.3 represents the explained variance from one of the multivariate outcomes studies. These studies ranged from analyses of overall satisfaction and cumulative GPA, to freshman commitment to attend the university "all over again," to examining self-reported intellectual and personal growth among graduating seniors. The most surprising finding from Figure 12.3 for the steering committee was the large influence of college experiences for most outcomes, and the relatively smaller influence of student precollege traits. Except for cumulative GPA (where SAT scores and high school grades are the best predictors), outcomes were determined most

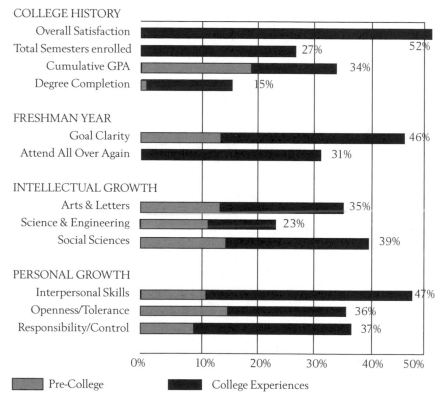

**FIGURE 12.3.** Outcomes measures for university undergraduates: the percent of variance explained by various measures of precollege characteristics and college experiences in multiple studies.

**TABLE 12.2**
**Results from Multiple Regression Analyses With Various Outcomes**

| Outcomes | Influential variables | |
|---|---|---|
| Type of outcome, population, and year of study | Most significant predictor of the explained variance | Other variables making important contributions to the explained variance |
| **Cumulative grade point avg.** | | |
| Freshmen (1986, 1990, 1994) | SAT<br>High school GPA | Student effort/conscientious-ness 20+ Hours employment off-campus (neg) Female |
| Seniors (1986, 1990) | SAT<br>High school rank | Student effort/conscientious-ness 20+ Hours employment off-campus (neg) |
| Final cumulative GPA at graduation (1994-1998) | Student effort/ conscientiousness | SAT, high school average, science major |
| All students (1997) | SAT | High school rank, female, classroom experiences, student effort/ conscientiousness |
| **Intellectual growth (seniors)** | | |
| All seniors (1994, 1997) | Classroom experiences | Peer relations, climate of tolerance, working off-campus (neg) |
| Seniors who entered as frosh (2000) | Classroom experiences | Student effort, peer relations |
| Seniors who entered as transfers (2000) | Classroom experiences | |
| Seniors who entered after work or military experience (2000) | Classroom experiences | Student effort, perceived climate of tolerance |
| Arts and letters (1990) | Classroom experiences | Diversity, social involvement |
| Arts and letters (2000) | Faculty relations | Classroom experiences, peer relations |
| Science and engineering (1990, 2000) | Classroom experiences | Faculty relations, high faculty contact—academic, participation in activities |
| Social Sciences (1990, 2000) | Classroom experiences | Faculty relations, high faculty contact—academic, peer relations |
| **Personal growth (seniors)** | | |
| Openness and tolerance (1990) | Classroom experiences | Social involvement, diversity, female |

*(Continued)*

**TABLE 12.2**
**Continued**

| Outcomes | Influential variables | |
|---|---|---|
| Type of outcome, population, and year of study | Most significant predictor of the explained variance | Other variables making important contributions to the explained variance |
| Openness and tolerance (2000) | Peer relations | Classroom experiences, faculty relations, diversity, |
| Interpersonal skills (1990, 2000) | Peer relations | Faculty relations, participation in activities, social involvement, male, science oriented |
| Responsibility/self-control (1990) | Peer relations | Student effort/conscientiousness, female, classroom experiences |
| Responsibility/self-control (2000) | Classroom experiences | Student effort/conscientiousness, faculty eelations, peer relations, employment hours |
| Overall satisfaction among seniors (1994, 1997) | Classroom experiences | Peer relations, faculty relations, participation in athletics, intramurals, student government |
| Freshman goal clarity (1986, 1990, 1994, 1997) | Classroom experiences Faculty relations | Student effort/conscientiousness, peer relations, social involvement |
| Institutional commitment and willingness to "attend all over again" | | |
| All students (1994, 1997) | Academic integration/growth | Social integration/growth, especially peer relations, financial need/aid, age |
| Freshmen (1986, 1990, 1994, 1997) | Peer relations | Classroom experiences, faculty relations |
| Seniors (1990, 1994, 1997) | Peer relations | Classroom experiences, faculty relations, male |
| Number of semesters enrolled (8 max.) (1998) | Classroom experiences | Peer relations, financial need (neg), high school class rank, female |

*Note.* Neg, negative.

by what happened to students after they arrived on campus. This was welcome news for the faculty and student affairs staff alike.

The group's next step was to determine which were the best predictors of each outcome. Table 12.2 summarizes in the first column the type of outcome studied, the student population and the year or years of the study. The middle column identifies the most important predictor of that outcome, and the third column lists other important predictors.

The first group of studies all examined the predictors of student academic performance (cumulative GPA) between 1986 and 1997. In six different studies, student SAT scores, either by themselves or in combination with high school GPA or class rank, were the best predictors of university cumulative GPA. The second most important predictor was self-reported student effort and conscientiousness. A frequently appearing negative influence on academic performance was working off campus, especially for 20 or more hours per week.

The remainder of Table 12.2 paints a consistent picture of what matters most—classroom experiences followed by peer relations, faculty relations, and student effort. Classroom experiences were the most powerful contributors to various measures of student outcomes in 21 of 33 studies at the university over the years. The classroom scale was a set of items developed at the university to reflect the vitality and quality of instruction, stimulating assignments that promote learning, and faculty preparation for class. Classroom vitality was the best predictor of intellectual growth in 10 of 11 studies, and in the 11th it was a significant secondary contributor. The vitality of the classroom experience was also the most important influence in one study of openness and tolerance, in one study of responsibility/self-control, in two studies of overall satisfaction, in four studies of freshman goal clarity, in two studies of student commitment, and one study of the length of enrollment.

Peer relations, a scale of items reflecting mostly the strength of student friendships, was the most powerful contributor in one study of openness and tolerance, in two studies of interpersonal skill, in one study of responsibility/self-control, in four studies of student commitment among freshman, and in three studies of student commitment among seniors. Peer relations were strong secondary contributors in several of the other outcomes studies.

These results in Table 12.2 were consistent with the student–institution fit literature (Pascarella & Terenzini, 1991; Strauss & Volkwein, 2002; Volkwein & Carbone,1994; Volkwein & Lorang, 1996). Measures of academic integration, especially classroom experiences, exerted the strongest influences on student growth and satisfaction. Classroom experiences were approximately twice as strong as peer relations and three times stronger than any other significant variables. In nearly all these studies, few student precollege characteristics proved to be significant. In 9 of 33 studies, small amounts of the variance were explained by financial need, ethnic diversity, and being female. Most other traits that students brought with them consistently failed to achieve significance.

The results of this research synthesis, which continued beyond the period of self-study and reaccreditation, had a far-reaching impact on the campus. Armed with such convincing evidence, the accreditation steering committee made several recommendations in the self-study that were quickly implemented. The convincing evidence about what matters most touched off a series of ongoing discussions ranging from the president's and provost's regular meetings with vice-presidents, deans, directors, and chairs to the university senate and its committees. Over the next few years several changes were implemented, and the most prominent of them follow:

1. *Greater faculty interest in student learning and growth.* In the previous two decades faculty were bombarded with information and views suggesting that what happened to students outside the classroom was more important than what happened inside it. The self-study brought the faculty role back into prominence, and generated greater faculty interest and participation in undergraduate affairs. Knowing the importance of the classroom experience gave faculty greater confidence and pride in their role in undergraduate education at the university.

2. *Alterations in new student orientation.* Prior to these findings the orientation program for new students was almost entirely a social experience aimed at getting students into clubs, activities, and residential life. The student affairs and academic affairs staffs worked with the faculty to restructure orientation so that the academic component dominated and was aimed at getting students off to a good start academically.

3. *New academic support services for students.* One of the studies of student attrition and academic probation found that a small number of undergraduate courses was responsible for the vast majority of failing grades among freshmen. (Students called them killer courses.) Working with the undergraduate council and the advisement center, the provost and student affairs vice-president gave greater attention to academic adjustment and advisement, including the establishment of a peer mentoring program, study skills workshops in the residence halls, and an academic early warning system in "killer courses" that was linked to tutoring programs.

4. *Residential living–learning communities established with faculty in residence.* The provost and student affairs vice president began a series of feasibility studies aimed at creating classrooms and faculty apartments in selected residence hall complexes. In each residential unit, the freshmen take at least one general education course together. The impact of these is being evaluated.

5. *Enhanced administrative decision making and strategic planning.* The president announced for the campus new planning and resource allocation criteria that gave top priority to the protection of academic and instructional resources.

6. *Greater attention to faculty development.* The provost allocated new resources for an instructional development center to work with faculty on their teaching skills and use of technology.

7. *Centralized institutional research.* Instead of institutional analysis being decentralized and spread among the vice-presidential areas, the president's executive team realized the benefits of a centralized office with coordinated data collection and analysis. Thus, the institutional research analysts in the separate vice-presidential offices were brought together under one director. It was decided that institutional research constitutes a strategically better, more balanced, and less narrow resource for the institution when the IR team reports to the president's office, but also directs its analytical service to the needs and priorities of the vice presidents. The centralized IR model is more efficient and effective because it takes advantage of the natural economies of scale associated with assessment research expertise, cross-training, and methodological diversity. Also, a centralized arrangement protects the institution better against staff turnover and the inefficiency of narrow specialization. The need for a person to be dedicated to a particular function or task (like enrollment management, or student climate research, or budget analysis, or instructional analysis) can be incorporated into a centralized office and, in fact, better support it, because of the additional expertise and backup that comes with cross-training.

Thus, as a direct consequence of the self study, the university had visible outcomes information to support campus planning and decision making, to measure attainment of campus and program goals, and to demonstrate institutional effectiveness for accreditation. The model-driven process of inventorying and analyzing existing campus data proved to be an effective strategy that supported constructive changes in undergraduate education at the university.

## CONCLUSION

Thus, we have seen in this chapter several examples of campuses that used existing and locally available data to respond administratively to policy problems. These examples demonstrate the value of starting with an outcomes model as an organizing framework both to inventory and to examine existing campus outcomes evidence, and to guide new data collection.

## FOR FURTHER READING

For additional reading on methods to be used in analysis of local data, see Terenzini (1989), Bauer (1998), and Upcraft and Schuh (1996). For specific examples of the use of campus data, see Banta, Lund, Black, and Oblander (1996).

## REFERENCES

Astin, A. W. (1984). Student involvement: A developmental theory for higher education. *Journal of College Student Personal, 24*(5), 207–308.

Astin, A. W. (1991). *Assessment for excellence: The philosophy and practice of assessment and evaluation in higher education.* New York: Macmillan.

Banta, T. W., Lund J. P., Black, K. E., & Oblander, F. W. (1996). *Assessment in practice: Putting principles to work on college campuses.* San Francisco: Jossey-Bass.

Bauer, K. B. (1998). *Campus climate: Understanding the critical components of today's colleges and universities* (New Directions for Institutional Research, number 98). San Francisco: Jossey-Bass.

Bean, J. P. (1980). Dropout and turnover: The synthesis and test of a causal model of student attrition. *Research in Higher Education, 12,* 155–187.

Bean, J. P., & Metzner, B. S. (1985). A conceptual model of nontraditional undergraduate student attrition. *Review of Higher Educational Research, 55*(4), 485–540.

Berger, J. B., & Milem, J. F. (2000). Organizational behavior in higher education and student outcomes. In J. C. Smart (Ed.), *Higher education handbook of theory and research* (Vol. XV, pp. 268–338). New York: Agathon Press.

Cabrera, A. F., Castaneda, M. B., Nora, A., & Hengstler, D. (1992). The convergence between two theories of college persistence. *Journal of Higher Education, 63*(2), 143–164.

Cabrera, A. F., Nora, A., & Castaneda, M. B. (1992). The role of finances in the persistence process: A structural model. *Research in Higher Education, 33*(5), 571–593.

Cabrera, A. F., Nora, A., & Castaneda, M. D. (1993). College persistence: The testing of an integrated model. *Journal of Higher Education, 64*(2), 123–139.

Cabrera, A. F., Nora, A., Terenzini, P. T., Pascarella, E., & Hagedorn, L. S. (1999). Campus racial climate and the adjustment of students to college. *Journal of Higher Education, 70*(2), 134–160.

Cabrera, A. F., Stampen, J. L., & Hansen, W. L. (1990). Exploring the effects of ability-to-pay on persistence in college. *Review of Higher Education, 13*(3), 303–336.

Feldman, K., & Newcomb, T. (1969). *The impact of college on students.* San Francisco: Jossey-Bass.

Fleming, J. (1984). *Blacks in college: A comparative study of students' success in Black and in White institutions.* San Francisco: Jossey-Bass.

Hall, R. H. (1992). *Organizations: Structure and process.* Englewood Cliffs, NJ: Prentice Hall.

Hurtado, S. (1992). The campus racial climate: Contexts of conflict. *Journal of Higher Education, 63,* 539–569.

Hurtado, S. (1994). The institutional climate for talented Latino students. *Research in Higher Education, 35,* 21–41.

Hurtado, S., Carter, D. F., & Spuler, A. (1996). Latino student transition to college: Assessing difficulties and factors in successful college adjustment. *Research in Higher Education, 21*(3), 279–302.

Loo, C. M., & Rolison, G. (1986). Alienation of ethnic minority students at a predominately white university. *Journal of Higher Education, 57,* 58–77.

Middle States Association of Colleges and Schools. (1996). *Framework for outcomes assessment.* Philadelphia, PA: Author.

Nora, A. (1987). Determinants of retention among Chicano students: A structural model. *Research in Higher Education, 26*(1), 31–59.

Nora, A. (1990). Campus-based programs as determinants of retention among Hispanic college students. *Journal of Higher Education, 61*(3), 312–331.

Nora, A., & Cabrera, A. F. (1996). The role of perceptions of prejudice and discrimination on the adjustment of minority students to college. *Journal of Higher Education, 67,* 119–148.

Pace, C. (1984). *Measuring the quality of college student experiences.* Los Angeles: University of California, Higher Education Research Institute.

Pascarella, E. T. (1985). College environmental influences on learning and cognitive development: A critical review and synthesis. In J. Smart (Ed.), *Higher education: Handbook of theory and tesearch* (Vol. I, pp. 1–61). New York: Agathon.

Pascarella, E. T., & Terenzini, P. T. (1983). Predicting voluntary freshman year persistence/withdrawal behavior in a residential university: A path analytic validation of Tinto's model. *Journal of Educational Psychology, 75*(2), 215–226.

Pascarella, E. T., & Terenzini, P. T. (1991). *How college affects students.* San Francisco: Jossey-Bass.

Ratcliff, J. L., Lubinescu, E., & Gaffney, M. (2001). *How accreditation influences assessment* (New Directions in Higher Education, number 113). San Francisco: Jossey-Bass.

Smedley, B. D., Myers, H. F., & Harrell, S. P. (1993). Minority-status stresses and the college adjustment of ethnic minority freshmen. *Journal of Higher Education, 64,* 434–452.

Spady, W. G. (1970). Dropouts from higher education: An interdisciplinary review and synthesis. *Interchange, 1*(1), 64–85.

Spady, W. G. (1971). Dropouts from higher education: Toward an empirical model. *Interchange, 2*(3), 38–62.

St. John, E. P. (1992). Workable models for institutional research on the impact of student financial aid. *Journal of Student Financial Aid, 22*(3), 13–26.

Stage, F. K. (1989a). Reciprocal effects between the academic and social integration of college students. *Research in Higher Education, 30*(5), 513–526.

Stage, F. K. (1989b). University attrition: LISREL with logistic regression for the persistence criterion. *Research in Higher Education, 29*(4), 343–357.

Stark, J. S., Shaw, K M., & Lowther, M. A. (1989). *Student goals for college and courses: A missing link in assessing and improving academic achievement.* ASHE-ERIC Higher Education Report 6. (ed317121) ERIC Clearinghouse on Higher Education, The George Washington University.

Strauss, L.C., & Volkwein, J. F. (2002). Comparing student performance and growth in 2- and 4-year institutions. *Research in Higher Education, 43,* 133–161.

Terenzini, P. T. (1989) Assessment with open eyes: Pitfalls in studying student outcomes. *Journal of Higher Education, 60,* 644–664.

Terenzini, P., Theophilides, C., & Lorang, W. (1984a). Influences on students' perceptions of their academic skill development during college. *Journal of Higher Education, 55,* 621–636.

Terenzini , P., & Wright, T. (1987a). Influences on students' academic growth during four years of college. *Research in Higher Education, 26,* 161–179.

Terenzini, P. T., Springer, L., Pascarella, E. T., & Nora, A. (1995a). Influences affecting the development of students' critical thinking skills. *Research in Higher Education, 36,* 23–39.

Terenzini, P. T., Springer, L., Pascarella, E. T., & Nora, A. (1995b). Academic and out-of-class influences on students' intellectual orientations. *Review of Higher Education, 19,* 23–44.

Tinto, V. (1987). *Leaving college: Rethinking the causes and cures of student attrition.* Chicago: University of Chicago Press.

Tinto, V. (1993). *Leaving college: Rethinking the causes and cures of student attrition* (2nd ed.). Chicago: The University of Chicago Press.

Toutkoushian, R. K., & Smart, J. C. (2001). Do institutional characteristics affect student gains from college? *Review of Higher Education, 25*(1), 39–61.

Upcraft, M. L., & Schuh, J. H. (1996). *Assessment in student affairs: A guide for practitioners.* San Francisco: Jossey-Bass.

Volkwein, J. F. (1991, November). *Improved measures of academic and social integration and their association with measures of student growth.* Paper presented at Annual Meeting of the Association for the Study of Higher Education, Boston.

Volkwein, J. F. (1992). *Albany outcomes model. Assessment Research Report, 12* (online). Office of Institutional Research, State University of New York at Albany. <http://www.albany.edu/ir/reports.html>.

Volkwein, J. F. (1999). *What is institutional research all about: A critical and comprehensive assessment of the profession* (New Directions for Institutional Research, number 104). San Francisco: Jossey-Bass.

Volkwein, J. F., & Carbone, D. A. (1994). The impact of departmental research and teaching climates on undergraduate growth and satisfaction. *Journal of Higher Education, 65*(2), 147–167.

Volkwein, J. F., King, M. C., & Terenzini, P. T. (1986). Student faculty relationships and intellectual growth among transfer students. *Journal of Higher Education, 57,* 413–430.

Volkwein, J. F., & Lorang, W. G. (1996). Characteristics of extenders: Full-time students who take light credit loads and graduate in more than four years. *Research in Higher Education, 37*(1), 43–68.

Volkwein, J. F., & Szelest, B. P. (1995). Individual and campus characteristics associated with student loan default. *Research in Higher Education, 36,* 41–72.

Volkwein, J. F., Szelest, B. P., Cabrera, A. F., & Napierski-Prancl, M. R. (1998). Factors associated with student loan default among different racial and ethnic groups. *Journal of Higher Education, 69*(2), 206–237.

Volkwein, J. F., Valle, S., Blose, G., & Zhou, Y. (2000, June). *A multi-campus study of academic performance and cognitive growth among native freshman, two-year transfers, and four-year transfers.* Paper presented at the meeting of the Association for Institutional Research Forum, Cincinnati, OH.

Voorhees, R. A. (1997). Student learning and cognitive development in the community college. In J.C. Smart (Ed.) *Higher education handbook of theory and research* (Vol. XII, pp. 313–370). New York: Agathon Press.

Weidman, J. (1989). Undergraduate socialization: A conceptual approach. In J. Smart (Ed.), *Higher education: Handbook of theory and research* (Vol. V, pp. 289–322). New York: Agathon Press.

*Part 5*
# COMMUNICATING YOUR RESULTS—
# ADDING TO THE KNOWLEDGE
# OF THE FIELD

*Chapter 13*

# REPORTING RESULTS

**Frances K. Stage,** *New York University*
**Kathleen Manning,** *University of Vermont*

When conceiving this book, the editors invited new and experienced research-ers to fulfill the promise of educational research as articulated by Keller in 1985 (see Preface). As such, the purposes of this book were to introduce re-search methods less commonly used but relevant to higher education, whet the readers' appetites for research, build enthusiasm for the possibilities of research on college campuses, and spur readers to develop their research skills to the fullest possible degree. Keller (1985) employed the metaphor of trees without fruit as a way to critique educational research as well as urge change in the quality and type of research conducted. The methods and approaches conveyed in this book carry Keller's message. Regardless of the method dis-cussed in the chapter, the authors communicated that quality, meaningful-ness, and ethical practice are of utmost importance. This concluding chapter expounds on that message of quality, usefulness, and relevance. In this final chapter we (a) revisit the main points of the methodological chapters, (b) review remaining research topics, (c) discuss researchers' obligations as they report research findings from their privileged positions, and (d) explore the possibilities for contribution to social change that research affords.

## SUMMARY OF MAIN POINTS

The content of this book illustrates the following important points about research.

1. Researchers are urged to determine their question prior to selecting the choice of method; this is reinforced by both the order and content of chapters 1 and 2. Although this may seem obvious, experience as dissertation advisors and researchers led the editors and chapter authors to the conclusion that the methods choice cart is often put before the research question horse.

2. There is a wealth of research possibilities and resources of which to take advantage. The range and creative means to pursue the methods discussed within the chapters indicate just how inventive researchers can be when pursuing their topics. The possibilities for breadth and reach of method, design, and dissemination are endless and stimulating.

3. Researchers can use multiple methods for the most applicable results. Thirty years ago, researchers had a somewhat narrow range of quantitative methods from which to choose. Fifteen years ago, a debate, often named the "paradigm wars," raged about the efficacies of quantitative versus qualitative methods. Today's researcher no longer has to settle for the previously oversimplified dichotomies of quantitative or qualitative and theory or practice. Educational research is coming of age in ways that make multiple, cross paradigm use of methods a possibility. Even critical approaches, mentioned briefly in chapter 2, once thought of as belonging strictly within the emergent research pardigm, are now sometimes combined with conventional approaches (Hurtado, 2002; Slaughter, 2002) or even conducted using entirely conventional methods (St. John, 2002; Stage, 2002).

4. Any research conducted becomes part of the continuum of theory and practice in higher education. Researchers can add to and enrich this theory base by positioning their research in the higher education literature. This process begins with a thorough pre-research review of the literature. It continues, most importantly, with discussion of the relevance of the research in light of the past and future theory within the field. Doctoral student researchers often underestimate the importance of their dissertation findings in the greater scheme of higher education theory.

5. This book provides an introduction to research methods often underused or newly introduced into the repertoire of educational methods. The more imperative purpose of this introduction is to urge the researcher, new or experienced, to expand expertise to other methods, and to develop and extend his or her expertise in the method selected. The Further Reading section of each chapter contains a wealth of sources and references for this purpose. The reader is urged to delve into these sources because the methods are often more complicated than they first might appear. Any investment of time by the researcher or respondents deserves the highest level of expertise possible. For new researchers, use of any research method

will be the first time he or she is exposed to that approach. For those of us who graduated many years ago from our doctoral programs, new ways to look at older research methods are always being introduced. An examination of these newer perspectives and ways to view the methods can vastly improve the research process and product.

The authors in the collection sought to convey several significant ideas about research in higher education settings. These points hold true regardless of the research experience but may have particular significance for doctoral students and new researchers.

Anna Ortiz discussed the fact that knowledge is a product of interaction among research participants. This cooperative approach between researcher and respondents adds to the quality of the research effort. She delineated carefully the complicated steps needed. Ortiz also debunked the assumption that one can "just do" ethnographic interviews or any research method, for that matter. Bridget Turner Kelly, in discussing focus groups, recommended that researchers, particularly doctoral students, avoid using a method chosen for convenience. Instead, the methodology must fit the research questions and purposes being pursued. The strengths and limitations of any method should be assessed for fit and appropriateness to the purposes of the project prior to their use. Ruth Russell and Agnes Kovacs discussed the ways in which researchers cannot help but affect the environments in which they conduct studies. As remedy, they discussed nonreactive (or unobtrusive) ways to collect data. The issue of research influence raises questions of bias and validity. Because the issue of validity differs between the emergent and conventional paradigms, the reader is advised to study the many sources available on this subject to gain a fuller understanding of these important issues of quality. Additionally, these authors raised interesting questions about the ethics of conducting research, whether obtrusively or unobtrusively.

Robert Schwartz, discussing historical methods, provided the beginning and experienced researcher a perspective on how specific research projects fit into the larger narration of previous and future efforts. Adding to the legacy of theory and practice is one of the most important roles of any researcher. Patrick Love, with document analysis, and Katie Branch, for visual methods, illustrated how the written and visual artifacts of everyday life can be mined as sources of significant meaning. These creative uses of data, different from the standard numerical type, point to endless possibilities of meaningful sources. Michelle Thompson introduced the reality that legal issues are an integral part of higher education practice. Thompson's caveats about dispensing legal advice can be generalized across all chapters and methods. Because research findings are applied in practice with human beings, researchers possess a weighty ethical responsibility to apply only the most competent use of methods to generate theory. Deborah Carter's chapter on secondary analysis of data illustrated an expedient, resource-conserving approach to research. In a time when universities are criticized for frivolous research expenditures, her economic approach is worth examining. Additionally, these rich sources of data allow the researcher to answer quantitative questions about diverse students who are not usually well represented in smaller studies. Teboho Moja reminded us that policy analysis can be used for research purposes as well as for policy formulation. She delineated stages that are useful in an analysis. Finally, Fredericks Volkwein, in his chapter on the usefulness of local data, enjoined us to be conservative in data collection efforts, to seek out sources of data on campus that can be used to triangulate with our data, or in some instances be our major source of data.

As researchers examine possible methods, we urge them to seek other avenues for information. Within this book, we have only introduced these data collection techniques. Lists of further readings as well as local experts on your own campus can add to your understanding of these topics. Additionally, attending research conferences provides a unique opportunity to discuss research problems and issues with the experts as well as other researchers with common ideas and interests. Although the issues discussed here are important considerations in any research project, several topics related to all the research efforts deserve more complete treatment. These include honoring various perspectives, dissemination of findings, and contributions to social change.

## HONORING VARIOUS PERSPECTIVES

Three issues apply when considering the range of perspectives in research. First, one must make the context in which the research was conducted explicit. Second, higher education research as a whole should attend to the diversity of higher education. Third, the researcher's perspective must be made clear so that the findings are understood in the context in which they were generated.

### Making the Context Explicit

In the name of value plurality and a full understanding of perspective, environment, and situation, the research findings must be embedded in the circumstances in which the research occurred. The institutional characteristic(s) (e.g., a publicly funded institution or a competitive liberal arts college), history, sense of place, and ways of being can be cited with the aim of generating a fuller understanding of the values in which the research was conducted. Often referred to as thick description, this understanding provides the readers with not only depth of knowledge but also a perspective from which they can apply (or not apply, as the case may be) those findings to another situation.

## Inclusive Research Practice

Women, people of color, ethnically diverse individuals, persons with disabilities, people from a wide variety of social classes, and those with a range of sexual orientations are full participants on today's college campus. If the research did not incorporate a representative or inclusive sample, the results cannot extended to a wider population. Increased diversity on college campuses adds the necessity that research (including the most esoteric studies) now must be representative across various groups. Unless the research is narrowly defined as part of its purposes and outcomes, including a broad range of respondents and honoring a wide variety of perspectives is an obligation.

Long gone are the days when homogeneous samples could imply practice or behavior across a range of groups. In addition to the dilemma of representativeness, all participants on college campuses, as members of that community, have the right to be invited as participants in research. This is particularly the case when the results of that research shape practice and policy that impacts their situation.

## The Researcher's Perspective

Research cannot help but be shaped by the values and assumptions of the researcher (Lincoln, 2002). In the name of positionality (e.g., race, gender, sexual orientation, class), the researcher needs to be clear about the perspective from which he or she generated the research questions, conducted the research, and wrote the findings. Qualitative research, in particular, uses several means, such as the subjective "I" and reflexivity, as means to be clear about the individual perspective from which the research was undertaken. The biography (often represented through a vita, short biography, or other means) is an important piece of the research report and can make a person's or persons' perspective(s) obvious.

## Representing the "Other"

When one acknowledges his or her position, it becomes clear that others fill different positions. Denzin and Lincoln (1998) wrote of the many ways of representing "the Other" in research. This representation can be accomplished in multiple ways ranging from accurately representing the voice of others, to actively training others to conduct research from their own perspective, deliberately chosen as different from the researcher's. "For some this means participatory, or collaborative, research and evaluation efforts. . . . For still others, it means . . . investigation wherein Others are trained to engage in their own social and historical interrogative efforts. . . . For yet other social scientists, including the Other means becoming coauthors" (p. 411). Regardless of the way in which the issue of "otherness" is considered, one has choices to make about the ethics of representing the other. This issue becomes particularly acute during the dissemination phase of the research project.

## DISSEMINATION OF FINDINGS

At the end of a research project, after the data are collected, analyzed, and compiled into findings, the researcher often struggles to consider the next steps. Readers are urged not to consider the research project over until the findings are disseminated to the widest possible audience. Only in this way can educational practice be improved.

Campus researchers have a wide range of possibilities for dissemination of their research findings to both practitioners and fellow researchers. The means to accomplish this are varied: case studies, refereed journal articles, books, and reports of empirical research, as well as visual and performance media and the popular press. The careful tracking of a project through a research journal, mentioned in chapter 1, can help with this process. Reference to the earliest notes might remind the author of intended audiences and outlets for dissemination. Decisions made throughout the research process, beginning with initial formulation of research questions, through the choice of method and the approaches taken for the analysis, provide a template for the researcher as he or she reports results. But even before the research process begins, initial motivation to conduct the research plays an important role in decisions regarding how the results are reported and made useful to a larger audience.

The options for dessemination, while constrained somewhat by the methodology chosen, are wider than those dictated by convention. Researchers are urged to think broadly about possible outlets and locales for dissemination. Often we do not think beyond our immediate obligation to report (e.g., a consultation report, dissertation, journal article), when our work might hold relevance for others who practice in the field or, if we are practitioners, for researchers.

As the time to write up the findings nears, much of the content has been determined, but the form of the report is less clear. One of the most important decisions in a research project is how to write up the research in an effective form. This final form should take into account not only the limitations but also the wide range of possibilities.

## Inclusion Considerations in Dissemination

In addition to the more grand purposes of education and educational research, two nuts-and-bolts ethical issues are to be considered when disseminating research findings: authorship and acknowledgments, and the education of young researchers.

### Authorship and Acknowledgements

Ethical practice in research entails several areas often not considered at first glance. These issues often present themselves during the dissemination phase, when authorship and public recognition of contributions come to the fore. The following questions should be considered when the research project begins so resolution at the dissemination phase is well understood: Who will be first author in any or all of the publications generated from the research project? What role did students play? Were they full-fledged collaborators deserving of authorship or assistants? How will their work be acknowledged?

### Education of Young Researchers

As researchers and educators, we are in the business of educating students and new professionals. Toward this end, each research project could involve undergraduate and/or graduate students in such a way that they gain experience in the research process. This is particularly important with undergraduate students because retention research indicates that such involvement increases faculty-student contact, augments the engagement of those students, and results in higher retention (Astin, 1993). But, with the pressures of dissertation research, research that leads to tenure, and other demands on the researcher, incorporating students can be difficult. Despite this, we urge that students be involved in the research learning process and acknowledged for their contributions.

## Forms of Research Reports

Journal articles, books, academic magazine articles, case studies, and conference proceedings represent modes most frequently thought of when considering research outlets. When finished analyzing data, many restrict their aspirations to producing a journal article, campus report, or conference paper. Creating an exhibit where people are likely to stop and read charts or illustrations is a less obvious way of communicating research results. Newspaper reports, personality profiles and biography, film documentaries, popular magazine articles, interviews, television or radio programs, and even obituaries are all ways that one can learn something about academic research. Some of the most novel ways of presenting academic research include creative writing. The 2002 American Educational Research Association conference included research presentations in the form of poetry, fiction, video, photographic and slide presentations, and plays (see American Educational Research Association, 2002).

The forms research takes can and often does vary widely. Readers are encouraged to use the venues for the research report to think beyond their original intentions in seeking audiences. By considering a variety of dissemination forms, researchers can broaden their audience, widen their influence, and serve others beyond their original intentions. In this section we discuss briefly some of the more conventional forms that are used for reporting research and then suggest venues that might not have been considered.

### *Journal Articles*

Likely, many readers will design a research project with the goal of writing a refereed journal article. The following simple steps are offered as ways to increase the reader's likelihood of success:

1. Visit a research library and examine several journals that cover topics similar to your own research topic. The field of higher education alone has approximately 100 journals!
2. Once you find a journal that includes reports of research results, look closely at the topics and methods of the articles reported. If your study uses quantitative methods, find a few that are similar in scope to yours. If you use qualitative methods, look for a journal that includes reports on studies that employ research designs similar to yours.
3. Read the articles carefully, making note of the conventions followed for stating the problem, relating results from other relevant work, describing the methods employed, presenting your results, and discussing findings.

The journal referee process can be a difficult one to navigate success-fully. This is particularly the case for high-quality journals with a low acceptance rate. It is important to avoid discouragement and to know that few, if any, articles are accepted without significant revisions. Even after the author receives a positive review from the editors, several more drafts must be generated before the final copy is definitively accepted. New and experienced readers are well advised to ask a friend, particularly a successful writer, to review a draft of the manuscript prior to submission.

## Books

Book-length manuscripts represent a significant investment of time and energy. Any research project that results in sufficient data and findings to fill a book is most likely outside the purview of a first research project. Furthermore, the book proposal process is time-consuming and often results in a wave of rejections before one or two acceptances are given. This venue is best left to an experienced writer who has had success with journal articles or book chapters. The reader is advised to read the variety of publications that discuss book prospecti, editing, and the writing process.

## Reports of Empirical Research

Research projects funded through federal grants or other means often require a written report. Although the dissemination of these reports is limited, this is a frequently used means of disseminating findings. The form of the report depends on the audience and the means of funding. The breadth of dissemination can be enhanced through an Internet website, which eliminates printing and mailing costs. Also, submission of the manuscript to the Educational Research Information Clearinghouse (ERIC; http://ericfacility.org), which regularly accepts research reports, can enhance availability.

## Popular Press

Although few academics are familiar or completely comfortable with the popular press, television, radio, newspapers, magazines, and popular books should be on the list of dissemination options. Frequently colleges and universities have information bureaus that can aid faculty and staff in finding outlets willing to publish articles highlighting research projects. Undergraduate students, useful barometers regarding general interest in academic work, can review research information as part of a class reading packet or course lecture. This activity can gauge student understanding and response.

### National and Regional Conferences

Conferences are excellent places to present papers, offer symposia, or conduct focused dialogues on research results. Conference presentations are often refereed and therefore of high quality. The reader is cautioned to investigate conference attendance well in advance as the call for papers and programs often has a minimum 6- to 9-month lead time.

### Classes

Research and teaching go hand in hand when findings are incorporated into a class. Students can learn from reading a research report still in its formative stages. Their interest can be piqued both by the research findings (which are more current than any reading assigned) and the research project. Guest presentations in colleagues' classes should also be considered.

### Consultation

Any high-quality consultation must be based on a solid base of research and knowledge about the field. Current research findings from others can be incorporated into knowledge shared through consultations. Additionally, the consultation provides an excellent laboratory in which to try out research findings and dissemination styles.

### Creative Outlets

Films, video, photo essays, art, performance art, and poetry are rarely considered by academics as ways to disseminate research. However, one can easily imagine research projects that lend themselves to these artistic displays. Collaboration with film, photographic, and other artistically gifted colleagues may be the best way to take advantage of these creative means of information sharing.

### Internet

The Internet presents endless possibilities for dissemination of research results. Web sites can be used throughout the entire research process to (a) build collaboration among participants, (b) post initial findings, (c) solicit reactions from various audiences, and (d) post the final research findings. Web sites among academics and students are commonplace. Although judging the quality of information posted on the Internet is often a challenge, research consumers are willing to take the risk of weeding through the wide range of information obtained resulting from powerful search engines. Given the pervasiveness and acceptance of the Internet, researchers can automatically plan to post research results, references to copyrighted publications, announcements about presentations, and other opportunities for dissemination.

## Dissemination and Accessibility

The obligation to spark or, at minimum, add to social change (discussed later) means that research should be disseminated to the places where it will do the most good. Often this means disseminating the research through less "academic" means (e.g., campus newspapers, association newsletters, letters to the editor). With the reward system for tenure and other academic assets focused on scholarly journals and less widely circulated publications, accessibility becomes a challenge. Researchers are urged to consider multiple means of dissemination with an eye for the ways in which more people can access the results. In chapter 1 we discussed a time period in which higher education research was likened to "trees without fruit." Now that we are producing fruitful work, researchers should feel an obligation to share that bounty, to disseminate their work so that others, who for one reason or another are not able to conduct research, may use it as well. This is particularly important when the research was funded through public monies.

## CONTRIBUTIONS TO SOCIAL CHANGE

Research presents challenge and opportunity to college campus constituents. As members of that community, researchers willingly participate in the goals of higher education. Among those purposes of higher education are social change, improvement in the quality of life for participants, the perpetuation of social justice, and education for participation in democracy. Nearly any research on the college campus directly or indirectly relates to those purposes. A study of stress of untenured faculty relates to a college's ability to deliver education to students. A study of part-time and commuter students' experiences with academic advising relates to access and equal opportunities for all students. Likewise, a study of student motivation in a chemistry class ultimately will improve the life of students and society when more succeed.

As research is undertaken, one must consider the privileged position from which that research is conducted. This position obligates us to give back to educational and social communities so others can benefit. Furthermore, educated people have an obligation to use that education to ends that improve social conditions. As one of the most diverse social institutions in the

United States, colleges and universities can advance social causes and improve the human condition.

## SUMMARY

The editors of this book embarked on the project with the idea, however modest of improving the quality and content of higher education research. We sought to introduce new and experienced student, faculty, and practitioner researchers to novel research ideas and techniques or older ones cast in a new light. We hope this book and the methods encouraged in it urge students, faculty, and practitioners to pursue less narrowly focused research efforts. Although many of these closely conceived studies discuss important aspects of educational practice, the broadly defined topics of higher education remain underresearched. Here we identify broad themes within higher education in order to spark further study and encourage more expanded efforts. To that end, we encourage research along the following themes:

How did higher education lose the public trust? What higher education activities are essential to regain that trust?

How do we enrich and deepen the executive leadership among boards of trustees, presidents, and academic leaders?

What are the issues attached to academic freedom? How is that freedom threatened? How might it be abused?

What research is needed to understand the dearth of involvement and lack of success in higher education among Native Americans?

Why is identity such a salient issue for traditional-age college students? What are equally salient issues for adult learners, commuters, and distance learners?

What research would help us better articulate the nexus between in and out of classroom learning for students?

What programs and initiatives improve the college-going and retention rates for African American males?

How is real institutional change linked to research, evaluation, and assessment activities?

How can we change our campuses so they are more receptive to all students, not just those who match the college ideal?

What occurs when you decouple the ideas of resources and excellence?

In what ways are students open to engagement and involvement?

How can higher education institutions encourage democratic citizenship among students?

The community of scholars and researchers in higher education is a rich, diverse, and intellectually gifted group. We invite you to join and maintain membership in this community. Improvement in practice, theory, and policy in higher education is greatly aided by the activities of a research community intent on enriching knowledge and a sound literature base. This community—with the larger community it serves and inform—is enriched when new and experienced researchers strive to say something important. The press of time, resources, and energy and, at times, well-meaning colleagues push research efforts in directions so that the finished product often falls short of the full potential of the researcher. In opposition to a merely adequate approach to educational research, the editors and authors of this book hold hope for the future of research and theory in higher education. We welcome your participation and look forward to the results of your efforts.

## REFERENCES

Astin, A. (1993). *What matters in college: Four critical years revisited.* San Francisco, CA: Jossey-Bass.

American Educational Research Association. (2002). Annual Meeting Program. Accesss March 9, 2003. <http://www.aera.net/meeting/previousmeetings.htm>.

Denzin, N. K., & Lincoln, Y. S. (Eds.). (1998). *The landscape of qualitative research: Theories and issues.* Thousand Oaks, CA: Sage.

Hurtado, S. (2002, November). *Toward a new conceptualization of college student success.* Paper presented at the annual meeting of the Association for the Study of Higher Education, Sacramento, CA.

Keller, G.(1985). Trees without fruit: The problem with research about higher education. Change, *17*(1), 7–10.

Lincoln, Y. (2002, November). *On the nature of qualitative evidence.* Paper presented at the annual meeting of the Association for the Study of Higher Education, Sacramento, CA.

St. John, E. (2002, November). *Diverse pathways to college: Untangling the influences of rinancial aid, high school curriculum, and postsecondary encouragement.* Paper presented at the annual meeting of the Association for the Study of Higher Education, Sacramento, CA.

Slaughter, S. (2002, November). *Using quantitative data for a critical analysis of faculty productivity.* Paper presented at the annual meeting of the Association for the Study of Higher Education, Sacramento, CA.

Stage, F. K. (2002, November). *Using quantitative data to answer critical questions.* Paper presented at the annual meeting of the Association for the Study of Higher Education, Sacramento, CA.

# AUTHOR INDEX

# SUBJECT INDEX